PRAISE FOR *The Cost of Courage*

"A very compelling story."
—ROBERT O. PAXTON, author of *Vichy France*

"Kaiser reveals the moral ambiguity of resistance when one's enemy is as ruthless as Nazi Germany...[He] makes the most of the inherent drama in the story he tells, but his touchstone is his relentless search for truth amid the fog of war...brilliant."
—JONATHAN KIRSCH, *Washington Post*

"Charles Kaiser relies on an old family friendship to unearth stirring stories of the brave French who risked their all to oppose the Nazis...Moving...Compelling...a story with the detailed intimacy of a journal and the powerful immediacy of a novel."
—NICK ROMEO, *Christian Science Monitor*

"In this poignant personal tale, Kaiser explores the emotions and breaks through the silences that haunted an amazing family after their experiences in the French resistance to Nazi occupation. The result is a compelling and heart-wrenching book about courage, love, and the complex shadings of heroism."
—WALTER ISAACSON, author of *Steve Jobs*

"*The Cost of Courage* is a mix of history, biography, and memoir which reads like a nerve-racking thriller."
—MARTIN PENGELLY, *The Guardian* (US)

"Charles Kaiser's *The Cost of Courage* combines a thorough and quite accessible history of Europe's six-year murderous paroxysm with a deftly told story."
—RONALD C. ROSBOTTOM, *Wall Street Journal*

"The Cost of Courage is good history, loving biography, excellent reporting. It turns out the cost of courage is beyond the means of most of us."
—EDMUND WHITE, author of *Inside a Pearl: My Years in Paris*

"'Ignorance is a formidable thing at a time like this,' André Boulloche wrote in a 1940 letter to his father. 'Whatever one decides to do, it's a descent into the unknown.' Kaiser places you in the middle of that 'unknown' with a mercurial intensity."
—MICHAEL UPCHURCH, *Seattle Times*

"Charles Kaiser deserves a Legion of Honor red ribbon for bringing to vibrant life the suspenseful, never-before-told true story of a family's courage, suffering, and ultimate triumph amid the existential dangers and challenges of the French Resistance. Chapeau!"
—HENDRIK HERTZBERG, author of *Politics: Observations & Arguments*

"Even now, almost three quarters of a century after the Second World War, the role played by the French Resistance in German-occupied and Vichy France is often overlooked. Charles Kaiser has not only unearthed the story of an extraordinary family, but set it against a world in which courage, selflessness, and resilience were of greater importance than personal survival and collaboration, however trivial. It makes for a fascinating book."
—CAROLINE MOOREHEAD, author of *A Train in Winter: An Extraordinary Story of Women, Friendship, and Resistance in Occupied France*

"Dramatic... *The Cost of Courage* admirably explores the dynamics of a painful reckoning."
—MATTHEW PRICE, *Newsday*

"A vivid family portrait that examines four siblings' heroic contribution to the French Resistance of World War II ... a riveting paean to unsung war heroes in occupied France."
— *Publishers Weekly*

"Remarkable ... a story of recovery and resilience ... *The Cost of Courage* is a poignant reminder that there are many untold stories of World War II, but that those who lived them will soon be gone."
— *BookPage*

"One legacy of the Nazi occupation of France was secrecy, a shield that long hid the heroism of resisters no less than the shame of collaborators. In this gripping true-life drama, Charles Kaiser reveals the long-buried story of one prosperous Parisian family that paid a high price for the bravery of its children. Until now, only through silence could they live with the painful cost of their courage."
—ALAN RIDING, author of *And the Show Went On: Cultural Life in Nazi-Occupied Paris*

THE COST OF COURAGE

THE
COST
OF
COURAGE

★ ★ ★

CHARLES KAISER

OTHER PRESS

NEW YORK

First softcover printing 2017
ISBN 978-1-59051-839-7

Production editor: Yvonne E. Cárdenas
Text designer: Julie Fry
This book was set in Galliard.

Opening photograph: German soldiers in their daily parade
down the Champs Elysées during the Occupation.

Closing photograph: Parisians celebrate the return
of Charles de Gaulle to Paris, August 26, 1944.

1 3 5 7 9 10 8 6 4 2

Library of Congress Cataloging-in-Publication Data

Kaiser, Charles.
The cost of courage / by Charles Kaiser.
pages   cm
ISBN 978-1-59051-614-0 (hardcover)—ISBN 978-1-59051-615-7 (e-book)
1. World War, 1939–1945—Underground movements—France—Biography.
2. France—History—German occupation, 1940–1945—Biography.
3. Audibert-Boulloche, Christiane. 4. Katlama, Jacqueline Boulloche, 1918–1994.
5. Boulloche, André. 6. Guerrillas—France—Biography. I. Title.
D802.F8K35 2015
940.53'440922 — dc23
[B]
2015008560

For Joe

&

For Christiane

naturellement

If mankind lasts because of the masses of people
for whom enduring has a higher value than acting,
its fate is determined by those who choose, act, and decide.
—Stanley Hoffmann, paraphrasing Paul Valéry

This is such a story of coincidences—or luck, or destiny.
—Eric Katlama

CONTENTS

Prologue

THE FIRST TIME I SAW PARIS, I FELL IN LOVE.

It was 1962, and I was eleven years old.

Her name was Christiane Boulloche-Audibert.

She was a beguiling thirty-eight-year-old brunette, the mother of four children, a campaigner for women's rights, and a hero of the French Resistance. She was strong and warm, percolating with life and love, and ten years younger than my own mother.

Her husband was Jean Audibert, a brilliant, high-spirited engineer with a belly-shaking laugh, a passion for fast cars, and a gigantic joie de vivre.

Jean had fought in the Free French Navy, and he witnessed the Normandy invasion from the sea—a good war, but not nearly as fraught as Christiane's. Their sons and daughters, each just a little bit older or younger than I was, were smart, political, precocious, and bilingual, which made them very much like everyone in my family.

I was the third of three sons. My father had just become a diplomat, and we were living in Dakar, in West Africa, where John F. Kennedy had made him his ambassador.

As a child, I was obsessed with the black-and-white images of World War II. To a young American who hadn't lived it, the war glowed with the romance of victorious history. When I met Christiane, the war was seventeen years behind her—an expanse that felt like a lifetime and a half to an eleven-year-old.

My uncle, Henry Kaiser, who moved in with Christiane and Jaqueline Boulloche at the end of 1944, when he was an American lieutenant stationed in Paris. He quickly learned everything that had happened to them while they were in the Resistance.

It did not occur to me that for Christiane, it felt more like the day before yesterday. And, as she admonished me twenty years later, to her it had never been romantic *at all*.

In the fall of 1944, just after the Liberation of Paris and the triumphant return of Charles de Gaulle, Christiane and her sister, Jacqueline, saw an ad in the newspaper seeking housing for U.S. Army officers. That ad created a bond that continues after seven decades.

My uncle, Henry Kaiser, was the lieutenant they took in, rent free, "in gratitude to the Allies," as Christiane always explained it. They installed him in an empty bedroom in their parents' sprawling apartment in the 16th arrondissement.

The most dramatic movie about the war was one I learned by heart but had seen only in my head. All of its images came from my uncle Henry, a charismatic storyteller with animated eyebrows and magnetic good looks. In an implausibly deep, tobacco-tinged baritone, he re-created the movie's layers of suspense for me, over and over again.

The film starred Christiane, Jacqueline, and their brother André, and its plot was exhilarating.

During the twelve months my uncle Henry lived in their apartment, he learned about almost everything the two sisters had endured during the four years the Nazis occupied Paris. There had been many narrow escapes. I reveled in their brave adventures and their incredible grace under pressure.

Years later, as the red wine flowed freely around the dining room table at their apartment in square Alboni in Paris, or the picnic table at their country house in Fontainebleau, where Christiane and Jean were joined almost every weekend by Christiane's extended family, Kaisers and Audiberts and Boulloches dissected everything from de Gaulle and Kennedy to *Jules and Jim*. But I don't remember anyone telling the stories I had heard from my uncle about the war. I may have assumed that it was not discussed because the grown-ups had already talked about it so often. But there was also the number tattooed on André's forearm—the first one I had ever seen—and André's grim demeanor, hinting at unvanquished demons.

Nevertheless, for a very long time, I did not realize that World War II was a taboo subject within Christiane's family. The ones who had been so magnificent in the Resistance never discussed their bravery with their own children.

They actually avoided anything that might remind them of those piercing years. Christiane had had many close friends in the Resistance, but after the war ended, she never saw any of them again. She blotted out that part of her life, as much as she could, after she and her sister decided that "it was necessary to turn the page."

I grew up inspired by the story of my remarkable French cousins, whom I thought of as a branch of my own extended family. Christiane was like a beacon. Her life proved that you could do the right thing, the most difficult thing, if you were determined to do it. Perhaps one wouldn't, but one always could—even under the most chilling circumstances.

But their own children were never really nourished by their parents' bravery. They admired it, they appreciated it, they were intimidated by it—but it never felt nurturing.

What they experienced most of the time was an amorphous black cloud, never fully visible, hovering somewhere above their parents' past.

It would take me five decades, including two and a half years living in France, to unravel the reasons for the heroes' silence.

The answer is *The Cost of Courage*.

Part I

One

IT IS a few minutes before four on a gray Paris afternoon when the black Citroën Traction Avant pulls up in front of a drab apartment building in the rue de la Santé on the Left Bank. The low-slung, front-wheel-drive Citroën is famous as the getaway car for French gangsters, but now it has acquired a more menacing pedigree: It is the official automobile of the German secret police.

Two Gestapo agents in black leather raincoats jump out onto the sidewalk. They pull a single prisoner, a short twenty-year-old Frenchman named Jacques, out of the car after them. The youth's nearly limp body broadcasts defeat, but he shows no obvious marks of a beating.

Two and a half miles away, a swastika sways in the wind atop the Eiffel Tower. It is the one thousand three hundred and eighth day of the Nazi Occupation of Paris. Dozens of other swastikas defile the French capital. Below them, street signs written in German punctuate the avenues with unfamiliar accents, humiliating Parisians at every carrefour.

The city's best restaurants, like Maxim's and La Tour d'Argent, are still flourishing, but now their customers are mostly German officers and their young French companions.

German street signs punctuate Paris avenues with unfamiliar accents, humiliating the French at every carrefour.

Starvation rations for the French have transformed apartment terraces into rabbit farms, as the urban dawn is heralded by roosters. More fortunate Parisians rely upon the generosity of country cousins, who have much more access to food.

Daytime Paris echoes to the sound of shoes with wooden soles clip-clopping down its narrow side streets and grand avenues. "If an old pair of shoes needs a new sole, you can't do anything about it, because there is no leather," said Pierre Mendès-France. "It's really very difficult to describe what life is like in a country where everyone spends all their time looking for things."

The nightly blackout means the only authorized light outdoors is the eternal flame under the Arc de Triomphe. Electricity and gas are both erratic. Heated apartments are a dimly remembered luxury from 1940. Only seven thousand cars circulate on the streets of the City of Light—many of them converted to run on wood. They are called *gazogènes*. Two million bicycles are the best way to get around aboveground. But a good bicycle can cost 10,000 francs—almost as much as a car did before the war. The only taxis are pedicabs pedaled by bicycle riders, or "taxis hippomobiles," pulled by a single horse. The fastest pedicab is propelled by veterans of the Tour de France.

Bicycle power also keeps the movie theaters open: four men pedaling a generator at thirteen miles an hour for six hours can produce enough reliable electricity for two full shows.

Jews and Communists are the first victims of the Occupation, but the dangers of resisting the Nazis are escalating for everyone at the beginning of 1944. Huge yellow posters plastered on the walls of the Métro proclaim that members of the Resistance are no longer the only ones facing German firing squads. A new edict ordains that their fathers, cousins, and in-laws will be executed as well.

And yet, in January, there is a new uncertainty bubbling underneath the humid winter air. All across Nazi Europe, the occupied are buoyed, and the occupiers menaced, by the event that everyone knows is coming, but no one knows exactly when or where: the Allied invasion of the Nazi-ruled continent.

Across the English Channel, massive numbers of British, American, Canadian, and French troops are gathering on the southern coast of England, where General Dwight Eisenhower is making the plans for a spectacular invasion of France. Thanks to a huge disinformation campaign, its location remains a secret six months before the assault begins. After four years of war, a cautiously optimistic Churchill believes that the biggest danger now facing the Allies is stalemate rather than defeat.

YESTERDAY, the young prisoner accompanying his German captors was a proud member of the French Resistance. Today, he is leading the German agents to the secret address he had sworn to conceal, so that they can arrest his boss, André Boulloche—a man he worships. If André is really there, the Germans have promised Jacques that he will be rewarded with his freedom.

But should he believe that?

Jacques is young looking, even for his age; especially today, he almost looks like a little boy. Deeply religious, he has joined the Resistance just three months earlier, after being recruited by his Sorbonne classmate, André's sister Christiane Boulloche. Christiane has no trouble persuading him to join their cause. When she asks him if he wants to work for her brother, the boy signs up immediately, without hesitation or reflection.

Jacques is the same age as Christiane, who turned twenty at the end of 1943. Christiane is smart, strong, and attractive. She also has a prominent nose that she thinks is unattractive. She worries, perhaps, that it makes her less glamorous looking than her older sister, Jacqueline, who has joined the Resistance with her.

Christiane's clandestine duties require her to ride her bicycle all over Paris, sometimes as much as sixty miles in a day. She picks up telegrams from secret drop-off points and decodes them, transports forbidden radio equipment, and sometimes smuggles guns through the capital, usually in a basket underneath eggs or vegetables.

All Boulloches share an innate sense of duty. When Christiane returns from the countryside after the armistice to find German soldiers goose-stepping through Paris, she is consumed by a single thought: "This is wrong." Before the war started, she had been certain: "We wouldn't just resist them, we would beat them. That's why the Occupation was a thunderclap."

Coupled with youthful fearlessness, and hero worship of her brother, that simple notion—"This is wrong"—propels her into the underground fight against the Germans. She is hypnotized and horrified by the Occupation. It swallows all of her attention.

The Boulloche sisters' very first act of resistance occurs when they are stopped by two German soldiers on avenue du Président Wilson. When the young Germans ask for directions to Place de la Concorde, the girls cheerfully dispatch them in the opposite direction.

There is no heat at her lycée, and Christiane wears gloves to turn the pages of the classroom dictionary. She is upset when one of her Jewish teachers loses her job, but she does not consider the plight of the Jews to be the most important thing. More than anything else, it is instinctive patriotism that pushes her into battle.

When the Germans are finally driven out of France, everyone's nightmare will be over.

Or so she believes.

As 1944 begins, her brother André François Roger Jacques Boulloche has been back in France for only four months. He is an engineer, a lawyer, and something of an adventurer. He and his sisters come from many generations of Catholic judges and prominent civil servants.

Iconoclasm is a leitmotiv in their family: Two Boulloche ancestors were members of the Cour de Cassation, the highest court in France, at the turn of the century. Both of them, remarkably, had been pro-Dreyfus: a belief that had made them strangers to their class—because they were partisans of the truth.

FOUR MONTHS EARLIER, in the second week of September 1943, André has taken off from England under a nearly full moon, with seven other passengers in a single-engine Westland Lysander. Many underground fighters are being parachuted into occupied France, but the plane carrying this group touches down on a secret airstrip in the Loire Valley, near Tours.

These landings are dangerous, because there is always a chance that the Germans have been tipped off. This one has been organized by Jean-François Clouet des Pesruches, who has arrived the night before from London, and it goes off without a hitch. Resistance members outline the tiny runway with flashlights pointed straight up at the sky. Foil extends over the tops of their torches, to make them invisible to everyone except the airplane circling above them.*

André is a handsome twenty-eight-year-old with brown hair and thick eyebrows that hover over a permanent glint in his eyes. Nearly six feet tall, he walks with a tempered, youthful swagger. Before the war, he was considered something of a dandy.

André has been ordered back to occupied France by Charles de Gaulle, to be the general's personal military delegate in Paris. Pseudonym, Armand, code name, Hypotenuse, André's charge from the renegade general† is to bring some order to the burgeoning Resistance movements now operating in eleven different departments in northern France.

During André's absence from France in 1943, there has been a dramatic increase in the membership of the Resistance. In the fall of 1942, the collaborationist Vichy government has taken one of its most unpopular steps, shipping off two hundred thousand Frenchmen to work in Germany. But with so many German soldiers fighting on so many different fronts, that isn't nearly enough slave labor to satisfy the voracious appetite of the Nazi war machine.

---

* Of the seven other men on the plane, one would be arrested eight days later, another was shot, and a third would die in a German concentration camp.

† A renegade is certainly what de Gaulle was considered when he left France in 1940, "when Vichy dominated the climate of opinion" and Germany's collaborators argued that to "remain in France was itself proof of honor," as Ian Ousby put it. "To go to Britain and accept British favors made the desertion far worse." (*Occupation*, p. 234) In 1942, the Institut d'étude des Questions Juives published posters depicting the general as a puppet of the Jews—"The Real Face of Free France." (Peschanski, *Collaboration and Resistance*, p. 173)

In February 1943, Vichy makes an even bigger blunder: It inaugurates the Service du Travail Obligatoire. The STO requires all Frenchmen between the ages of eighteen and twenty to work in Germany for two years. Faced with the prospect of forced deportation, thousands of these young men simply disappear into the mountains, where, by June, they have vastly increased the number of *Résistants*. They and their place of refuge both become known by a Corsican word for mountainous scrubland: Maquis.

As one historian put it, "The concept did not exist in January 1943; it was everywhere by June."

In September 1943, after a nine-month absence, André has returned to France on that Lysander. He is carrying 500,000 French francs in cash. Like everyone in the Resistance arriving from England, he also carries a cyanide pill in his pants pocket. It will stay there, always, unless he is arrested. When he touches it with his index finger, it feels like his insurance against torture. Or, perhaps, like his destiny. Either way, he knows he will swallow it if he is captured by the Germans. In this period, the average life of an agent is just four months before he is arrested.

A certain fatalism fuels André's fearlessness. "I never felt the slightest hesitation on his part," said his sister Christiane. But there is one irony that probably escapes him: The only thing that could impinge on his heroism might be his own survival.

NOW, IN JANUARY 1944, André is inside his secret headquarters on the top floor of an apartment building on the Left Bank. With him are his "right hand," Charles Gimpel, and his assistant, Geneviève.

Gimpel has arrived one month earlier, carrying another 100,000 francs from England. During his brief time in Paris, Gimpel has already set up an excellent liaison organization with the southern zone, and he has arranged for a large number of radios to be

The ranks of the Maquis jump sharply after the forced deportation of French workers to Germany. The poster says "French and German workers unite!"

brought up from the south to transmit messages from Paris to London.

Because their junior aide, Jacques, has been absent for only a day, neither Boulloche nor Gimpel suspects that he has been arrested.

They certainly haven't imagined that Jacques has violated the cardinal principle of the Resistance. No matter how badly you are tortured, you must try with all your might not to divulge anything important for forty-eight hours after your arrest.

After you have been missing for two days, your comrades are supposed to assume that you have been arrested, and relocate immediately to a new clandestine location. Only then, after the captured agent has endured two days of unimaginable affliction, is he authorized to tell everything he knows.

If the system works the way it's supposed to, by then his information should be largely worthless anyway.

Jacques adores his boss, André. But almost immediately after he is grabbed by the Germans, the young agent realizes that he will never be able to remain silent after his captors begin to beat him, or semidrown him, since a form of waterboarding is one of the Gestapo's favorite methods of torture.

He sees only one way out. In a small cell with another Frenchman, he whispers, "Strangle me so I won't talk! If you don't, I will tell them everything."

But the boy's cell mate is incapable of providing such grisly mercy.

Soon after that, the young Sorbonne student begins to give up all of his secrets, including the location of André's secret apartment.

Barely an hour later, Jacques is squeezing into the narrow elevator in the apartment house on rue de la Santé on the Left Bank with two Gestapo agents. When it reaches the fifth floor, the three men exit silently onto the landing.

Jacques has been brought here to perform the secret knock. The young Frenchman points at the door of the doomed apartment, then walks toward it to carry out the sordid duty: one sharp rap of his fist, a beat, then two softer knocks on the door.

Inside the apartment, André recognizes the cloak-and-dagger sequence and stands up from his desk to acknowledge it. When he opens the door, he sees two Germans in black leather raincoats pointing identical Walther PPK pistols at his heart.

"HANDS UP!" they shout.

"WHAT'S GOING ON?" André screams back.

Instinct propels the Frenchman toward the staircase as the Germans open fire. Two bullets strike the Resistance fighter just below the chest. One agent rushes toward him to check for a weapon as the other one storms the apartment to capture his confederates.

If he hadn't been wounded, André thinks, this part would have been easy: He would have swallowed the fatal pill right away. But now he is writhing on the floor, with blood spurting out of his stomach—and the cyanide never leaves his pocket.

For a very long time, he will wonder whether this was the right decision.

BACK ON THE SIDEWALK in front of the apartment building, the German agents shove André into the backseat of the black Citroën, next to Jacques. Then they speed away through the darkening streets of the Paris dusk.

Jacques is in a state of total collapse; he is weeping and howling and begging his boss for forgiveness. For the rest of his life, André will carry a hideous memory of these moments.

This part of André's trauma ends a few minutes later, when he is dumped off at La Salpêtrière, which the Germans have taken over as a prison hospital, where his wounds will be operated on.

For the moment, the Gestapo men prefer to keep André alive, because they won't be able to torture him unless they first make an effort to nurse him back to some semblance of health.

Despite his promised reward, Jacques is soon shipped off to Germany, where he will die in a concentration camp.

FOR JUST ONE HOUR, the Gestapo leaves the secret apartment unoccupied and unwatched.

Forty-five minutes have passed since the first German team has departed with André and his betrayer. Now Jacqueline, André's sister and confederate, is at the apartment's front door. She is there to make dinner for everyone, because—naturally—the women are expected to cook. (In prewar France women don't even have the right to vote—a privilege de Gaulle will finally bestow upon them after the Liberation.)

Jacqueline performs the secret knock. Hearing no answer, she lets herself in with her own key. At first, the empty apartment doesn't make her anxious. Gradually, she senses a certain disarray, but if there is blood on the floor of the hallway outside, she hasn't noticed it. She walks into the kitchen and begins to peel some potatoes. Then she strikes a match to light a fire beneath them.

Suddenly, she realizes she is missing a vital part of the meal. One immutable fact of Parisian life has not been altered by the Nazi Occupation: Frenchmen still require wine with their dinner. So Jacqueline leaves the potatoes simmering on the stove and walks out the front door.

She skips the elevator and bounces down five flights of stairs to the street. Then she walks around the corner to the neighborhood *épicerie*. There she buys a few more groceries and the vital bottle of *vin rouge*.

She will always remember this as the best-timed shopping trip of her life. When she returns to the apartment house, she notices something out front that had not been there four minutes earlier: another black Citroën Traction Avant.

Jacqueline tiptoes into the apartment house. The passengers from the car out front have just closed the door of the elevator behind them. Now it is only one floor above her. Her body stiffens as she watches the wooden cabin rise slowly through the narrow open shaft. Second, third, fourth...finally, it stops at the fifth floor.

Where her potatoes are cooking.

Later, she will wonder what the Gestapo men think when they discover her potatoes on top of the kitchen stove.

But right now, she is already sprinting toward the Métro.

I have to save my sister. That is her only thought.

Most of the time, Jacqueline and Christiane don't tell each other where they will be during the day. But today Jacqueline happens to know that her little sister has taken the afternoon off to listen to some Bach at the Palais de Chaillot.

But the concert hall is on the Right Bank, at Trocadéro—fourteen Métro stops away.

Jacqueline sprints eight hundred yards to the Métro Glacière. She is pretty enough to turn heads anytime, but the sight of her racing through the Métro, her arms full of groceries, makes her uncomfortably conspicuous.

She is out of breath when she reaches the platform—just as the train DIRECTION ÉTOILE pulls into the station.

The train's doors close behind her; then the trip seems to take forever: Denfert-Rochereau, Raspail, Montparnasse, Pasteur—still seven more stops to go.

Jacqueline is hardly religious, but she is praying anyway—praying that she will somehow be able to intercept her sister before she returns to the secret apartment, where the second wave of the Gestapo is now waiting to capture both of them.

But can she possibly get there before the concert ends?

And even if she arrives before the final notes, how will she ever be able to pick her sister out of the crowd? She has no idea where Christiane is sitting, and the Palais de Chaillot is one of the largest concert halls in Paris.

Now the train is rumbling out of its underground tunnel to travel over the Seine, to Passy. Just one more stop to go. Then it dives back underground to pull into Trocadéro.

Jacqueline knows every inch of this station: It is the one she grew up with, the one closest to her parents' apartment.

She runs toward the exit for Palais de Chaillot. Now she is dashing past the statues of Apollo and Hercules, still carrying her groceries. As she enters the lobby, she can just make out the sounds of Bach still seeping out of the hall.

I haven't missed the end of the performance!

But how will she ever be able to snatch Christiane out of the crowd?

Happy accident? Or intuition?

To the end of her life, Christiane will never be able to answer that question. Before today, she has never left a concert early. But this afternoon, something suddenly makes her stand up to leave the hall — *ten minutes before the concert has ended!*

When she reaches the empty lobby, she walks straight into the arms of her frantic sister.

"We can't leave by the front door!"

That is Jacqueline's only greeting: She thinks that the Gestapo may have followed her here.

Deciding that they have nothing left to lose, they approach the box office.

Jacqueline tells the ticket seller that she needs to speak to the manager. He may betray them, but they see no other choice.

When the manager appears, Jacqueline exclaims, "We can't leave by the front door." Nothing more.

The manager looks at her silently, his face revealing nothing.

Now he will save them ... or turn them over to the Germans.

He turns around and walks out of the box office.

Then he leads the terrified (but still very attractive) young women to the stage door.

Jacqueline repays his kindness by thrusting the groceries and the bottle of wine she has carried halfway across Paris into his hands. They will only slow them down now anyway. Outside, they scour the street for Gestapo men, but no one looks particularly menacing.

BACK ON THE MÉTRO PLATFORM at Trocadéro, Christiane tells her sister she has another problem: She is carrying dozens of coded telegrams in her purse, having spent most of the day retrieving them from secret drop-off points all across Paris. Just three days earlier, André had finally managed to open a direct communications link to his handlers in London.

Christiane never considers throwing away the incriminating cables; she must find somewhere to hide them. She settles on the apartment building of a sympathetic cousin, who lives on avenue Marceau. When they get there, Christiane runs inside and shoves the telegrams under the carpet in the elevator cabin. Without telling her cousin, of course. Later, she will retrieve them, after the immediate danger has passed.

By now it is after eight o'clock, and the sisters still have no idea whether André, or anyone else, has been arrested. They decide to return to the Glacière Métro stop. They think they might catch their brother before he returns to the secret apartment, so they plant themselves at the station's two exits.

Then they stay there until the last Métro.

Exhausted and depressed, they finally return to their parents' apartment across the Seine, which is where they are still living, right next to the Palais de Chaillot. Fortunately, their parents are asleep, so they don't have to decide whether they should tell them anything right away about what has happened.

Two

Dignity is incompatible with submission ... I am a man who feels the necessity of engagement.
—André Boulloche

THE NEXT DAY, the Boulloche sisters are in shock. They still don't know the fate of their brother and the rest of their confederates. They don't even know if any of them was in the secret apartment when the Gestapo arrived, but they do know that André, his right-hand man, Charles Gimpel, his assistant, Geneviève, and Jacques may now be under arrest.

And if the Germans have taken them, today they are almost certainly being tortured.

In any case, the sisters must assume the worst and immediately evacuate all the clandestine locations known to their brother and his assistants. After two days, their co-conspirators are supposed to have found new hiding places, and the knowledge of the prisoners should be useless to their captors.

In the afternoon, the sisters finally learn the dreadful news from Marie-Hélène Lefaucheux, a friend who is on good terms with the chaplain at La Salpêtrière. Marie-Hélène suspects that the chaplain is playing a double game with the Germans, but his information is usually reliable.

The chaplain tells Marie-Hélène that André, Gimpel, and Geneviève have all been arrested, and that André has been shot. Marie-Hélène immediately relays the terrible news to André's sisters.

In a family full of secrets since the war began, the biggest secret of all is the fact that André has been back in Paris since September. For four months, the two girls have been spending their days with André, and sleeping at their parents' home at night, without ever telling their mother and father that their youngest son has returned—because that is what André has ordered them to do.

But their brother has also said that if he is arrested, they must tell their parents immediately, because his capture could mean they would now be in danger.

So now they finally reveal that André has been in Paris for four months, working for the Resistance. And today he is in a prison hospital, with a gunshot wound in his stomach.

Their parents are horrified.

But their mother also says this about her children's decision to fight the Germans: "That's what I would have done."

Perhaps she means that is how she would have acted if she had been sixteen or twenty when the war began, instead of fifty-one.

The last time the whole family had been together was a dinner at the parents' apartment in the spring of 1942. That evening, twenty months earlier, Christiane had felt terrible anxiety when she said goodbye to her two brothers.

When will I see them again? she wondered.

And even earlier, during the German invasion of France in 1940, her father had thought that his whole family would never be reunited in the same room again.

For the next three weeks, Christiane and Jacqueline go to the apartment of a sympathetic woman friend who lives on boulevard Saint Michel. Her husband is a mining engineer who is away, working in the north most of the time. When he returns home one weekend, he makes it clear that he completely disapproves of what

the two sisters are doing, because he's not in the Resistance himself. But he does not betray them.

After three weeks at their friend's house, they briefly return
home to their parents' sprawling apartment, because they think the
danger has disappeared. "In general," Christiane recalled, "things
happened very quickly." Then they decamp permanently to a series
of secret apartments on rue de Lille and avenue Mozart.

Her parents don't feel that they are in danger, partly because
they assume the Gestapo has been unable to learn their son's
real identity.

Three

I think I was marked by the debacle of 1940 for my whole life. I saw all the egotism and all the cowardice. I had an unreasoning patriotism. For me war is fought to the end—to the death.

—André Boulloche

W HEN WORLD WAR II BEGINS with Hitler's invasion of Poland, on September 1, 1939, André and his older brother, Robert, have already been mobilized to serve in the French Army. Christiane is just fifteen years old. She has spent the summer across the channel in Kent, living with an English family so that she can learn the language. Before she leaves France, her father warns her that she may have to come home early. A couple of days before the war begins, he telephones her in England to summon her back to Paris.

Remembering how the capital was bombarded during World War I, Jacques Boulloche decides to move his wife and daughters to their country house in Fontainebleau, forty-five miles south of Paris. The fifty-one-year-old father is still in his government job in the capital, which puts him in charge of all French highways. Since 1937 he has been *inspecteur général des ponts et chaussées* and *directeur des routes du ministère des travaux publics*.

IN 1939, the catastrophe of the First World War is still a scorching memory for every French person over twenty-five. More than 1,357,000 French soldiers died in the "Great War"—and a staggering 76 percent of the 8,410,000 Frenchmen who fought it were killed, wounded, taken prisoner, or missing in action.

That was more than one-fifth of the population of France.

Those casualties transform postwar France into a nation of old people and cripples and women without men in the 1920s. Every surviving municipality has a monument commemorating its losses in the Great War, but scores of villages are wiped out altogether, after a whole generation of their young men has been annihilated.

The worst legacy of World War I is the obsequious approach Britain and France adopt toward Hitler's Germany. Between 1935 and 1939, British and French leaders bungle every opportunity to rein in the Nazi leader before another all-out war becomes inevitable.

In 1935, a year after promoting himself to the new office of Führer, Hitler abrogates the military provisions of the Treaty of Versailles and begins Germany's massive rearmament program. In March 1936, he violates the treaty again, by reoccupying the Rhineland on France's border.

At that moment, Britain and France could easily have rolled over Hitler's troops, but both countries are paralyzed—still reeling from the Great Depression, and their losses in World War I.

The depth of antiwar feeling in France and Britain is suggested by the reaction of a clergyman in Liverpool after Germany reoccupies the Rhineland. When the British government declares that the Rhineland should be occupied by an international force until the dispute with Hitler can be resolved, the canon gives orders that no more prayers are to be offered up for the British government. "To continue an enforcement of the spirit of inequality upon Germany is a proposal unworthy of our creed and of our country," the canon thunders. "To renew an occupation of their homeland is a proposal monstrous and unjustifiable; it is an unnecessary degradation of the soul of a great people. To add to it that we shall do it again at the dictation of France is to lend aid to malice and to surrender right to vengeance. We cannot pray a blessing upon such proposals."*

The views of a large portion of the British upper classes are reflected in a repellant ode to Hitler that appears in *Homes & Gardens* in November 1938. The article oozes admiration for the Führer's modesty: His gardeners, his chauffeur, and his pilot are "not so much servants as loyal friends." Air-Marshall Göring is a delightful "bon viveur" [*sic*] and the Führer himself is a "droll raconteur" who prefers the "society of brilliant foreigners, especially painters, singers and musicians."

The dread of anything that might provoke a new world war is equally powerful in France. In 1938, the famous anti-Semitic novelist Louis-Ferdinand Céline predicts that a new conflict with Germany will bring twenty-five million casualties, and the "end of the breed...We'll disappear body and soul from this place like the Gauls."

These overwhelming feelings of fearfulness culminate in the tragedy of Munich. The British and French prime ministers, Neville Chamberlain and Édouard Daladier, meet there in September 1938. They agree to the dismemberment of Czechoslovakia and give Hitler the right to occupy the Sudetenland and all of its fortifications.

When Chamberlain returns to London, he is hailed as a conquering hero when he calls the accord "peace for our time."

The *Manchester Guardian* is one of the very few British newspapers to identify the agreement's real significance: "Politically Czecho-Slovakia is rendered helpless, with all that that means to

---

* The British diplomat and politician Duff Cooper, who quotes this passage in his autobiography, points out that by this time "anybody who read the newspapers" was already aware "not only of the hideous persecution of the Jews which [Hitler] had initiated, but also of the blood-bath of June 1934 [Night of the Long Knives] in which he had slaughtered without trial so many of his own closest associates." (*Old Men Forget*, p. 197)

the balance of forces in Eastern Europe, and Hitler will be able to advance again, when he chooses, with greatly increased power."

Four days after the agreement is announced, Winston Churchill rises in the House of Commons to give one of the most brutal and prescient speeches of his life. After "immense exertions," said Churchill, the most that Chamberlain had "been able to gain for Czechoslovakia in the matters which were in dispute has been that the German dictator, instead of snatching the victuals from the table, has been content to have them served to him course by course." Churchill continued:

All is over. Silent, mournful, abandoned, broken, Czechoslovakia recedes into the darkness... Not only are they politically mutilated, but, economically and financially, they are in complete confusion. Their banking, their railway arrangements, are severed and broken, their industries are curtailed, and the movement of their population is most cruel...

When I think of the fair hopes of a long peace which still lay before Europe at the beginning of 1933 when Herr Hitler first obtained power, and of all the opportunities of arresting the growth of the Nazi power which have been thrown away, when I think of the immense combinations and resources which have been neglected or squandered, I cannot believe that a parallel exists in the whole course of history...

We are in the presence of a disaster of the first magnitude which has befallen Great Britain and France. Do not let us blind ourselves to that. It must now be accepted that all the countries of Central and Eastern Europe will make the best terms they can with the triumphant Nazi power. The system of alliances in Central Europe upon which France has relied for her safety has been swept away, and I can see no means by which it can be reconstituted. The road down the Danube Valley to the Black Sea, the road which leads as far as Turkey, has been opened...

Many people, no doubt, honestly believe that they are only giving away the interests of Czechoslovakia, whereas I fear we shall find that

*we have deeply compromised, and perhaps fatally endangered, the
safety and even the independence of Great Britain and France . . .*

*Do not suppose that this is the end. This is only the beginning of
the reckoning. This is only the first sip, the first foretaste of a bitter
cup which will be proffered to us year by year unless by a supreme
recovery of moral health and martial vigour, we arise again and
take our stand for freedom as in the olden time.*

THE CONVICTIONS EXPRESSED in the home where the Boulloche
children grow up are closer to Churchill's than to Chamberlain's.
The most important intellectual influence on the Boulloche brothers and sisters is their father, Jacques, who was born in 1888.

Jacques's reputation for resilience begins when he is still a child.
One August night, eleven-year-old Jacques boards a train in Paris
with his family to travel to the fashionable beach at Dinard, 250
miles to the west on the Côte d'Émeraude in Brittany.

At one o'clock in the morning, he pushes on an unlocked door
and tumbles off the train into the summer darkness. Miraculously,
he lands in a hedge, which cushions him from serious injury.

Jacques brushes himself off and walks along the tracks for fifteen minutes, until he stops to knock on a stranger's door to
request assistance. The next day, his terrified mother is immensely
relieved when she learns that her son is alive and unharmed.
Partly because of the prominence of the boy's father, who sat on
the Cour de Cassation, Paris newspapers duly report the event for
posterity.

As the family patriarch, Jacques sees the Second World War
coming much sooner than most of his contemporaries. He was
brought up by a German governess, he speaks German fluently,
and his highway work takes him to Germany frequently during the
1930s. As early as 1937, he is convinced that another war with Germany is inevitable—and he is pessimistic about the outcome.

One of his favorite sayings is well known to his children: "One German is okay. Five or six? That's a catastrophe!" (Churchill had his own version of this sentiment: "A Hun alive is a war in prospect," he told visitors to Chequers in October 1940.)

Jacques won the Legion of Honor for his service as an officer, fighting the Germans for four years during World War I. Often he was so tired that he fell asleep in the saddle of his horse.

At three o'clock in the afternoon of November 11, 1918, the day the armistice was declared, he celebrated with a letter to his mother: "The great day has finally arrived—the day of glory and happiness. Everyone is more or less crazy with joy!" Four days later, he joked in a letter to his father that he is about to get Occupation duty in "Bochie"—the land of the *Boches*, an epithet for the hated Germans.*

Jacques returned home for leave from time to time, and two of his children, André and Jacqueline, were born while he was at the front. Jacques almost never speaks about his wartime experiences, except to say that he loathes all career military officers. He regards them as "imbeciles," and he is proud that he knows of none among his ancestors.

The Boulloches are upper-middle-class Catholics, fierce republicans whose forebears have been prominent lawyers, judges, and civil servants in Paris since the revolution. The family traces its ancestors back to Normandy in the sixteenth century. They migrated there from Scotland, where they had been "Bullocks" or "Bullochs."

Whenever the Boulloches stand up for what they believe in, they often stand apart. The Boulloche children are all mindful of their family's dual pedigrees of patriotism and iconoclasm.

---

* At the end of World War I, Canadian general Andrew McNaughton said of the Germans, "We have them on the run. That means we will have to do it over again in another 25 years." Or, as satirical songwriter Tom Lehrer put it in 1965, "We taught them a lesson in 1918—and they've hardly bothered us since then."

Their grandfather was the chief magistrate of France, the president of France's highest court, the Cour de Cassation. His brother, their great-uncle, was his colleague on the same supreme court. After the Jewish army officer named Alfred Dreyfus was convicted of treason in 1894, these two Boulloche judges maintained the tradition of the Boulloche "exception," by insisting that Dreyfus was innocent.

While most of the haute bourgeoisie joined in the anti-Semitic frenzy that produced the Dreyfus prosecution, these Boulloches made themselves traitors to their class by defending the Jewish officer. Characteristically, there was no self-congratulation when Dreyfus was finally exonerated. "We triumph," declared the chief judge, "but in such sad company."

THE CHILDREN OF JACQUES AND HÉLÉNE BOULLOCHE enjoy an unusual amount of freedom. A young friend often at their dinner table remembered Jacques as a "calm and liberal man," while his wife was "a lover of fine music."

Unlike their cousins, who go to Catholic schools, Robert, André, Jacqueline, and Christiane all attend public schools. Their parents encourage intellectual independence, and outsiders are startled by the outspokenness of the children, whose exuberance is sometimes more than their charming mother can control.

When she is still very young, Christiane wonders out loud, "How will we feel if we find ourselves in front of Buddha instead of God when we get to heaven?" It is the sort of question that delights her parents.

André excels at mathematics at the Lycée Janson de Sailly in Paris, and he is one of the only students who can hold his own discussing philosophy with the teacher after class.

Precocious but unpretentious, his contemporaries give him the nickname "Boull." He wins most of the academic prizes, while keeping his classmates amused with risqué magazines like *La Vie Parisienne*, illustrated with photos of scantily clad young women. Boull even provides forbidden alcohol, the perfect accompaniment for the magazines. Trains, planes, and automobiles are some of his other passions.

As a teenager, André is struck by the power of money to corrupt, and the young idealist even dreams of returning France to a barter system. At eighteen, he follows his father's footsteps into the French elite, when he is admitted to the country's most celebrated *grande école*, the Ecole polytechnique, or l'X, and, again, like his father, becomes an engineer.

After that he spends two years at Ecole Nationale des Ponts et Chaussées (National School of Bridges and Highways), while simultaneously studying for a law degree—because every Boulloche male is still expected to continue centuries of family tradition by studying the law, whether or not he plans to practice it.

THE BOULLOCHES are "social Catholics," but they are not particularly observant. They blend a soft anticlericalism with a sharp republican spirit. No priest ever joins them at the dinner table, and by her seventeenth birthday, Christiane is certain there is no God.

The children grow up surrounded by books and music. Their parents' favorite writers are Proust and Rimbaud, literary tastes that make them slightly avant-garde. Jacques plays the piano, Hélène is an accomplished violinist, and each of the children also plays an instrument.

Jacques is kind but serious—almost austere—while Hélène is more playful. Christiane thinks her mother has only one real passion in life: her husband.

When Christiane is just sixteen months old, her parents leave for a long trip to Indochina, depositing their children with their very stern grandparents. It is a dramatic and difficult change for

College chums: André Boulloche is on top smoking a pipe. On his left, André Rondenay steadies himself by holding on to a lamp. Everyone is wearing the uniform of L'Ecole polytechnique. Several years later, Rondenay succeeded Boulloche as de Gaulle's military delegate in Paris, after Boulloche was arrested.

the older children, who are suddenly forbidden to laugh at the dinner table.

In a letter home during their stay in colonial Saigon, Hélène jokes to her ten-year-old son André that she is disappointed when a Chinese man hosting a party is not smoking opium when she meets him, although "he did have his pipe next to him!"

When the parents finally return, Hélène is furious when she hears Christiane calling her nurse "Mother."

Their father is famous for his genuineness, and his children inherit that trait, together with a profound sense of duty. "It was not taught," Christiane remembered. "It was implicit. There was no discussion at all. But it was in the air—that's for sure."

THE FINAL FRANCO-BRITISH BLUNDER in the run-up to World War II is the failure of the two countries to forge an alliance with the Soviet Union against Hitler. After Britain and France bungle the Russians' feelers, Hitler seizes the opportunity to secure his eastern flank. On August 23, 1939, archenemies Hitler and Stalin astound the world by announcing a nonaggression pact.

Ten-year-old Stanley Hoffmann, who would grow up to become a brilliant political scientist and an expert in French history, was vacationing in the Alps with his mother when news of the pact arrived in the tiny village where they were staying. "It was as if the plague had suddenly struck," Hoffmann remembered. Even at his young age, he "understood at once that this meant war—that Hitler had free hands for his next aggression and that Britain and France could no longer weasel out."

The West considers Stalin's decision to make temporary peace with Hitler typical "Communist duplicity." But as the historian James Stokesbury points out, for Stalin it was a "simple either-or proposition": "Either he could ally with Britain and France, in which case there would be a war, a war that Russia was expected to fight while Britain and France sat and waited it out, after which, when Germany and Russia had destroyed each other, France and Britain would move in and pick up the pieces; or, he could make a deal with Hitler, they could divide Poland between them, Hitler would (probably) turn west, and Germany, France, and Britain would fight it out, after which Stalin would move in and pick up the pieces."

The secret protocol of the Hitler-Stalin pact—widely rumored but publicly denied—divides Finland, Estonia, Latvia, Lithuania, Poland, and Romania into separate spheres of influence for Germany and the Soviet Union. Freed of fears of a battle with the Communist monolith, Hitler invades Poland nine days later, on September 1. Blackout conditions begin in London the same day. On September 3, Britain and France both declare war on Germany. The *New York Times* proclaims, "Germans Rush Gayly to Arms, Believing Poland Will Be Crushed in 10 Days."

The prediction is nearly correct. By the end of the month, Germany has conquered Poland, and Hitler divides up the country with Stalin. Organized Polish resistance is over by the first week in October.

Four

*Throughout the '30's, France and Britain had been slow, often
indecisive and hopelessly outmaneuvered by Hitler's devilish strokes.
The ponderous bourgeois gentlemen in heavy suits and hats
who led the Western democracies didn't have a chance against
the cunning gangster.*
—Stanley Hoffmann

THE CONCLUSION of the German campaign in Poland in
the fall of 1939 marks the beginning of the Phony War. This
period of relative calm will last seven months on most of the European continent. Churchill calls it the Twilight War. In France it is
drôle de guerre (funny or strange war); in Germany, *Sitzkrieg* (sitting war—a pun on *Blitzkrieg*.)

While Russia invades Finland at the end of November, and Germany and Britain engage in occasional skirmishes at sea, French
and German troops remain mostly silent, as they gape "at each
other from behind their rising fortifications" on France's eastern
front, throughout the winter of 1939.

After her father moves his wife and daughters out of Paris in
the fall of 1939, Christiane Boulloche embraces her new life at
the lycée in Fontainebleau. Her classes are smaller than they were
in the capital, and she excels with very little effort. Her parents
agree to board a French officer who teaches at the artillery school

in Fontainebleau, and his twenty-something students are frequent guests at the Boulloche dinner table—a beguiling circumstance for a fifteen-year-old girl.

At the end of 1939, most French officers still believe in France's military superiority, and that is the opinion Christiane hears at her dinner table. Like most French people (except de Gaulle), the Boulloches still hope that they will be protected by the Maginot Line, the massive fortifications France has built above- and below-ground along the German border between 1929 and 1940. They also think that when the war finally comes to France, it will be a short one.

Christiane enjoys the period before Germany invades France. It feels like a "new and exciting adventure." But she is jealous of her brothers, because they are actually able to *do something*, by being in the army. Predictably, her brother André is dissatisfied with his calm life as a lieutenant with the 6th *régiment du génie* (engineers) on the eastern front. Starving for action, he snares a transfer to the aviation officers' school in Dinard.

As the Phony War continues through the winter, more and more children are evacuated from the northeast corner of France in anticipation of the expected invasion. While their parents stay behind to work, the children are relocated to places like the golf club in Fontainebleau. The children's presence, and a nightly blackout, are the only things Christiane experiences that make the possibility of an actual war seem real. Jacqueline, who has recently graduated from Sciences Po (the institute of Political Science in Paris), spends her days working with the refugee children from the north.

The eight-month-long lull between the time Britain and France declare war on Germany and the moment when full-scale hostilities begin does not work to the Allies' advantage. After Hitler and Stalin announce their nonaggression pact in August 1939, the French Communists take their cue from Moscow and end their active opposition to the Nazis. They denounce the war as "an imperialist and capitalist crime against democracy."

Meanwhile, morale plunges among French troops, who are undermined by shortages of socks and blankets, as well as simple inaction. Even the weather conspires against the French: The winter of 1939–1940 is the coldest France has shivered through since 1893.

In November 1939, Jean-Paul Sartre writes in his diary that the men who were mobilized with him were "raring to go at the outset," but three months later they are "dying of boredom."

WHEN THE GERMANS finally storm into Holland and Belgium on May 10, 1940, the impact is felt almost instantly in Fontainebleau. Christiane experiences the effects of the crushing advance of the enemy, as thousands flee in front of the German blitzkrieg, traveling in horse-drawn carriages and cars overflowing with exhausted women and children.

No one has expected the Germans to roll over the French Army so quickly, not even Germany's own generals. In England, Neville Chamberlain resigns as prime minister, as his dream of "peace for our time" evaporates, and the king summons Winston Churchill to Buckingham Palace to form a new government to fight the war.

Churchill is appalled by the speed of the German onslaught. The new prime minister learns that German tanks are advancing at least thirty miles a day through the French countryside, passing through "scores of towns and hundreds of villages without the slightest opposition, their officers looking out of the open cupolas and waving jauntily to the inhabitants. Eyewitnesses [speak] of crowds of French prisoners marching along with them, many still carrying their rifles, which were from time to time collected and broken under the tanks... The whole German movement was proceeding along the main roads, which at no point seemed to be blocked."

With hundreds of thousands of refugees now surging southward, Jacques Boulloche once again tries to move his wife and daughters out of danger. This time he sends them to an aunt's house in Perros-Guirec, in Brittany, in the northwest corner of France, far from the Germans' invasion route. Christiane is miserable because she has a new puppy that she isn't allowed to bring with her, and she never sees her dog again.

But when the three Boulloche women flee Fontainebleau at the end of May, they are much more fortunate than the refugees who had been housed at the golf club. The cars carrying those children are bombarded from the air, and scores of them are killed.

As France's army is being pulverized at the end of May, a gigantic crowd gathers in front of Sacré-Coeur on the hill above Paris to pray for victory. At the end of the emergency service, fifty thousand voices belt out "The Marseillaise." More than six million French citizens have already abandoned their homes.

Across the channel in London, a thirty-year-old foreign correspondent named James Reston writes in the *New York Times* that a German invasion of the British Isles is now considered nearly certain.* Looking down from a plane, the writer-pilot Antoine de Saint-Exupéry observes that the mobs of refugees below look like a massive anthill, kicked by a giant.

ON JUNE 3, more than one hundred German bombers attack Paris. The French authorities claim they have shot down twenty-five of the planes, but the bombardment kills more than 250 Parisians and wounds 600 more.

---

* In the underground bedroom Churchill slept in during much of the war, his bed faced a map that highlighted all the possible invasion points of the British Isles.

"This is what we dreaded for so long, and what we hoped might never happen," the *New York Times* declares on its editorial page the next day.

It seems worse, somehow, than any of the other crimes perpetrated by Germany in this war...Great cities...are more than aggregations of men, women and children. They are the treasure-houses of the Western spirit. Whoever strikes at them strikes at all that man has built through ages of sacrifice and suffering...

Free men will not endure these things without a new resolve to destroy the forces of evil that have sent the German bombers on their errand. The great columns of smoke and flame that rose above Paris yesterday...were also the first fires of a wrath such as our world has never known. If this kind of fiendishness continues, if Paris and London are to become shambles of ruined buildings and murdered civilians, the fires of hate will not be quenched in our time. The anger of civilized peoples will burn so fiercely that it will consume the hateful German system which has loosed these horrors upon the world.

The *Times* is almost alone in its prescience. Certainly no one in France is optimistic about the eventual defeat of the Nazis the day after the bombardment of Paris.

SIX DAYS LATER, the French government prepares to evacuate Paris. Jacques Boulloche, the director of the national bureau of highways, is ordered to leave the capital for Royan, three hundred miles to the south on the western coast of France. That evening he heads for his country house in Fontainebleau, but his car breaks down on the way, and he doesn't get there until four o'clock in the morning.

The next day he opens his fountain pen to write a letter to his wife:

The Boulloche country house in Fontainebleau, where Jacques Boulloche retreated as the Germans advanced on Paris in 1940.

I can't describe my feelings when I got here, considering all that we've had to abandon. And yet, we are among the lucky ones... The peace of the garden and the fragrant smells make the unfolding tragedy seem like nothing more than a bad dream...

The same day as Jacques writes to his wife, Norway surrenders to the Nazis, and Italy declares war on Britain and France.

The capital Jacques has left behind is filled with smoke from burning archives and incendiary bombs. On June 10, the French government declares Paris an open city, meaning it will no longer be defended—after the Germans have already passed through the city's gates. There are twenty thousand people jammed outside the doors of Gare d'Austerlitz, trying to force themselves onto trains leaving the capital.

The *New York Times* reports on June 13, "The German guns are battering at the hearts and minds of all of us who think of Paris when we try to define what we mean by civilization... Of all cities it expresses best the aspiration of the human spirit."

Paris falls the next day, on June 14. By then, its population of three million has shrunk to eight hundred thousand.

Jacques Boulloche is distraught. His boys are at the front, and his wife and daughters are hundreds of miles away in Brittany. He is terrified that he may never see any of them again. He and his wife have an exceptionally strong bond. They are so close, their children sometimes complain that it's hard to find any room for themselves in between them.

On the afternoon of June 15, Jacques sits down at the desk in his room at the Grand Hôtel de Paris in Royan to write another anguished letter to his wife:

My Beloved,

Everything is finished. Will we ever see each other again?

In case you are reunited someday with the children, I have included a message for them in this letter.

I don't know what to say, except that I adore you, and I can't stop thinking about you. Stay calm, courageous and proud.

I love you, and I still hope that someday we will be reunited.

Jacques

And this is what he writes to his children:

If I never see you again, know that my last thoughts will have been about the four of you.

I hope you will once again see a free and joyous France.

I love you with all my heart.

Your Father

Jacques

Samedi soir, 15 Juin,
Royan, Grand Hôtel de Paris.

Mon aimée,

Tout est fini - Nous reverrons nous?

Si les enfants sont un jour réunis auprès de toi, je mets dans cette lettre un mot pour eux -

Je ne sais que te dire, si ce que je t'aime infiniment, et que ma pensée ne te quitte pas. Reste calme, courageuse, et fière -

Je t'embrasse, et j'espère quand même que nous serons un jour réunis

Jacques.

In a letter to his family, Jacques Boulloche pours out his fears about what the German invasion will bring.

Five

Had all of us in France meekly, lawfully carried out the orders of
the German master, no Frenchman could have ever looked another
man in the face. Such submission would have saved the lives of many—
some very dear to me—but France would have lost its soul.
—Commandant le Baron de Vomécourt

ALTHOUGH the German campaign in France lasts less than six weeks before the armistice is declared, the French still suffer enormous casualties. There are ninety thousand French soldiers killed and two hundred thousand wounded. Another two million soldiers are taken prisoner, and a million and a half of them are sent to Germany. These French prisoners will remain on the far side of the Rhine until the war ends, almost exactly five years later.

The same day Jacques Boulloche sends his farewell letters to his family, President Roosevelt rejects the Allies' plea to America to enter the war against Germany at once. Meanwhile, French prime minister Paul Reynaud, who had been an early opponent of appeasement, informs the British that he intends to split his government and lead half of it abroad.

On June 16, Churchill makes a dramatic gesture to try to convince the French to continue the fight against the Germans. The new British prime minister proposes the merger of France and Britain into an "indissoluble" Franco-British union. A single War

Cabinet will direct the affairs of the new nation, to "concentrate its whole energy against the power of the enemy, no matter where the battle may be."

But defeatist members of the French cabinet recoil at the idea of a union with their historic rival. They predict that within three weeks, England will "have her neck wrung like a chicken."* A French minister of state even declares, "Better to be a Nazi province. At least we know what that means."

Marshal Henri-Philippe Pétain, the eighty-four-year-old hero of World War I whom Reynaud had summoned out of retirement a few weeks earlier, leads the fight against a merger with Britain. When Reynaud is unable to convince his colleagues to embrace Churchill's bold idea, the French prime minster resigns, and Pétain succeeds him as the head of the French government.

Charles de Gaulle had been wounded three times during World War I, and he spent almost three years in German prison camps. Since the 1930s, he has been a voice in the wilderness, warning of France's unreadiness to confront the Germans. He has published a book advocating the mechanization of the army and the offensive deployment of tanks, but his fellow officers ignore his advice. A prescient Reynaud has been the only politician to support him.

De Gaulle has fought as long as he can to keep France in the war. But after Pétain becomes France's new leader, de Gaulle finally slips away from his office in Bordeaux, on June 17, to be driven to a nearby airfield.

At nine A.M., he takes off for England in a plane provided by the British. Churchill observed that the solitary French general "carried with him in the small airplane the honor of France."†

---

* This led, of course, to Churchill's famous riposte eighteen months later: "Some chicken. Some neck!"

† Later, de Gaulle said of France's collapse in 1940, "We staggered, it is true. But was this not, first of all, a result of all the blood we had shed twenty years before in others' defense as much as our own?" (*Complete Wartime Memoirs*, p. 461).

That evening, Marshal Pétain goes on the radio to tell the French Army to surrender. Christiane listens to Pétain's broadcast with her aunt and five of her aunt's six children. The young teenager feels like the sky is falling on her head. She is especially angry when her elderly uncle declares that England will never be able to continue the fight alone. She has no idea that he is echoing the majority view inside the French government.

Christiane considers her uncle appallingly defeatist: "In spite of everything, I never stopped believing in a miracle—that somehow our army would rise again." But she is also aware of the state of the French Army: "Not defeated. Crushed."

The following evening, Churchill allows de Gaulle to use the BBC to broadcast his first appeal to the French people. This time Christiane is mesmerized. The general's words have a profound effect on everyone who still believes that the Germans may someday be defeated:*

Has the last word been said? Must we abandon all hope? Is our defeat final and irremediable? To those questions, I answer No! . . . I ask you to believe me when I say that the cause of France is not lost.

And then the prickly iconoclast minted the phrase that made it possible for all unvanquished French citizens to continue to fight for the honor of their fallen nation:

Whatever happens, the flame of French Resistance must not, and shall not, die!

Christiane has never heard of de Gaulle before tonight. Although he had become undersecretary of state for war on June 6, he had only been a colonel before the war.

When he is introduced on the BBC, Christiane asks herself, "General of Gaul—what rank of officer is that?" As soon as she hears him, she immediately agrees with her male cousins: We must

---

* De Gaulle spoke on June 18, but Christiane thinks she didn't hear the broadcast until it was repeated the following evening.

all decamp to England! But none of them is old enough to cross the channel without an adult.

AT THIS POINT, her older brother André really isn't any more political than Christiane is. But he shares all of his sister's instinctive patriotism.

On the night of June 17—the same day de Gaulle decamps for London—André distinguishes himself by helping Lieutenant Jean-Pierre Berger blow up the bridge at Marcigny-sur-Loire, between Digoin and Roanne, which slows the German advance a bit.

As the French government is suing for peace, André retains an unquenchable appetite for action. He decides that he must leave France to avoid surrendering to the enemy. Together with ten of his comrades-in-arms, he sneaks onto a boat leaving Port-Vendres on the Mediterranean coast the day before the armistice is announced.

From the moment he heard Pétain on the radio saying, "We must stop fighting," he categorically refused to accept defeat and had only one desire: "to continue and then to resume combat." André doesn't base his actions "on a critical analysis of the situation, or a particular political belief...but simply on an elementary conviction: *that dignity is incompatible with submission.*" Like so many of those who are praying that the Germans' victory is only temporary, he blends optimism with fatalism. He thinks that "we [will] win in the end, and that it [is] the duty of all Frenchmen to fight for this victory"—but he also thinks it's unlikely that he will live long enough to witness the German defeat himself.

André and his compatriots decide that North Africa is the best place to continue the battle against the Germans. But when their cargo freighter reaches Oran in French Algeria, the welcome they receive from the French colonial authorities is not at all what they expect. Instead of being greeted as heroes, they are treated practically like traitors.

That is because, between the time they leave France and the time they reach North Africa, the new government headed by Pétain has discarded Reynaud's idea of sending some officials abroad to wage the war in exile, as Belgium, Holland, Poland, and Norway already have—to continue the fight against the Germans from London. Mostly because the Pétain government wants to rid itself of some unwelcome dissenters, on June 21, twenty-four deputies and one senator are allowed to sail away from France to North Africa on an armed auxiliary cruiser, the *Massilia*.

When news of the armistice is picked up on the *Massilia*'s radio two days later, the anti-Nazi legislators on board plead with the captain to change his course for England. But the captain is taking his orders from the new French government, and he continues on to Morocco. When the *Massilia* reaches Casablanca on June 24, the whole party of government officials is put under ship arrest for nearly three weeks, while Pétain's cronies debate what to do with them. Finally, they are sent back to France.

"I embarked on the *Massilia* never dreaming the *Massilia* would become a trap," remembered Pierre Mendès-France, a French prime minister in postwar France. "But quite soon the politicians who had remained in Bordeaux realized they could exploit this and present the departure of the *Massilia*, with a number of politicians on board, as a sign of panic—an escape, a surrender... And paradoxically a certain number of them—Viénot, Jean Zay and myself—were charged with desertion, when our idea had been to go on fighting."

Churchill noted with disgust that these patriots were "disposed of as the Vichy Government thought convenient to themselves, and agreeable to their German masters."

By now the new French government has accepted the terms that Hitler's generals have dictated to them in a railway car at Rethondes, near Compiègne. With revenge at the heart of his brutal campaign, Hitler chooses the exact spot where French General

Ferdinand Foch had accepted the surrender of the Germans at the end of World War I, just a quarter century earlier.

To encourage their rapid acceptance by the French in 1940, the Germans do not make the terms especially harsh. The southern portion of the country will be left unoccupied while the Germans are granted an occupied zone in the north that includes Paris. (The unoccupied zone will also free up more German troops for the expected invasion of Britain.) The French Army will be demobilized, except for a force of one hundred thousand to ensure internal order. The fleet will be disarmed and the ships will be docked in their home ports, and the Germans promise they will not touch them. One and a half million French prisoners will remain in captivity until a peace treaty replaces the armistice (which never happens). The cost of keeping German troops in France will be paid for by the French government.

THREE DAYS after the armistice is declared, Hitler sneaks into Paris for an early-morning visit. He flies into Le Bourget airport with a small entourage that includes Albert Speer, the Third Reich's official architect. The civilians accompanying him all wear borrowed uniforms, because Hitler has demanded that they dress as soldiers for the trip.

Thirteen years earlier, a hundred thousand Parisians had mobbed Charles Lindbergh at the same airfield to celebrate his triumphant arrival from New York.* But today, there are no crowds to greet the Führer.

Three large Mercedes sedans whisk his party to the ornate Paris Opera House. This is the German leader's favorite building in the French capital. As a student he even studied its architectural plans, and his French guide is impressed when the dictator asks him what

---

* At the height of his fame, Lindbergh became one of Hitler's most naïve supporters.

Fascist sympathizers show their enthusiasm inside the French Chamber of Deputies after the rebroadcast of a speech by Hitler in July 1940.

has happened to a particular room. The guide explains that it no longer exists, because of a renovation.

At the end of the opera tour, one of Hitler's aides offers the guide a 50-mark tip. Albert Speer watches as the Frenchman quietly refuses the gift—twice.

Choosing the obvious tourist stops, Hitler continues on to the Eiffel Tower, the Arc de Triomphe, and Les Invalides. Inside the monument to the French emperor, he stands for a long time gazing silently at Napoleon's tomb. Perhaps he is already contemplating a Russian invasion—and vowing to make his more successful than Napoleon's.

Hitler poses in front of the Eiffel Tower, but he never gets to the top, because the French have cut the cables to the elevators before his arrival. The elevators will remain out of commission until the end of the war.

Three hours after he lands, Hitler climbs back onto his plane to return to Germany. He has spent less than half a day inspecting his most glorious conquest.

He will never enter the City of Light again.

ANDRÉ AND HIS COMRADES reach Algeria the same day Hitler visits Paris. They are disgusted when they are greeted like deserters instead of patriots. Two of them make contact with the British consul. But when they ask the diplomat for help to get to England, he urges them to wait out the war in Morocco instead.

André is completely baffled by his predicament. He is desperate to continue the fight, but he has no idea how to do that. Should he stay in Morocco until the war is over? Or should he return to France to confront the enemy?

On July 6, 1940, the twenty-four-year-old lieutenant sits down at his desk to describe his anguish in a letter from Rabat. The letter smolders with passion and uncertainty.

My Dear Father,

I can finally write to France with a small chance that my letter will actually reach you. I won't try to tell you how I've experienced the past month — I can't find the words to describe it. Once again, it seems as though we have reached the depths of degradation and debasement, but day after day, our descent continues. What a struggle it will be to pull our country out of this abyss!

All I can tell you is that I came to North Africa so that I would be able to battle the enemy, by joining an organized resistance, but you know as well as I do how vain that hope was...Ignorance is a formidable thing at a time like this. Whatever one decides to do, it's a descent into the unknown. I desperately want your advice right now. I've been reduced to imagining what it might be, but I can't be sure you would approve of the course that I've chosen.

Now I am posted at a base at Rabat, without any real respon-
sibilities. I'm suffering terribly from inaction... There is one ques-
tion in particular for which I need your advice... Should I return
to France?... Everyone here agrees our country is in terrible disar-
ray, and people like me may not be experienced enough to help put
it back together. Some people think I should stay here to gain some
seasoning, so that I can be more effective when I return home.

Personally, I prefer the opposite course. The ghastly state my
country was in when I left makes me want to return as soon as pos-
sible. It can only be saved by a complete moral resurrection, some-
thing that will require the work of all men of good will... I think I
can contribute a great deal. And if more troubles lie ahead, isn't
it my duty to be present?

This is the question that has really gotten under my skin. I
never thought it would be so difficult to determine one's duty, once
one had put aside all personal considerations. And yet, for the last
two weeks, I have been at war with myself.

I am impatient for news about all of you... If the only thing
that Frenchmen still have is the affection of our families, at least
ours won't be the most badly divided.

André

André's final prediction did not turn out to be prescient.

His father's response has not survived. But ten weeks after writing his letter, André has returned to France to resume his fight
against the Germans.

Six

The Resistance was irresistible.
—André Postel-Vinay

THE FEARS Jacques Boulloche described in his letters of a permanent separation from his family were premature. At the end of the summer of 1940, his wife and daughters return to the French capital from Brittany, and they move back into the family's spacious apartment.

Jacques's youngest daughter, Christiane, has a visceral reaction to what she sees in the newly occupied capital. The French *tricolore* has been banned. In its place there are huge swastikas swaying in the wind, freshly painted street signs in German—"black on yellow," she remembers clearly—and German drummer boys in front of Wehrmacht soldiers goose-stepping down the Champs-Élysées. "There would be parades in the morning and they would sing. And they sang well—that was especially annoying!"

Christiane is stunned by all of this. She sees it as "the visible proof of our defeat. Seeing the Germans in Paris is ghastly. You feel like you are no longer at home. We were touching the reality of the Occupation with our fingers. It was a succession of shocks."

A German soldier complained to an attractive Parisian girl that her city seemed sad. "You should have been here before you got here," she replied.

This is when Christiane begins to ride a bicycle, when there is no longer any heat in her parents' apartment, and when she begins to feel hungry all the time. Jacqueline goes to work for an organization that sends packages to French soldiers who are imprisoned in Germany.

Jacques and Hélène Boulloche share their children's revulsion at the German Occupation. As early as July 1940, Jacques writes to his wife that the new anti-Semitic campaign is going to make life difficult for one of his colleagues. Three months later, the government publishes its first "Jewish law," which excludes Jews from the higher levels of public service, as well as professions like teaching and the press, where they might influence public opinion.

Back at her Paris lycée in the fall of 1940, Christiane and her friends take up a collection for Mademoiselle Klotz, a much-loved history teacher, who is fired after the publication of the new law. Christiane is shocked by the persecution of the Jews, especially when one of her classmates, Janine Grumbach, is forced to start wearing a yellow star.

Beginning in October 1940, all foreign Jews can be interned at the discretion of prefects. On November 1, even in the unoccupied zone, every Jewish-owned business must display a yellow poster in the window: ENTREPRISE JUIVE.

By the start of 1941, some forty thousand Jews are held in seven main camps, in atrocious conditions. Some three thousand Jews perish in the French camps even before the Final Solution has begun.

In June 1942, every Jew over the age of six in the occupied zone is ordered to wear a star over the heart, and they are forced to buy three of them from their local gendarmerie. Adding insult to humilliation, those purchases are deducted from their clothing coupons. In July, they are banned from all public places: cinemas, main roads, libraries, parks, cafés, restaurants, swimming pools, and phone booths, and they can only ride in the last car of the Métro.

By 1941 the swastika was everywhere in Paris. Here the former (British) WHSmith had become a German bookstore on the rue de Rivoli.

Christiane considers all of this outrageous, and she thinks that her parents are helping some of their Jewish friends to escape. Her family is also directly affected by the new law, because one of her cousins, a surgeon named Funck-Brentano, has a Jewish wife, and she is forced to go into hiding.*

---

* The doctor joined the Resistance in 1943. But when he was interviewed by the government after the war about his clandestine activities, he never mentioned the fact that he had a Jewish wife. (French National Archives, box 72AJ80)

IN SPITE OF their shared hatred of the *Boches*, the two halves of the Boulloche family choose very different paths after the fall of France. Unlike their three youngest children, neither Jacques nor Hélène will ever join the Resistance.

Jacques and Hélène both turn fifty-two in 1940, and they share the caution of middle age. Jacques helps some Jewish friends to go into hiding, but he is always discreet. He is also careful not to do anything that might jeopardize his family's safety, or weaken the nation, to which he and his ancestors have devoted decades of service.

As the British historian Julian Jackson observed, "Conduct which might be described as collaboration could incorporate a myriad of motives including self-protection, the protection of others, even patriotism."

Christiane doesn't consider her father "pro-German at all." She thinks he merely wants to make France work for the French, "not for the Germans." The Boulloches defiantly listen to the BBC at home. They know that if the British don't stay in the fight against Hitler, their only hope for the future will be extinguished.

Jacques Boulloche never confronts the German occupiers directly. He keeps his government job, and he commutes to Vichy, the seat of the collaborationist government. His family notices he is always particularly depressed when he returns from Vichy. He never tells his children whether he has signed an oath of loyalty to the Vichy government, but he is almost certainly required to do so.

Jacques and Hélène's oldest son, Robert, serves in the army during the German invasion, but he avoids capture after the armistice. Now he has returned to his job as an inspector for the Finance Ministry, in Toulouse.

Robert shares his parents' prudence and their commitment to the French government. Like his father, Robert probably sees some

Jacques and Hélène Boulloche. Jacques was the family patriarch, who kept his job as the director of the national bureau of highways after the Occupation began. Like her husband, Hélène never joined the Resistance. But when her daughters told her that they had, she said, "That's what I would have done."

value in keeping France functioning for the French, despite the invasion of the Germans.

A twenty-seven-year-old bachelor, Robert is not as good-looking as his younger brother, André. But he has a terrific sense of humor, a passion for art, and an impressive collection of original paintings.

At the end of 1940, Robert becomes the first member of his family to be asked to join the Resistance. The invitation comes from André Postel-Vinay, who had met Robert two years earlier, when the two of them took the exam to become finance inspectors together.

Postel-Vinay is a strikingly handsome twenty-nine-year-old, with delicate features set off by a broad forehead and an aquiline nose. As a lieutenant in the 70th Régiment d'Artillerie in 1940, he is

Robert Boulloche was the oldest son in the family, and shared some of his parents' caution. He declined André Postel-Vinay's invitation to join the Resistance at the end of 1940—but he predicted that his younger brother would be eager to join the fight against the Germans.

celebrated for his bravery and his exceptionally accurate shooting. On June 17, he is captured by the enemy, but he manages to escape a week later. After three days on foot, he makes it back to his parents' home in Paris, utterly exhausted.

The apartment is empty, because his parents are in Brittany. The next morning, he is awakened by a German military ceremony taking place in the street below. When he goes to the window, he has the same reaction as Christiane and thousands of others. He is appalled by the savage sight of German soldiers holding gilded crosses in the air as they parade down the street.

LIKE JACQUES BOULLOCHE, Postel-Vinay had seen the war coming many years earlier. After the Night of the Long Knives in 1934, when Hitler ordered the execution of Ernst Röhm, the gay commander of the Nazi SA, two army generals, and at least a hundred others, Postel-Vinay decided that "war is the only way to communicate with the Nazis—because even among themselves, they behave like butchers."

(In a speech to the Reichstag after the bloody massacre, Hitler freely admitted that what he had done was completely illegal. The legislature quickly passed a law that retroactively legalized his butchery.)

After France's collapse in 1940, Postel-Vinay thinks that any victory over the Nazis will take a very long time, if it ever comes at all. But he is propelled by the conviction he shares with the small number of very early *Résistants*: He believes that his life will have no meaning until he finds a way to fight for the Germans' defeat.

By October 1940, he has linked up with one of the earliest British Resistance groups in the Paris region, which is helping downed British airmen escape back to England through Spain. Then he connects with a group of French officers from the army's intelligence service, the Deuxième Bureau, who are collecting information on German troop movements and relaying it to London.

Postel-Vinay also makes contact with a group of anti-Fascist intellectuals at the Musée de l'Homme in Paris, who have begun to organize in the summer of 1940. Most of them are leftists, and some of them aren't French, including the group's most active member, Boris Vildé, a linguist with anarchist leanings and Estonian origins.

The group at the Musée de l'Homme is one of the very first Resistance groups. In December 1940 it starts to publish the newspaper called *Résistance*. During the next three years, dozens of other clandestine newspapers will appear all over France. Delivering some of these publications is one of Christiane Boulloche's earliest acts of resistance.

When Postel-Vinay asks Robert, his former classmate, if he will join the Resistance to collect intelligence about the Germans for the British, Robert shows no interest. He doesn't seem to think the work will be very useful, and as the oldest son in his family, he probably shares some of his parents' caution.

André Postel-Vinay in his army uniform.
He convinced André Boulloche to
join the Resistance at the end of 1940.

Robert tells Postel-Vinay he won't become a clandestine enemy
of the Germans. Then he makes a fateful prediction: "I know someone who will jump right in."

"Who's that?" asks his friend.

"My little brother, André," Robert replies.

ANDRÉ BOULLOCHE has managed to return to France from
Morocco at the beginning of September 1940. He is demobilized in
Marseille, then quickly makes his way back to Paris, where a family
reunion takes place, as joyful as it is unexpected.

He rejoins the Department of Bridges and Highways, where he
worked as an engineer before he was mobilized, and he is posted
to Soissons, where he is named *adjoint ingenieur-en-chef* (deputy
chief engineer). This puts him sixty miles northeast of Paris.

When Robert takes him to meet Postel-Vinay, André responds
just as Robert had predicted: He immediately joins the under-

ground. For the first time since the armistice, he has finally found a way to fight the Germans.

On the surface, André doesn't seem very emotional. But Postel-Vinay quickly discovers that beneath a placid exterior, André is full of zeal. The two of them agree about everything that matters at this ominous moment. Neither can bear France's defeat, they share a profound horror of Nazism, and they both feel a compulsion to do something about it. "It was absolutely unbreathable," said Postel-Vinay. "André was very passionate, and he couldn't sit still."

Although Postel-Vinay is four years older than his new recruit, the two men share another quality that pushes them into this treacherous adventure: the impetuousness of youth.

"For the two of us, the Resistance was a kind of lifesaver," Postel-Vinay explained, "because without it, life no longer had any meaning." Their decision to join the Resistance is so instinctive, and so immediate, they barely consider the possible consequences for themselves, or for anyone else.

THE DECISION of these two young technocrats to join the secret war against the Germans at the end of 1940 is very unusual for Frenchmen of their class. There is hardly any other milieu more unprepared for clandestine activity than bourgeois civil servants, and at this point there is only a small number of Frenchmen actively challenging the German Occupation.

Unlike so many early members of the Resistance, these fiercely committed young men are not outsiders at all: they are neither Jewish nor foreign-born nor Communist. But they share a larger idea about human progress, which makes them passionate about the horror and the absurdity of Nazism—and the perils it poses for everyone.

By now the Third Reich has conquered Austria, Poland, Czechoslovakia, Holland, Belgium, Luxembourg, Denmark, and

Norway, as well as France, and most people consider it invincible at this stage of the war.

However, there remain a couple of skeptics. When the Russian foreign minister, Vyacheslav Molotov, visits Hitler in Berlin in November 1940, the Führer tells him the British are finished. "Then whose bombers are those overhead?" Molotov asks. "And why are we in this bomb shelter?"

Over the next eighteen months, André Boulloche convinces his boss, Pierre Pène, and a fellow engineer, Jean Bertin, to join him in collecting information about German troop movements in the region. He reports on the work of the Germans who are constructing a secret headquarters in a tunnel at Margival, outside Soissons. This is supposed to become Hitler's headquarters when he invades Britain, but he will not visit it for the first time until 1944, after the Normandy invasion.

Through his own contacts and those of his colleagues with local builders, André obtains the plans of more than 150 structures being built by the Germans, and he believes that they are reaching London.

He also marks off parachute fields and sets up arms depots. To make himself a better secret agent, he memorizes a book that interprets every insignia of the German Army. The book is easy to get when the Germans first arrive in France. It disappears when the Germans realize how useful it can be to their enemies.

Employing primitive spy craft, he sends Postel-Vinay letters written with lemon juice, which only becomes legible when the pages are heated over a candle. Twice a month he goes to Paris to give his information to one of Postel-Vinay's contacts, who is supposed to transmit it to London. These trips also make it possible for him to visit his parents. But he never discusses his clandestine activities with his family, partly because he doesn't want to influence his sisters.

MEANWHILE, in London, Charles de Gaulle is cementing his position as the leader of the Free French. Once France has signed an armistice, the British no longer worry about offending the new French government, and Churchill is ready to grant de Gaulle formal recognition. At this point de Gaulle is still a little-known, recently promoted general, and Churchill hopes that he will attract other, more famous French personalities to his cause in London. But that never happens.

At the end of May 1940, eight hundred small boats had loaded 338,000 men into larger ships during the legendary evacuation of Allied troops from Dunkirk, including 500 French officers and 18,000 French sailors, to prevent them from being captured or killed by the Germans. But all but 50 of these officers and 200 of these sailors will return home to occupied France, rather than stay in Britain to fight the Germans.

"Their idea was to get out of the war no matter what, as quickly as possible," recalled Sir Edward Spears, the wartime liaison between Churchill and de Gaulle. "We had 15,000 French sailors at Liverpool. I went to speak to them. I tried to persuade them to continue the fighting. Impossible . . . As for what might happen to England, they couldn't care less. That was the way it was—we were defeated, and if the French army was defeated, it was impossible to imagine that the English would survive."

Only one deputy, one admiral, and one leading academic remain with the Free French in London, and de Gaulle notices that all of his earliest supporters are either Jews or Socialists.

A man of mythic pride, de Gaulle is infuriated by his total dependence on the British. His relationship with Churchill vacillates between prickliness and open hostility. But both men share "a love of drama and a deep sense of history"—and they recognize that they need one another. Like André Boulloche and

Postel-Vinay, de Gaulle experienced the defeat of 1940 as a searing humiliation. Some thought de Gaulle felt like a man who had been skinned alive.

There was one other thing de Gaulle had in common with the Boulloches' ancestors—the general's father had also believed that Dreyfus was innocent.

One thing that provokes the suspicion of antifascist Frenchmen in London is de Gaulle's initial reluctance to publicly embrace republicanism. This hesitancy makes some people doubt his commitment to democracy in a postwar France. Early Free French broadcasts from London are introduced with the motto "*Honneur et Patrie*" (Honor and Country), rather than the traditional republican "*Liberté, Egalité, Fraternité.*"

But the general sees his position as tactical: Especially at the beginning, he tries to avoid all political labels so that he can attract the widest possible support. Not until November 1941 does he finally embrace "Liberty, Equality, and Fraternity"—to remain "faithful to the democratic principles...which are at stake in this war of life and death."

The BBC broadcasts quickly become a vital part of the Allied propaganda effort aimed at France. For millions of French people, listening to the outlawed BBC is the main act of rebellion they engage in.

The British give the Free French five minutes on the BBC every night. At the same time, French-language broadcasts of the BBC expand gradually from two and half hours daily in 1940 to five hours in 1942. As the size of the organized Resistance increases in France, these broadcasts also include a growing number of coded messages, which communicate everything from the location of new arms drops by parachute to the launching of the Allied invasion in Normandy.

AT THE END OF 1940, just as André Boulloche starts collecting information for the Resistance, de Gaulle creates a department in London responsible for "action in the occupied territories." The agents who are eventually recruited are hardly professionals. Almost anyone who volunteers is accepted, once he has satisfied British intelligence that he isn't a double agent.

Most of de Gaulle's earliest recruits are from French units that were evacuated from Norway or Dunkirk. At the end of June, his ranks are swelled by the residents of Sein, a rocky island off the western tip of Brittany near Audierne. The Germans don't reach the island until July, and by then two small fleets of fishing boats have put to sea with 133 men aged fourteen to fifty-one—virtually all the able-bodied men from the island.

Each of the emigrants carries a little food, a liter of wine, whatever money their family has—and the family shotgun, if there is one. After they dock at Falmouth, de Gaulle welcomes them in London. They will become some of the earliest recruits of the Free French. "The island of Sein stands watch duty for France," the general proclaims.

A week later, a French Army captain named André Dewavrin, who had fought in Norway in the spring, presents himself to de Gaulle at his temporary headquarters at St. Stephen's House on the Victoria Embankment in London. Nearly all of what Dewavrin knows about spying he has learned by reading thrillers.

De Gaulle is impressed anyway—and at this point he doesn't have a lot of alternatives. He promotes Dewavrin to major and puts him in charge of what will eventually become the Bureau Central de Renseignements et d'Action (BCRA) or Central Bureau of Intelligence and Action. The BCRA is the product of a merger of two organizations de Gaulle has started after his retreat to London: the Deuxième Bureau (intelligence) and the Troisième Bureau (operations). The original task of the Deuxième Bureau is to gather as much information as possible about German preparations for what is considered an almost inevitable invasion of England.

Dewavrin gives himself the code name of "Col. Passy," and he eventually dispatches more than 350 agents to occupied France. Because he depends on the British for transportation and radio equipment, he has to work with the newly created Special Operations Executive, which has an RF (République Française) section to work with the Free French, as well as its own French section (section F), which carries out independent operations in France. There is constant tension among all three bureaucracies, but by the end of 1941, Col. Passy has already managed to send twenty-nine of his own agents to France.

Seven

Never in the field of human conflict was so much owed by so many to so few.
—Winston Churchill, addressing Parliament, August 20, 1940

And while I am talking to you mothers and fathers, I give you one more assurance. I have said this before, but I shall say it again and again and again: Your boys are not going to be sent into any foreign wars.
—President Franklin D. Roosevelt, campaign address,
October 30, 1940

Throughout 1941, André continues his work as a highway engineer and a secret agent. The two jobs go well together, because his official responsibilities make it easy for him to travel without arousing suspicion. In his clandestine life, he alternates between diverting supplies destined for the Germans and accumulating a private stock of gasoline for his Resistance unit. He also continues to collect intelligence about German troop movements, to forward to London.

The war news since the fall of France has been relentlessly bleak. The Battle of Britain begins immediately after the Nazis conquer France. Between July and September 1940, Hitler's Luftwaffe targets Royal Air Force airfields and radar stations, to soften up Britain for what many people still think of as a certain German invasion.

On July 3, the great British iconoclast George Orwell writes in his journal: "Everywhere a feeling of something near despair among thinking people because of the failure of the government to act and the continuance of dead minds and pro-Fascists in positions of command. Growing recognition that the only thing that would certainly right the situation is an unsuccessful invasion; and coupled with this a growing fear that Hitler won't after all attempt the invasion but will go for Africa and the Near East."

Enraged by an RAF bombing attack on Berlin, Hitler switches his targets in the fall to London, Coventry, Birmingham, Liverpool, Manchester, and other British cities and ports. Beginning on September 7, London is bombed every day (or night) for fifty-seven days in a row. On September 12, the British government issues an invasion alert, but the scare fades quickly.

On November 14, St. Michael's Cathedral in Coventry, mostly built in the fourteenth and fifteenth centuries, is almost completely demolished by a German bombardment. By this time the British have already broken the German codes. Some historians believe that no extraordinary measures were taken to protect Coventry, to prevent the Germans from realizing that the British were reading their most secret messages.

Between July and December, German bombs kill 23,002 and wound 32,138 in Britain. Nearly 3,000 Britons are wiped out in a single day at the end of December. But despite the loss of 1,173 RAF planes and 500 pilots, Britain survives the German onslaught. In the spring of 1941, the bombing campaign finally tapers off. Britain's spirit, stoked by Churchill's extraordinary oratory, is still intact. As Orwell and others had predicted, Hitler has turned his sights elsewhere, abandoning his cherished plan to conquer the British Isles.

THE BATTLE OF BRITAIN is broadcast directly into American living rooms by Edward R. Murrow. The newly minted radio correspondent for CBS News becomes the most celebrated broadcaster of his generation practically overnight. Just thirty-two in 1940, Murrow is a master of vivid images, all of them rendered in the rich baritone of a Broadway actor. Fearless and theatrical, Murrow transfixes his listeners with live reports delivered from London rooftops, as German bombs fall all around him:

This is Trafalgar Square. The noise that you hear at the moment is the sound of the air raid sirens...The searchlight just burst into action off in the distance. One single beam sweeping the sky above me...There's another searchlight...You see them reach straight up into the sky, and occasionally they catch a cloud and seem to splash on the bottom of it...One of the strangest sounds one can hear in London these days—or rather these dark nights—just the sound of footsteps walking along the street, like ghosts shod with steel shoes.

Blessed with a story that doesn't require objectivity, Murrow becomes a good friend of Winston Churchill and a lover of his daughter-in-law, Pamela Digby Churchill.

When he returns to America for a visit in 1941, he is greeted at the dock by a crowd of fans and reporters. CBS celebrates him with a banquet for eleven hundred at the Waldorf-Astoria. Three years later, Murrow will dine with FDR at the White House on the night of the Normandy invasion.

In the fall of 1940, Murrow's reports inspire considerable sympathy in America for the beleaguered British. But when Franklin Roosevelt decides to seek an unprecedented third term that year, he feels compelled to promise a reluctant country that he will stay out of the growing European war. "Your boys are not going to be sent into any foreign wars," he pledges to a Boston audience a few days before he is reelected in November.

At the same time, Roosevelt continues to withhold American recognition of the Free French and de Gaulle. Churchill's relationship with de Gaulle is always prickly; Roosevelt actually loathes the Frenchman. As Eisenhower puts it delicately in his memoirs,

Roosevelt "could not agree to forcing De Gaulle upon anyone else."

Or as the historian Ian Ousby slyly summarized their relationships, "The familiar slur of enemy propaganda that [de Gaulle] was merely the tool of Britain or the Allies certainly found no answering echo in the hearts of Churchill or Roosevelt."

At the beginning of 1941, Roosevelt still sees some value in maintaining relations with Vichy France, and he names Admiral William D. Leahy to be his ambassador there. Leahy even arrives with a 1941 Cadillac limousine to present to the Vichy president, Marshal Pétain. The historian Robert Paxton called the fancy American automobile "a very, very explicit act of support."*

American public opinion begins to rally to de Gaulle long before the president does. In a rift with Churchill, Roosevelt hopes to keep France neutral by cozying up to the Vichy regime. His actions are befuddling to the budding Resistance movement.

THE MORALE of the French Resistance gets a huge boost from the rupture of the Hitler-Stalin nonaggression pact on June 22, 1941. That day the Führer announces that he is invading the Soviet Union, on a line stretching from Norway to Romania. Hitler's announcement includes what the *New York Times* calls one "vitally interested statement," which is also a tiny source of hope—a public suggestion that German military forces will not be strong enough in the west to conquer the British Isles, as long as so many Soviet troops are stationed on Germany's eastern flank.

The invasion transforms the attitude of Communists in France, most of whom have refrained from joining the Resistance up until now, because of the nonaggression pact. Now they will become some of the Nazis' fiercest enemies.

---

*When de Gaulle liberates Paris in August 1944, he makes sure that he enters the city in a Hotchkiss, a large French limousine. (Collins and Lapierre, *Is Paris Burning?*, p. 182)

The new military campaign also buoys every French citizen who remembers the importance of June 22, 1812, from history class at the lycée. That was the date Napoleon launched *his* invasion of Russia. Now, millions are praying that Hitler will replicate Napoleon's disastrous experience on his journey toward the Urals.

Eight

*This was our obsessive fear: that we would be tortured into giving names
if we were captured by the Germans. Compared to that nightmare,
death hardly seemed like a menace at all.*
—Christiane Boulloche

ANDRÉ POSTEL-VINAY, the man who has recruited André
Boulloche into the Resistance, is lucky because his two bosses
at the Finance Ministry know about his work as a secret agent, and
never object to it or betray him. Thanks to their complicity, he is
able to work practically full time against the Germans.

By the middle of 1941, Postel-Vinay has begun to wonder whether
the information he is collecting is actually reaching London. To
find out, he includes a request in one of his coded radio messages,
asking the BBC to confirm the arrival of his dispatches by broad-
casting "CBA-321." One night, just back from a trip, he flips on the
radio. Through the garbled sounds of the jammed transmission, he
manages to make out the magic combination: "CBA-321." At that
moment, those syllables feel like a miracle "from the great beyond."

Most of the newly organized Resistance units are dangerously
porous organizations, easily infiltrated by double agents. Even the
Resistance leaders who are trained in Britain before their repatriation to France receive only the most rudimentary instruction in the
dark arts of espionage.

Pierre d'Harcourt introduced Postel-Vinay to the first two Resistance units he works with. In July 1941, d'Harcourt is captured by the Gestapo in a Paris Métro station. When he is cornered by the Germans, d'Harcourt tries to run away and tumbles down a stairway. As he falls, he tries desperately to destroy the secret documents he is carrying with him. At the bottom of the stairs, the Germans fire on him, shooting him through the foot, the leg, and the lung.

Postel-Vinay learns the identity of the "charming accomplice" of the man who has denounced d'Harcourt. Postel-Vinay thinks that this accomplice is also aware of his own work in the Resistance, so now he feels like he is perilously balanced on a tightrope. And yet he still doesn't want to "interrupt" himself.

His behavior suggests a kind of fatalism that is familiar to his co-conspirators.

Two months after d'Harcourt is shot, the Gestapo raids the apartment of Captain d'Autrevaux, the number-two man in the French military intelligence unit Postel-Vinay has been working with. D'Autrevaux happens to be away when the Germans arrive, and he manages to escape to the unoccupied zone in the south. After that, three of his associates ask Postel-Vinay to start relaying their information to London. Postel-Vinay considers this a wonderful development: He finally feels like he is making a difference.

But then another danger sign appears. In November, an agent named Wiltz, who has been d'Autrevaux's closest collaborator, misses an appointment with Postel-Vinay. Almost immediately, Postel-Vinay receives word that Wiltz has been arrested. Now he begins to feel like he is back in the infantry, surrounded by artillery, the sounds of their explosions steadily approaching.

LATE IN THE MORNING OF DECEMBER 13, Postel-Vinay arrives home at his parents' apartment on avenue de Villars, adjacent to Les Invalides, which houses Napoleon's tomb. As he walks through the front door of the building, he spots two young men coming down the stairs in front of him.

He immediately recognizes the first one: a tall, thin, blond Englishman he knows only as Paul. Paul has been an aide to Patrick O'Leary, the head of one of two Resistance groups Postel-Vinay has been working with all year.

O'Leary pretends to one and all that he is a French-Canadian officer. In fact, he is a former surgeon in the Belgian Army, whose real name is Albert-Marie Edmond Guérisse.

After serving with the Belgian Army during the eighteen-day campaign of 1940, he escaped to England, where he secured a British Navy commission as a lieutenant commander. On April 25, O'Leary was on the HMS *Fidelity* when it overturned in a squall off the French coast near the eastern end of the Pyrenees, but he managed to swim to shore.

Identifying himself to the gendarme who arrested him as Albert O'Leary, an evading Canadian airman, he was sent to St. Hippolyte du Fort near Nîmes, to be with British officers. There he met Ian Garrow, a tall, dark-haired captain in the Highlanders in his early twenties, who quickly helped O'Leary escape.

O'Leary then joined one of the most effective networks of the war devoted to the repatriation of downed Allied pilots. After Garrow is arrested in October 1941 O'Leary takes charge of the operation, which becomes known as the PAO line (for his initials) and, more famously, as the Pat or O'Leary line. It eventually helps an astonishing six hundred pilots to escape from occupied France.

Postel-Vinay has met Paul once before, in Marseille. Although Paul is introduced to him as a fellow *Résistant* who is working for one of the best Resistance organizations, Postel-Vinay is immediately suspicious of him. He listens as the Englishman delivers a speech filled with beautiful principles — but everything he says rings false in the Frenchman's skeptical ears.

Now, in Paris, Paul is accompanied by someone Postel-Vinay has never seen before: a stocky, gray, sinister-looking fellow, who keeps his hands shoved deep into the pockets of his shabby raincoat.

"That's him," says Paul, motioning toward Postel-Vinay.

"My chauffeur," Paul explains, indicating his unpleasant companion.

Postel-Vinay has other reasons to suspect the Englishman. A few weeks earlier he had heard about a fistfight between Paul and his boss, O'Leary. The word on the street is that the fight was about money. Postel-Vinay knows that O'Leary has an impeccable reputation, so he assumes that Paul must have been in the wrong.

He also knows that Paul usually works in the unoccupied zone. So it feels odd to see him here in the north, where his pidgin French and pronounced English accent can hardly provide him with much cover if he is detained by the Germans.

Pondering all of this, Postel-Vinay realizes that these two have just been knocking on the door of his parents' apartment.

"Let's talk outside," Postel-Vinay suggests, hoping to get them away as quickly as possible. He leads the way, as Paul and the other man follow silently.

On the sidewalk, Paul explains that Patrick O'Leary's organization has been split into two parts: one to look after downed British airmen, and the other to collect intelligence for the British. Paul says he is working with the intelligence unit, and the stranger accompanying him is actually his new boss.

"Bring all the information you've collected to tomorrow's meeting," says Paul. "Even the stuff you've already sent to Marseille. We have a new radio post here in the occupied sector, so you won't need to go to Marseille anymore.

"I'll be back to pick you up at nine tomorrow morning," Paul continues, "with a beautiful fake identity card on the windshield of my car." Since Germans are almost the only people allowed to drive in Paris now, this boast hardly bolsters Postel-Vinay's confidence. Yet he agrees to meet Paul anyway.

In the afternoon, Postel-Vinay gets a visit from Bernard Vernier-Palliez, a young man who has studied for a job in the Foreign Ministry and has been recruited into the Resistance by André Boulloche, after André is signed up by Postel-Vinay. Vernier-Palliez is transporting a case filled with weapons, including a German Mauser—a job often consigned to Resistance women, because women are less likely to be suspected as arms smugglers.

Vernier-Palliez asks Postel-Vinay if he can keep the weapons for him for a while. Once again, Postel-Vinay agrees, even though he strongly suspects that this is not the ideal moment to perform this favor.

Then he spends the rest of the day gathering all the information he can for tomorrow's meeting.

Of course Postel-Vinay knows that Paul may be planning to betray him. But his judgment is clouded by exhaustion, and he continues to behave as if he isn't in serious danger. Part of him thinks it's a terrible idea to meet Paul tomorrow. But is that because he has real reasons to fear a trap? Or is it paranoia, the product of constant danger? During the last twelve months, he has taken many risks, and he has often thought that he was in danger. But he has always come through okay. Perhaps this is making him believe too much in his own luck.

Postel-Vinay thinks it is difficult to believe in the perfect treason until you have experienced one yourself. He imagines the ideal traitor would do you in with grinning flair. But he finds it hard to imagine such a person in real life. Paul's story about the organization being split in two does sound plausible. And the new radio transmitter he described in the occupied zone is exactly what Postel-Vinay has been looking for.

There is one other large question weighing on him, the same one that troubles many of his fellow young *Résistants*: If he runs away, will his parents be arrested in his place? Those big posters in the Métro are constant reminders that every relative of a *Résistant* is now subject to arrest.

Postel-Vinay sleeps badly. The next morning, his sister, Marie-Hélène, is the first person to arrive at their parents' apartment, at eight thirty. Like the Boulloche sisters who work with their brother André, Marie-Hélène participates in her brother's clandestine activities. Until today she has always managed to bury her fears about her brother's fate. But after he tells her about Paul's visit, she begs him not to meet with him again.

Postel-Vinay does his best to calm her down. Then his sister leaves the room to speak with their parents. At that moment, Postel-Vinay turns around to remove a loaded six-shot Enfield pistol from the closet. He slides it into the inside pocket of his overcoat. In his other pocket, he places a bulky envelope with all the intelligence he has gathered for Paul.

When his sister returns, he tries to mock her fears. But then he blurts out, "If Paul betrays me, I'll kill him! And then I'll kill myself." He thinks this is the first really good idea he has had all morning.

As soon as he walks out into the street, a black car pulls up beside him. Paul's "chauffeur" is in the driver's seat, with Paul next to him. When he tells Postel-Vinay to climb into the empty back-seat, that somehow feels reassuring.

Now they are driving through the place de la Concorde, then past Madeleine and Saint-Lazare. They pause for a moment in front of a Métro entrance. The perfect moment to jump out, Postel-Vinay thinks to himself. But his hand never touches the door handle.

A few minutes later they are passing the cemetery in Montmartre. Finally, they arrive at the Terrass Hotel, a venerable institution with panoramic views of Paris. Paul and Postel-Vinay climb out of the car, leaving the chauffeur behind.

As Paul guides him up to the second floor, Postel-Vinay thinks he sees the hotel clerk giving them an odd look. But then they walk into an empty, ordinary-looking hotel room, and Postel-Vinay decides it's a good sign that the chauffeur hasn't accompanied them. When the door is closed behind them, he hands Paul the fat envelope filled with intelligence reports.

The documents include information about German troop movements, detailed blueprints of airports used by the Germans, a plan of the port of Brest, and descriptions of the results of British bombardments of military targets.

He asks Paul about the location of the new radio transmitter, but Paul deflects his question.

Suddenly the door bursts open, and the chauffeur runs in with three accomplices. All four of them are pointing their pistols at Postel-Vinay. Just like André Boulloche, who is carrying a cyanide pill when he is arrested and has always planned to kill himself if the Germans capture him, Postel-Vinay is carrying a revolver for the same purpose. He reaches into his pocket so that he can shoot himself. But first he thinks, *I must shoot Paul!*

Before he can fire a single shot, four gun barrels are pressed against his chest. One of the men grabs his Enfield revolver, which is still in his pocket, as another one slams on the handcuffs.

Postel-Vinay feels himself entering a new universe, separated by a vast distance from the world where he lived before—somewhere dangerously close to hell.

He is impressed when one of the men throws Paul on the bed and starts slapping him. These men obviously take pride in their work, because they are trying to make it look as though Paul isn't the one who has betrayed him. The man attacking Paul seems to be enjoying the violent pantomime, but Postel-Vinay doesn't think any less of him for that.

PAUL'S REAL NAME is Harold Cole. Trained as an engineer, he was known in England before the war as a con man and a burglar. As a sergeant with the British Expeditionary Force in France, he had absconded with the sergeant's mess funds. When he turned up in Lille after the armistice, he identified himself as "Captain Harold Cole" of the British Secret Service.

During the fall of 1941, Cole had actually helped thirty-five British airmen escape. But on December 6—one week before he met Postel-Vinay in Paris—Cole had been arrested by the Germans in Lille. Probably to avoid a threatened execution, it was at this moment that he switched sides to the Nazis.*

ALTHOUGH HE IS UNABLE to shoot himself at the moment of his arrest, suicide remains Postel-Vinay's urgent priority. Three days after entering the Prison de la Santé, he breaks away from the guards and flings himself over a railing, down two stories into the center of the prison courtyard. The violent plunge breaks most of the bones in his body, but he survives his own suicide attempt.

Now he decides to feign madness, and the Germans transfer him to the Quentin Pavilion in l'hôpital de la Pitié.

André Boulloche is tipped off to Postel-Vinay's new location by André's cousin, Funck-Brentano, his only relative with a Jewish wife. His cousin also happens to be the chief surgeon at l'hôpital de la Salpêtrière next door to the one where Postel-Vinay is a prisoner. With the help of a young doctor, the surgeon locates an underground passage that connects the two hospitals.

After months of work, which includes help from his brother Robert, Jacques Postel-Vinay (a close cousin of the prisoner),

---

*After the war, Cole was shot and killed after exchanging gunfire with a French police inspector in January 1946. "A Soldier in Four Armies: He Betrayed Them One After Another," reported France-Soir. (Murphy, *Turncoat*, p. 258)

André's fellow *Résistants* Bernard Vernier-Palliez and Hubert Rousselier, as well as the fabrication of a number of keys, they finally manage to reach the cellar beneath Postel-Vinay's cell. There they remove a floorboard above them and try to communicate with Morse code. But Postel-Vinay only remembers enough of the code to respond with a simple SOS.

Postel-Vinay considers this attempt to free him crazier than his own decision to feign madness. Even if his rescuers manage to open a hole for him to escape through, he will never be able to perform the gymnastics required for an escape, since he can barely walk.

Before they can proceed to the next step, he is moved again, and the escape effort is abandoned. Postel-Vinay thinks it's a miracle that his would-be rescuers haven't themselves been captured during their attempts to free him.

Nine

POSTEL-VINAY has undergone two surprisingly civil interrogations by his German captors after his attempt to kill himself. He is completely baffled by the gentleness of his interrogators. But he concludes that logic is just as irrelevant as justice in his present circumstances.

Put into multiple casts by the Germans after his misadventure, he endures excruciating pain. But after his second interrogation, Postel-Vinay feels gigantic relief. He deduces from his interrogators' questions that his parents probably haven't been arrested, and he concludes that the Germans have failed to find his blue notebook—the one that includes the names of some of his confederates—because he is never asked any questions about it.

His ultimate nightmare—that he might have endangered his family or his comrades—has "miraculously disappeared." As a result, he regains some of his will to live, even as he remains certain that the Germans will eventually execute him. "The fear of talking stopped haunting me. Now I was sure I would be able to die in peace."

A month or two after the arrest, his mother makes contact with a German officer who is a chaplain to find out if her son is alive. The next day, the chaplain comes to Postel-Vinay's cell and extends his hand, covered in a field-gray glove, and declares, "Take this hand. Your mother touched it yesterday. She loves you very much. She is really very courageous."

Even more remarkably, a month later, one of Postel-Vinay's interrogators authorizes one package from his parents, every fifteen days, containing food, books, pencils, and paper. He begins to write poems, deep into the night, and goes to sleep with "the joys of an author's vanity, and duty accomplished."

Then around April 15, 1942, he receives a visit from a German officer and a white-haired man whom Postel-Vinay at first mistakes for an artist. In fact, his visitor is Clovis Vincent, the prewar head of neurology at the hospital who has retained his post during the German Occupation. Gradually, Postel-Vinay realizes the famous doctor has been sent there by his family to urge him to feign insanity, to avoid a firing squad.

Part of him remains eager to die. But is it fair to spurn his parents' attempt to save him? He knows their hope isn't completely far-fetched: Even one of his interrogators has mentioned the possibility that he will be tried by a tribunal rather than face summary execution.

Finally he decides it is too selfish to reject his parents' plan. He has already made them suffer too much. So he embarks upon "a ship of fools" to try to deceive his captors.

For the first stage of his fake madness, he pretends to suffer from terrible migraines. Then, toward the end of April, the casts are finally removed from his legs. They are skeletal, with no trace of calves, and his ankles are frozen in place. Postel-Vinay is certain he will never again be able to walk more than a few yards.

Realizing that his fake migraines and fraudulent tics will never get the attention of guards already numbed by the genuine traumas of his fellow prisoners, Postel-Vinay decides his only option is to attempt suicide—again.

At the beginning of May, he begins to search for the right instrument of destruction. The only one he can find is a short nail at the end of his bed. Blunt, rusty, and slightly twisted, it is hardly ideal, but it's all he has.

His first thought is to plunge the nail into his right eye (which doesn't see very well anyway), but he quickly realizes that he lacks the resolve to mutilate himself that way.

Once a week he is given a Gillette razor for ten minutes so that he can shave himself. On June 20, he shoves the handle of the razor into a bar of soap, then plunges the naked edge of the blade into his left forearm. He means only to cut some veins, but instead he hits an artery and severs some tendons.

When his captors return to his room a few minutes later, they instantly take him away to the operating room. There the surgeon spends an hour and a half repairing the artery and the surrounding tendons—without offering any anesthetic.

On August 1, he is ordered to get dressed. Then he is removed from his cell and taken outside. Waiting for him in the street is the familiar Citroën Traction Avant used by the Gestapo. Postel-Vinay is pushed into the backseat. Then he watches the streets go by—boulevard de l'Hôpital, boulevard Saint-Marcel, boulevard Arago, rue de la Santé. Now he knows he is being sent back to the place where his misfortune began—the Prison de la Santé.

After a month back in his old prison, on August 31, a guard opens his cell and tells him to gather all of his belongings, which at this moment consist of a single toothbrush. Is he being sent to a concentration camp? Or to the "next world"? He has no idea where he is going, but—to his own surprise—Postel-Vinay feels no fear.

This time, a windowless gray van awaits to take him to his next destination. Ten minutes later, he knows there will be no deportation or execution today. He has been returned to the Quentin Pavilion in the l'hôpital de la Pitié—to a cell just down the hall from the one he left four weeks earlier.

The following afternoon, on September 1, he is moved again. This time there is an ambulance downstairs, attended by a male nurse and a German soldier. Postel-Vinay lies down on the ambulance bed and the soldier closes the door. Ten minutes later, he has arrived at a new, unfamiliar building. He is led to something that looks like a shower room, and the nurse locks the door behind him.

Through the window he peers into a garden, where he sees other inmates walking around, who are obviously crazy. He doesn't know it yet, but he is actually in a psychiatric institution: l'hôpital Sainte-Anne, in the 14th arrondissement of Paris.

Nothing happens for two more days, and Postel-Vinay becomes increasingly nervous about the performance he has planned. He must convince his captors that he is truly crazy. Meanwhile, he is praying with all his might: "Here I am at the end of my strength. Help me God!"

Finally, on the afternoon of his third day at Sainte-Anne, a nurse leads him into the office of a German psychiatrist.

"So," the doctor asks, "what's wrong?"

"What's wrong?" he replies. "I know where I am. I'm in an insane asylum! My parents always thought I belonged here, but they are the ones who are crazy!"

Postel-Vinay continues his charade for several minutes, but to no avail. Finally, his German interrogator speaks again. "Monsieur Postel-Vinay, now I'm going to tell you what I think. You have played your role very well. But you are not crazy."

"Of course I'm not crazy," Postel-Vinay replies. "It's only my parents..." But suddenly the doctor's face darkens, and he stands up. Postel-Vinay stands up with him. At last the prisoner lets down his guard: "Whatever I did, I did for my country."

"Ah, yes," the German replies. "That is exactly the way I understand things."

The doctor walks him back out into the hallway, noticing that he is still suffering tremendously because of his barely healed ankles. "You really walk as badly as that?" he asks. "I will order an ambulance to take you back to Quentin."

The doctor deposits him on a bench and returns to his office. Postel-Vinay looks around him. He is in a narrow hallway, surrounded by other patients, all wearing the blue uniforms provided by the hospital. One door off the hall leads to a room where he can hear German being spoken—that must be a guard post. At the far end, another door leads to the garden—and possible freedom? But a soldier is guarding that exit.

After all he has been through, the odds against an escape seem overwhelming. But a primal instinct propels Postel-Vinay off the bench, toward the door to the garden. He pauses at the exit for a couple of seconds, like a man looking to see if his car has arrived.

Then the miracles begin: The guard makes no attempt to bar his way.

Why not? The soldier is only supposed to stop the patients in blue uniforms, and no one else? Postel-Vinay is very disheveled, but he *is* dressed like a civilian. *Oh, saintly German discipline!* he thinks silently to himself.

As he continues down the steps into the garden, he thinks he hears the soldier being called back into the guard room. But he does not turn around. He spots an archway in front of him and a workman—a Frenchman—coming toward him from that direction.

"Where's the exit?" Postel-Vinay asks, as casually as possible.

"Take your first left and follow the long alley to the end."

Surely there will be another guard at the end of the alley, but Postel-Vinay isn't about to stop now. And when he reaches the street, there is no soldier.

He listens for someone running behind him and watches for the ambulance that has been dispatched to return him to his cell. But there is no one and nothing, except for two small children walking toward him on rue Cabanis, to his right.

Now seconds matter.

"Listen, kids, I've just escaped. The Germans will shoot me if they catch me. Give me enough money for the Métro. I'm wounded, without a cent, and I can barely walk."

The children are wide-eyed, astonished—and speechless. But they immediately start searching their pockets for change. Between them they have 23 centimes, just enough for one Métro ticket. They give him all of their money and point him to the closest Métro station—Glacière.*

Postel-Vinay is self-conscious about the way he walks and looks; surely his appearance will draw unwelcome attention. He is unshaven, his suit is unpressed, there are no suspenders to hold up his pants, and no laces in his shoes. He looks like a young hobo, and the unhealed bones in his ankles are incredibly painful.

If his life did not depend on it, he could not possibly walk more than a couple of blocks by himself. But his life *does* depend on it, and somehow, he summons a supernatural force from within that propels him down into the Métro Glacière.

If I were them, I would certainly alert all the subway station chiefs to look for me, and I would stop the trains on the nearest line. But the trains keep running.

Underground there are throngs of Parisians—and plenty of German soldiers. Postel-Vinay gets on the train DIRECTION ÉTOILE. He travels five stops, then gets off at Montparnasse. Randomly, he decides to go north, DIRECTION PORTE DE LA CHAPELLE—anything to get off the line he started on.

The passages between the Métro lines suddenly feel incredibly long. When he reaches the platform, he thinks he's Jean Valjean, the forever-on-the-run protagonist of *Les Misérables*—and the Nazis are all Javerts. When the train arrives, it is full of more German soldiers.

He changes lines two more times and hobbles out at Trocadéro. He decides to telephone an old friend and fellow *Résistant*, Pierre Heeley. But he has no coins in his pocket. So he settles his gaze on a "perfectly suitable older woman."

---

* The same station Jacqueline ran to when she had to rescue Christiane from the Palais de Chaillot.

"Excuse me, madame. I am an escaped prisoner of war. My feet are wounded from walking and I want to telephone a friend. Could you give me just enough for one call?"

Like the children on the street a half hour earlier, she says nothing; just hands over the necessary coins and disappears. Postel-Vinay makes his call, but there is no answer. Then, wretched luck: His coins are not returned to him.

Now he sees a man in a Métro uniform approaching him, and this time he is certain he is done for.

"Excuse me, sir," says the Métro man. "A woman I know told me who you are. I can help you. First of all, take twenty francs—in coins, because it will be more useful to you that way. If you can't reach one of your friends, come back here around eleven thirty tonight. I'll be here until midnight. I won't take you to my house, because of the curfew; I'll put you in a broom closet. You'll have a bad night, but when the first Métro comes in the morning, I'll come and get you."

Postel-Vinay thanks the stranger with all his heart, and just as quickly, his benefactor disappears. In a city filled with noncombatants—Frenchmen who are neither resisting the Germans nor collaborating with them—there are a remarkable number of secret heroes. And when a downed British or American pilot knocks on a stranger's door in the countryside, 99 percent of the time, he will be hidden rather than betrayed.

Postel-Vinay takes the Métro to rue de la Pompe to see if there is anyone in the apartment of his friend Pierre Heeley. But the shutters are closed; he must be away on vacation, or on a voyage.

Now he is so exhausted and so thirsty that he commits what he knows is a "folly": He steps into a bistro in his hobo garb to order *un demi*. It tastes like "the most delicious beer ever drunk."

He must call someone who will recognize his voice so that he won't have to say his name over the telephone, especially if he's speaking to someone in the Resistance. His friends Henry and Suzanne Rollet were part of the underground fight long before

Postel-Vinay was arrested, so he settles on them. He returns to the phone booth at Trocadéro.

"Hello! Henry! Yes, my friend, I am completely cured, and I'm spending a few days in Paris. Could I come see you tonight?"

"What a great surprise," Henry replies. "But of course—with joy. We'll wait dinner."

"Thank you so much. I'll be there, but it will probably take me an hour."

The Rollets live at 68, rue Nollet, in the 17th arrondissement. Postel-Vinay will have to change at Étoile, then take the train to Rome. In between Boissière and Kléber—back on the line he first jumped on after his escape—the train rumbles to a halt. Again, he's sure the Germans have discovered him, but again, the interruption means nothing.

When he steps out of the Rome Métro, he proceeds in the opposite direction from his destination. He confuses rue des Dames, rue de Saussure, and rue Lebouteux, and suddenly he is in a new nightmare. Then he finds himself back in front of the Rome Métro. Parisians sitting outside a café stare at him. If they notice him this time, it's because they noticed him a few minutes earlier. "Who is this young tramp who can barely stand up and doesn't even have a cane?" he imagines them wondering.

Without his glasses, he can barely read the street names on the sides of the darkening buildings. He takes a left on rue Boursault, and a right on rue de La Condamine. Finally he is going in the right direction, and he spies his destination: 68, rue Nollet.

Utterly exhausted, he must still climb five flights of stairs. With one more supreme act of will, he makes it up to his friends' apartment.

"What a joy!" Henry declares.

"No! Look at the shape I'm in." Then he adds the caution every escapee seems to offer whenever he reaches safety: "I'm not even sure the Gestapo hasn't followed me here."

"Ridiculous," Henry says. "I've opened my last bottle of champagne, it's cold and we will drink it with dinner."

That night, Postel-Vinay has the soundest sleep of his life. The next morning, he wakes up with an incredible feeling: "Beloved liberty! Liberty miraculously reconquered, but still so fragile..."

TWELVE DAYS after Postel-Vinay's escape, his friend Henry Rollet makes contact with Patrick O'Leary, the head of one of the two Resistance organizations Postel-Vinay worked with before his arrest. O'Leary has always promised that he would get him out of the country if it became absolutely necessary, and he is a man of his word. His message to Postel-Vinay is that he must reach Marseille in four days, on September 18, where he will contact Georges Zarifi, at 12, allée Léon Gambetta.

Henry organizes Postel-Vinay's escape from Paris meticulously. The first leg is a bicycle ride to Pont Saint-Michel station—a departure point chosen to avoid the larger stations, which are more dangerous because they are more heavily patrolled by the police.

At the end of a bridge over the Seine, he is met by Henry and another co-conspirator, Jean Vialla, who takes Postel-Vinay's bicycle and rides away on it. Then Henry guides him down the stairs into the station.

They change trains at Juvisy and Brétigny. At six the next morning they arrive at Coutras. Now, the hard part: He must cross the line between occupied and unoccupied France. He has no idea when or how he will do it; he only knows that he must meet a guide in the café in the train station at ten o'clock. Then he is supposed to ride a bicycle for twelve miles. But will he have the strength to do that?

The café isn't open yet, so he and Henry sit in the waiting room, a dirty, poorly lit room, with a stone-cold stove in the corner on a black and chilly morning. Suddenly two policemen walk in. Is *this* the end of his voyage? Postel-Vinay remembers the name on his false identity card in his pocket: Fernand François Claude André Duval, an engineer, born July 4, 1912, in Algiers. But the policemen never approach him. Instead, they sit down and talk quietly.

Fifteen minutes later, they stand up to leave.

Exactly on time, the young guide arrives at the café with two bicycles. Postel-Vinay and Henry say their goodbyes, and Postel-Vinay begins to pedal painfully behind his guide. Often he has to get off and walk to climb a hill. The weather is clear and fresh and dry. After about two hours, his guide finally dismounts and tells Postel-Vinay to do the same.

They walk through a silent forest until they reach a clearing; a farmhouse lies beyond it. The guide tells Postel-Vinay to wait outside while he goes in to meet the residents. A moment later he signals him to follow him into the house.

The farmer and his wife greet him like a son. On the dining room table, among other marvels there is a huge smoked ham. They explain to him that he will be crossing the border between the two zones that evening—in an oxcart with a secret compartment!

After a magnificent lunch, Postel-Vinay retires for a nap in a large bedroom upstairs. Three hours later, he is awakened by the farmer's wife: Time to go.

The farmer removes a plank from the oxcart to reveal his hiding place. It's so narrow he's grateful that his months in prison have made him so thin. After a short ride, the oxcart comes to a halt, and the plank beneath him disappears so that he can climb out.

The farmer kisses him on both cheeks and sends him on his way. After a couple of hundred yards on foot, he reaches the zone libre. And his next guide—"small, round, and dark"—appears out of the darkness to lead him to the automobile he has borrowed from a local doctor.

Another two hundred yards and they reach the car. "I will take you to Ribérac," the new guide explains. "You will spend the night in a hotel there. At seven o'clock in the morning you'll catch a bus for Brive, and from there, the train to Marseille."

The next day, he travels for sixteen hours, reaching Marseille Saint-Charles station at eleven fifteen, just forty-five minutes before the curfew. Outside the station, there is a taxi driving by—and it stops for him!

Two more miracles.

"I've sprained my ankle and I need a hotel for the night," Postel-Vinay tells the driver.

"Well," he replies, "all the hotels in Marseille are full. But I'll help you out. I know a woman who will put you up in her house. And it will be cheaper than a hotel! Will that suit you?"

"Perfect!"

The driver delivers him to a mansion that shows no sign of being a commercial establishment. The proprietress welcomes him and gives him a room with a big bed and a lovely bathroom. Not even a registration form to fill out!

He leaves the house the next morning and walks out into a beautiful Mediterranean light "that chases away unhappiness." It is Friday, September 18, 1942. He asks another "suitable-looking" passerby for directions to allée Léon Gambetta, the home of his fellow *Résistant* Georges Zarifi.

Georges is an old friend, who has been in the Resistance as long as Postel-Vinay. He is about twenty-five, thin and athletic, a member of the French national tennis team. He comes from a wealthy family from Greece.

When Postel-Vinay reaches Georges's house, he is welcomed by his father. As with so many other young *Résistants*, it is never entirely clear how much his parents know about what Georges is doing. So Postel-Vinay assumes his father's ignorance and repeats his usual story about having just sprained his ankle. The father greets him warmly and tells him Georges will be back home for lunch.

When Georges arrives a few hours later, he tells Postel-Vinay that he has arranged for him to leave for Gibraltar—with forty other escapees!

The next morning when he arrives at nine o'clock at Saint-Charles station, Postel-Vinay is reunited with Patrick O'Leary, a man he particularly admires for his judgment and his organizational talent—qualities that he did not find often enough among many other Resistance leaders. O'Leary himself is in charge of the operation. The escapees break off in groups of three or four to take their places on the train. The RAF pilots with him have fake papers identifying them as deaf-mutes, so they won't betray themselves with their accents. The others include French and Polish agents, and even one German, Paula, who has been Patrick's secretary.

The train takes them to Perpignan in the south of France, not far from the border with Spain. Postel-Vinay's ankles begin to give out on their walk to the beach, and two big Canadian airmen carry him between them.

Hiding behind a dune, he is approached by an RAF pilot from New Zealand—whom Postel-Vinay has actually rescued one year earlier from the farmhouse where he had been hiding after his plane was shot down. This pilot had also stayed with Suzanne and Henry Rollet in Paris—the same couple who harbored Postel-Vinay for a few days right after his escape.

At two A.M., the boat that will take them to Gibraltar finally appears offshore, and a smaller boat reaches the beach to pick them up. A Polish sailor loads Postel-Vinay into the first vessel, then helps him on the larger ship a couple hundred yards later. The trip takes three days, and Postel-Vinay suffers from terrible seasickness until the weather finally calms.

A fellow passenger tells him he must make contact with de Gaulle when he reaches London. Some Frenchmen are working directly for the English, but Postel-Vinay must work for the Free French! Postel-Vinay says he had already decided to do that.

On the morning of the third day, they are met by the British vessel that will take them on their last leg to Gibraltar. Calm seas ensure an easy transfer. One of the British officers on board immediately offers Postel-Vinay his cabin; the Frenchman is moved by this "instant act of kindness."

The following afternoon, he finally reaches Gibraltar—"English territory." He quickly makes contact with Captain Jacques Vaudreuil (real name: François Thierry-Mieg), who has been de Gaulle's personal representative in the British colony since October. One of Vaudreuil's aides warns Postel-Vinay that a vetting awaits him at Patriotic School in England—a prospect that fills him with disgust. After all he has suffered at the hands of the Germans, he must now endure a new challenge from the British.

He understands the necessity of trying to ferret out double and triple agents, but he still resents the idea that he will have to prove himself again.

THREE WEEKS LATER, on October 15, 1942. Postel-Vinay takes off from Gibraltar in a twin-engine DC-3, which delivers him to an airfield in the English countryside. From there, a bus takes him to a police station in a London suburb, where a charming British officer listens to Postel-Vinay's unbelievable tale of escape.

The Englishman listens politely—and doesn't seem to believe a single word Postel-Vinay tells him. Then he dispatches him to Patriotic School for further interrogation.

This is the first stop for every self-described *Résistant* arriving in England during the war. Patriotic School has been created to distinguish between genuine Allied sympathizers ("sheep") and double agents who are really working for the Germans ("goats").

The London Reception Centre had been established at the Royal Victoria Patriotic School in Wandsworth by the British intelligence agency MI5 at the beginning of 1941. During the course of the war, thirty-three thousand refugees will pass through the center, where they are "questioned about their methods of escape, the routes they had followed, safe houses, couriers, helpers and documentation. Their statements [are] meticulously indexed and cross-checked against those of their companions and earlier arrivals. Intelligence [is] extracted and circulated to Whitehall departments."

Those identified as "goats" are shipped off to Camp 020, which oversees 440 prisoners during the course of the war. After an early instance of a violent, unauthorized interrogation, a strict rule against torture is enforced—because the British believe non-coercive interrogations are the ones most likely to produce accurate information. This is also the conclusion of more sophisticated Allied interrogators almost everywhere during World War II.

Patriotic School is an austere place, lightened a bit by a library that reminds Postel-Vinay of a London club. It is filled with refugees from every country invaded by the Nazis, many with escape stories just as implausible as his own. After eight days of waiting, his interrogation by the British finally begins.

The examination lasts five days: two or three hours in the morning and another two or three hours in the afternoon. He has to recount all of his experiences in the Resistance twice—first chronologically, then divided up among the various branches he has served in.

When he describes his escape from the mental hospital in Paris, he mentions the 23 centimes he received from the boys in the street. "And then I took my second left—"

"That's impossible!" his interrogator interrupts. "The rue Cabanis, where the hospital exit is, ends at the rue de la Glacière. So there is no 'second left'!"*

---

* Postel-Vinay's daughter, Claire Andrieu, points out that this is either a mistake by the interrogator, or something misremembered by her father, because "the rue Cabanis does not end at the rue de la Glacière, it ends at the rue de la Santé. But my father's argument remains correct—he did indeed take his second left." (e-mail to the author from Claire Andrieu, September 30, 2014)

They agree to examine a map of the neighborhood together.

"Look here," says Postel-Vinay. "There is another street—the street that starts right in front of the exit of the hospital. When I turned right into the street, I left this other street on my left. So for me, that was my first left. Rue La Glacière was my *second left*."

"Good answer," says the British officer. "Quite plausible. We will meet once more tomorrow morning, but it should be brief."

The Frenchman has climbed over his final hurdle before freedom.

At nine o'clock the following morning, Postel-Vinay walks into his inquisitor's office. "I have nothing else to ask you," says the Englishman. "But I have three things to tell you. First, you will leave us this morning. The BCRA is sending a car for you. Second, the head of Patriotic School, Major Y, is waiting to meet you in his office. And third...I am proud to know you!"

Major Y offers a parting glass of champagne—"a good champagne." Then Postel-Vinay climbs into the waiting car, which delivers him to BCRA headquarters in London at 10 Duke Street. There he meets Pierre Brossolette, and then, Charles de Gaulle himself.

The general asks just one question: "What would the effect be on the French if they learned there was a grave difference between me and the English?"

Postel-Vinay replies that this would be very dangerous, because it would reinforce German propaganda that England is France's real enemy.

Then de Gaulle tells him that he is making him associate director general of the newly created Central Bank for Free French colonies. Postel-Vinay is not enthusiastic about this, but de Gaulle has made his decision. Although he will no longer be fighting the Germans directly, the young Frenchman comforts himself with the thought that at least he will be working for the greater good of France. And de Gaulle has guaranteed that he will spend the rest of the war out of danger.

Ten

LESS THAN A MONTH after Postel-Vinay arrives in London, General Dwight Eisenhower oversees an invasion of North Africa, with 110,000 troops, who land near Casablanca, Oran, and Algiers on November 8, 1942.

Franklin Roosevelt favors the invasion because he thinks it's a political imperative to engage German troops as soon as possible, and North Africa is the only feasible place to do that at the end of 1942. The big question is whether the French troops in the African colonies will fight the Allied invasion. As Operation Torch begins, Roosevelt issues a statement saying that he hopes it will "prove the first historic step to the liberation and restoration of France."

As André considers where to go at the end of 1942, he is buoyed by the news that the French troops led by Vichy generals in North Africa have offered only a day or two of token resistance to the American assault. On November 11—which happens to be Christiane's nineteenth birthday—Admiral François Darlan, the senior French officer in North Africa, signs a cease-fire ending French fighting in the area.

Hitler reacts to the cease-fire by instantly ordering the German Occupation of the free zone in the south of France—a clear violation of the armistice he had signed in 1940. After that the free zone becomes known as the southern zone. De Gaulle observed that by not firing a single shot to resist the Occupation of the south, the

Vichy regime "dissipated the lying pretense of independence which [it] had claimed in order to justify its capitulation" in 1940.

The arrival of the Germans means that the French fleet at Toulon, commanded by Admiral Jean de Laborde, is now in danger of falling into the hands of the Nazis. It would be a huge prize for the Germans: three battleships, eight cruisers, seventeen destroyers, sixteen torpedo boats, sixteen submarines, and seven dispatch vessels, as well as some sixty transport ships, tankers, mine sweepers, and tugs.

For the next two weeks, Admiral Laborde is lobbied fiercely by the Germans, by de Gaulle, and by Admiral Darlan, who wants Laborde to sail his fleet to North Africa, where Darlan has just reached an armistice with the Allies. But Laborde remains paralyzed, and on November 26, the Germans storm Toulon to seize all of his ships.

To prevent the ships from falling into the hands of the Germans, Laborde orders what de Gaulle describes as "the most pitiful and sterile suicide imaginable": Laborde commands his sailors to scuttle the entire fleet. Just one destroyer, one torpedo boat, and five tankers are still intact by the time the Germans gain control of the port.

Now the Allies must decide which Frenchman will be allowed to lead the French overseas territories. De Gaulle is the only general who has sided with the British from the start, but he has been kept in the dark about the North African invasion, and he certainly has no friends among former Vichy officials.

The Americans flirt with General Henri Giraud but then settle on Admiral Darlan. Eisenhower agrees to recognize him as head of the French state in return for committing French troops to the war against the Germans. But de Gaulle's representative in Algiers reports back that despite the announced collaboration, Eisenhower's general staff has "stressed their desire to enter into direct relations with General de Gaulle."

There is an immediate uproar in Britain and the United States over the decision to embrace Darlan, a man who has openly connived with the Germans. "There was a tremendous outcry in the American press," said Robert Paxton. "Why are we working with these collaborators? That was one of the things that Roosevelt did that was most openly and bitterly criticized" in America.

The conflict is resolved when Darlan is murdered on Christmas eve. His assassin is a passionate young man named Fernand Bonnier de la Chapelle, acting on behalf of either the Count of Paris or de Gaulle's allies, depending on which version of events you choose to believe. The killer is almost immediately executed by French authorities, thus guaranteeing a permanent mystery.

In his memoirs, de Gaulle gives such a convoluted description of the assassin's possible motives that he (perhaps unconsciously) encourages the idea that his allies were responsible for the assassination. That is particularly so when he writes, "If the tragic character of Darlan's disappearance from the scene could not fail to be condemned by many, the very fact that he was forced from the stage seemed in accord with the harsh logic of events. For history, in its great moments, tolerates in positions of authority only those men capable of directing their own course."

Suspicion falls on de Gaulle because Darlan's assassination makes it possible for de Gaulle to immediately outmaneuver Giraud—and seize the reins of French power in North Africa.

Eleven

AT THE BEGINNING OF 1944, just over two years after Postel-Vinay's capture, André Boulloche has landed in the same prison hospital his boss was held in—after he has fumbled his own suicide at the time of his arrest. André has lost a great deal of blood when he is shot, but he survives the drive to l'hôpital de la Salpêtrière. The Germans operate on him immediately. They want him alive—but only so that they can make him talk. After the operation, they put him alone in a prison hospital room, without any postoperative care.

André thinks that the gunshot wound has probably saved his life. At the moment he was fired on, he had the cyanide pill in his pocket. He had always promised himself that he would swallow the pill when he was arrested, the denouement he had expected.

But in the instant after the Germans shoot him, he decides he will not kill himself.

Everything is ruined anyway, he says to himself. *Let's see what the next twenty-four hours bring.* Afterward, he remains certain that he would have swallowed the cyanide if he had been arrested unhurt.

Lying in bed, alone in his prison hospital room, André begins to ponder all the peregrinations that have led him to this wretched outcome.

First there was the abortive trip to North Africa, immediately after the armistice, where he found it was impossible to fight against the Germans. Then his return to France and his civilian job with the government, his recruitment into the Resistance by Postel-Vinay at the end of 1940, and Postel-Vinay's arrest at the end of 1941.

He had taken over for Postel-Vinay in the northern region after his boss was captured by the Germans. He made contacts with other leaders of the secret army and recruited three more of his government colleagues to fight the enemy. Throughout 1942, he continued to smuggle arms and to collect information about German troop movements to send to London.

Toward the end of 1942, André learns that the Gestapo is about to arrest him. When the news of the Allied invasion of North Africa reaches France in November through the always-jammed transmissions of the BBC, he tells his family that he has decided to return to Morocco.

AFTER SAYING GOODBYE to his family in Paris on December 1, 1942, André boards a train for Nevers in Burgundy, 150 miles south of the capital. His Resistance colleague Bernard Vernier-Palliez puts him in touch with a sympathetic garage owner who helps him cross the demarcation line into the newly christened southern zone on foot.

André arrives in Toulouse on December third. From there he travels to Pau, in the foothills of the Pyrenees, thirty miles from the Spanish border. Then he makes his way to Tardets-Sorholus, where an inn owner is another Resistance sympathizer.

At seven o'clock in the evening on the day after Christmas, André and twelve others meet up with a guide who leads them through the snow, on an unmarked path, over a six-thousand-foot mountain in the Pyrenees. When they reach the Spanish border seventeen hours later, the guide leaves them.

The Frenchmen continue on their own, finally reaching a hotel in the Irati forest at four in the afternoon. They are arrested almost immediately by the Spanish authorities. André pretends that he is a Canadian named Nicolas Boulloche. His fellow *Résistant* Vernier-Palliez identifies himself as an American.*

On January 1, they are transferred to a prison in Pamplona. There André meets other escapees, who convince him that he should try to make it to England, where de Gaulle is, instead of North Africa.

One month later, two pieces of very encouraging news reach the French refugees: British forces in North Africa have begun an assault on the German troops under the command of General Erwin Rommel ("the Desert Fox"). And as February begins, the last elements of the German 6th Army surrender at Stalingrad. That marks the end of what many strategists consider the decisive battle of the European theater.

On March 13, German officers make their first attempt to assassinate Hitler. A bomb disguised as two bottles of brandy is put on board the Führer's personal Focke-Wulf 200 Condor plane. The detonator activates, but cold temperatures prevent the plastic explosives from blowing up.

On March 20, André is moved to Jaraba, where he reconnects with André Rondenay, who had been his fellow student at the Lycée Janson de Sailly, as well as at the elite Ecole polytechnique, a decade earlier.†

The twenty-nine-year-old Rondenay is the son of a French general who served as the commandant of the military school at Saint-Maixent. The son is a charismatic fighter and a legendary forger. Fifteen months earlier he had created fake documents that enabled him to walk out the front gate of a German prison camp where

---

* An ironic choice for Vernier-Palliez: Four decades later he will become France's ambassador to the United States.

† Neither man can imagine that one year from now, Rondenay will succeed André as de Gaulle's military delegate in Paris, after André is arrested.

he was incarcerated. Now he presents André with the impeccable identity card of a German officer, to assist in *his* escape.

From Jaraba, André is once again transferred to Pamplona. On the evening of April 5, the Spanish guards there are distracted long enough to allow André and a fellow prisoner named Jean Martin to escape. It takes them several days to walk more than a hundred miles to Ariza. There they board a train to Madrid. In the Spanish capital, they locate another contact given to them by Rondenay, who introduces them to the British consul.

Ten days later, they are driven to an address that has been provided by their British contact. At the beginning of May, they cross the Spanish frontier into Portugal, reaching Lisbon on May 3. Two days later, they board a plane for Bristol, England.

There is exciting news from North Africa as soon as André reaches England. On May 7, American and British forces capture Tunis and Bizerte, and 160,000 German and Italian soldiers surrender. Six days later, German Afrika Korps commander General Dietloff Jürgen von Arnim surrenders another 275,000 troops.

Like Postel-Vinay before him, André is dispatched to Patriotic School as soon as he lands in England. Once he has convinced the British that he is indeed a "sheep"—a genuine enemy of the Germans—he seeks out Charles de Gaulle at his headquarters in London.

André is excited at the prospect of the massive invasion to be led by the Americans, although his British handlers have noted that his "deep satisfaction" with the growing strength of the Allies "is mingled with a fear of eventual blunders by American authorities, due to a lack of understanding of aspirations in the occupied countries."

André tells de Gaulle that he wants to return to France with the forthcoming Allied invasion. But the French general is still desperately short of men to send into occupied France. The fifty-two-year-old general tells the twenty-seven-year-old engineer that he requires him in occupied Paris as soon as possible, so that he can be the general's military delegate, coordinating all Resistance activity in northern France.

Flattered by the general's invitation, André immediately accepts his commission. André is assigned to the action division of the intelligence section of BCRA, which coordinates with the British foreign intelligence agency, MI6, while the action section focuses on sabotage operations in France. To prepare him for his return to Paris, the French send him to the British espionage school, where he is given the agent name Roger Doneau.

The first officer to work with him is Lieutenant Colonel Hutchison. He describes André as a "capable type, enthusiastic, straightforward, intelligent. Has a pleasing personality and is helpful, in a quiet way, towards his less brilliant comrades. Is modest. Not very communicative about himself. Should turn out to be A.1 from security point of view."

His next instructor echoes Hutchison's assessment: "An outstanding man. He has considerable previous experience but has shown himself very keen to learn. He is very pleasant to work with." The base commandant also finds him "very quick to learn. Is intelligent and possesses powers of Leadership. Should do well."

André goes on to win superlatives in almost every clandestine competition: "physical training, very fit and enthusiastic; fieldcraft, excellent; weapon training, a good shot; explosives & demolitions, very competent, previous experience stands him in good stead; signaling & communications, very good; he has an incisive brain and completely understands the requirements of any given situation."

He earns a General Agent Grading of "A" for "Outstanding," and his intelligence rating is 9, which also puts him in the top category: "Superior Intelligence."

BUT NONE OF THESE QUALITIES is enough to prevent André's capture by the Germans less than four months after his return to Paris.

Lying in his prison hospital bed in January 1944, recovering from his gunshot wounds, André reflects on his many narrow escapes. Still delirious in his postoperative state, he decides that he still has the strength to liberate himself.

Unlike Postel-Vinay, who tried to plunge to his death, André believes that he can ascend to freedom. The wounded man will use his bare hands to scale the curtains in his room, which lead to the skylight above him—and a faint possibility of escape, if he can shatter the glass to reach the roof.

André starts slowly, gripping the curtain with one fist right above the other. Superhuman determination carries him up a couple of yards; then he loses his grip and crashes down on the floor.

As soon as he hits the ground, he realizes that he has popped most of the stitches in his stomach. Despite excruciating pain, he manages to pull himself back onto the bed.

The Germans don't discover his ruptured wound until their next examination, eight days later. Then they do a very poor job of suturing him a second time. For a long time afterward, his organs are covered by a frighteningly thin layer of skin.

A week after his arrest, his sisters decide to organize André's escape. Their cousin, the surgeon Funck-Brentano, works in a hospital right next to the one where André is a prisoner. He is the surgeon who had assisted André in his unsuccessful attempt to liberate Postel-Vinay from the same prison hospital two years before.

Funck-Brentano has worked with André ever since his return to Paris, sometimes performing forbidden operations on Resistance members who have suffered gunshot wounds. Gradually he becomes so involved in the secret war that he acquires his own code name: Paulin.

With the surgeon's help, a group of André's friends locate the underground passage that connects the two hospitals, and an escape attempt is organized at the end of January. Christiane and Jacqueline rent an apartment near the hospital so that they can receive their wounded brother after his escape.

The two sisters spend a horrible night together in the apartment. With their stomachs in knots, they are so scared the neighbors will hear them that they don't dare even to turn on a water tap.

Their surgeon-cousin takes the first Métro at dawn so that he will be at the secret apartment when André gets there. But by the time he arrives, the sisters already know that the escape has failed.

The plotters have been unable to penetrate the floor of his prison hospital room from the basement below. Hearing the awful news, Christiane and Jacqueline fall into each other's arms and dissolve into tears.

Their cousin, fearing a trap, immediately flees the apartment.

ANDRÉ'S FIRST INTERROGATION by the Gestapo occurs at the hospital at the end of January 1944.

This is the baffling part of his story.

André and his chief aide, Charles Gimpel, have been arrested together on January 12, 1944.

Gimpel is brutally tortured by the Germans, but he survives the torture—and never talks.

Unlike Gimpel, André is shot at the time of his arrest, and that may explain why he never suffered the same way his deputy did—if André has told the truth about the way he was treated.

It is possible that by the time he had recovered enough from his gunshot wounds to be interrogated, whatever information he had was no longer worth much, because by then his unarrested comrades had all moved on to new secret locations.

Or else the Germans felt they had already learned whatever

they needed to know from Jacques, the Sorbonne student who had betrayed him and brought the Gestapo to his door.

Later, André tells his sister that his interrogators read him excerpts of their interview with Jacques, including this passage: "I was recruited by Christiane Boulloche. She lives with her parents and her sister Jacqueline at 28, avenue d'Eylau, third floor on the right. Her brother is my boss. He is living in a clandestine apartment on rue de la Santé in the Thirteenth."

When his German interrogators demanded confirmation of Jacques's words, André said that he used a formula that failed for scores of others but somehow worked for him: He identified himself as a French officer on a military mission. Therefore, under the rules of war, he cannot speak.

"If you found yourself in the same circumstances," he tells the German officers standing over him, "you would certainly do the same, and remain silent."

After that, André always said, the Germans stopped trying to interrogate him that day.*

The strongest counterevidence to this claim appears in the secret British file about André's wartime activities, which was declassified almost six decades later, at my request. There was only one item in the file that contradicted anything that he had told his family.

It is this entry from 1946: "in spite of [his wounds] *and of cruel tortures* [emphasis supplied], he gave away no compromising information." (Later, for his valor he was awarded the King's Medal for Courage.)

In February, André is moved to Fresnes, one of the largest prisons in France, in the town of Fresnes, Val-de-Marne, just outside Paris. Most of the other prisoners are fellow Resistance members,

---

* André's brother-in-law, Alex Katlama, told his son, Michel, that André hadn't been tortured because he had been wounded: "My father told me that they didn't torture him because they were worried he would die, or he wouldn't be able to take it." (author's interview with Michel Katlama, March 14, 1999)

and many of them have already been tortured. On February 15, he undergoes his second interrogation. By then he has been a prisoner for just over a month. The Germans read him a list of names and ask him to identify the ones he knows. Once again he refuses to cooperate.

By now his information is so old, most of it is probably worthless anyway. That could be why he again avoids being tortured.

"The Gestapo wasn't always logical." That is his sister Christiane's only explanation for the way her brother says he was treated. Or, as Postel-Vinay put it, pondering his own survival without ever being tortured, "Perhaps I was wrong to look for logic in an organization in which ability, incoherence, chance, barbarism and political rivalries were constantly warring for the upper hand."

TIPPED OFF that her brother has been moved to Fresnes, Christiane tries to deliver packages to him there. Occasionally they are accepted, but usually they are rejected.

One night in March, André reconnects with fellow prisoner Gilbert Farges, a former rugby player whom he had met a few times before. They stay up all night talking about their families, their arrests, and the "loving attention" they have both received from the Gestapo. Despite their circumstances, they also talk about the future, and their determination to escape. About this André is "inflexible, inexhaustible—and full of imagination."

By dawn, Farges and Boulloche have become good friends. For André, this will quickly become a lifesaving friendship.

On April 7, André is moved to the transit camp of Royallieu, in Compiègne, fifty miles north of Paris. Compiègne has been the hunting grounds of the kings of France since the eighth century. In 1944, it becomes the final stop for thousands of French patriots hunted down by the enemy, before they are deported to Germany.

Despite his badly tended wound, André is already becoming a leader of his fellow prisoners, through his dignity, his serenity, and his intellectual strength. In Fresnes, he had been kept in an underground cell. Now, for the first time in months, he can occasionally see the sun.

To Gilbert Farges, Compiègne feels like "semiliberty" compared to Fresnes: "The simple fact of seeing the sky and the sun, of being able to walk around and talk, feel like precious gifts. But we were barely nourished and many of us were already in terrible health."

André reconnects with another important person here: Charles Gimpel, his deputy in Paris before their arrest, now a fellow prisoner. As Gimpel's British handlers noted before his return to France, Gimpel is "an excellent man," "physically well above average," with "an excellent brain," an "outstanding" personality and a "keenness on the job" that is "infectious." (After the war, the British also award Gimpel the King's Medal for Courage.)

During their walks outside in the prison courtyard, the men are buoyed by glimpses of squadrons of American B-17 Flying Fortresses and B-24 Liberators filling the sky on their way to Germany.

Another fellow prisoner, Michel Bommelaer, finds it incredibly moving "to watch these heads from a mortuary...following the planes as they flew east, where a promised land of unimaginable cruelty awaits us."

In the third week of April, Christiane gets a tip that André is about to be shipped off to Germany. Hoping to catch a final glimpse of him, Christiane and Jacqueline travel with their parents to Compiègne, where they spend the night in a squalid hotel. The next morning, they spot André in the courtyard, hunched over because of his badly tended wound. When André sees them, Christiane tries to throw him a loaf of bread with a file hidden in the middle of it, but the Gestapo shout at her and push her away.

At this moment it occurs to André that this may be the last time that he will ever see his family. But despite his family's horror over his departure, there is also an element of hope: "When we learned one of our comrades would be deported, we were relieved," Christiane remembered. "Because it meant that they hadn't been tortured to death."

André boards the deportation train on April 27, 1944—forty days before the Allied invasion at Normandy. Gilbert Farges pushes him into a corner of the car to make it easier to protect him. Then Farges asks Rémy, a beefy man from the Basque region, to stand next to both of them. From then on, André leans on one of these two men, doing anything he can to conserve his energy.

Seventeen hundred prisoners are put in seventeen cattle cars: one hundred crammed into each car. Their destination is Auschwitz. Among them are thirty-nine employees of the French national railroad, two poets, twenty priests, and members of sixty-four different Resistance organizations.

Most of them are younger than thirty-five. The youngest prisoner is fifteen, the oldest, seventy-one. They range from laborers and journalists to businessmen, politicians, and policemen.

Among the more famous are Pierre Johnson, inspector general of Compagnie Transatlantique shipping company, who is a great-great-nephew of the nineteenth-century American president Andrew Johnson, and Count Paul Chandon-Möet, a champagne magnate, who will die a few days before his prison camp is liberated by the Allies.

Also on board is Charles Porte. Porte was the police commissioner of Chartres when Jean Moulin, the head of the Resistance, was prefect of Eure-et-Loir. Porte had been responsible for security for the inaugural meeting of the Conseil national de la Résistance, which Moulin presided over on May 27, 1943. Porte will survive deportation and return to France after the war.

During four horrific days and three terrible nights, the prisoners struggle to survive without food or water. Dozens of them succumb before the train reaches the death camp. The cars are so crammed with humanity, no one ever has enough room to sit down. André is guarded the whole time by Gilbert Farges and Rémy, both of whom are big enough to protect him; fortunately, Farges is as wide as he is tall. André's organs are kept inside by that very thin layer of skin, and a blow to his stomach would surely be fatal.

When thirst and hunger take hold, many of the prisoners become delirious, touching off terrifying scenes of madness. "As time passed, the temperature mounted, asphyxiation was winning, and a devouring thirst installed itself with dementia and violence," Farges remembered.

As one prisoner after another dies, their corpses are piled on top of one another in a corner to make more room for the survivors. "The crazy people become dangerous to the point where they try to open their own veins or those of others to drink their blood."

Rémy tells Farges, "We will not let your friend André die because of these maniacs." Somehow, through it all, André retains a strong spirit. "That was essential," said Farges. Occasionally, André is able to snatch a breath of fresh air from the cracks in the car. Just once, the Germans offer a bucket of water, but the prisoners are so frantic that it gets turned over before anyone can take a drink.

As their journey approaches the end, the survivors are nearly naked after stripping themselves because of the scorching heat. As the train reaches Silesia, the temperature drops, and the fetid air inside becomes slightly fresher. By the time they reach Auschwitz, it is freezing, and the ground is covered with snow.

When the doors of the cars are finally flung open, the prisoners are greeted by Gestapo men armed with revolvers and machine guns, others with vicious dogs pulling at their leashes, and the notorious capos, prisoners who are violent criminals used by the Germans to assist them with their punishments.

As he climbs out of the train, one of the Frenchmen jumps on a guard, causing his gun to misfire; the man is immediately shot dead by another German.

The prisoners are put in two separate barracks in Birkenau, the main extermination camp at Auschwitz. There each one is tattooed with a number on his forearm. Finally, the day after their arrival, they are given their first drink of water in five days.

After that, under the watchful eyes of the capos—"precarious survivors, brutal, hostile thieves who also know fear in this atmosphere of death"—all of the hair on their bodies is shaved.

Auschwitz is an unusual destination for these political prisoners: The convoy of April 27 is one of only three trains of non-Jews to be sent there from France during the entire war. André believed that these seventeen hundred prisoners were brought to Auschwitz to be exterminated in retaliation for the death of Pierre Pucheu. A former minister of the interior in the collaborationist Vichy government, he had been executed by the Free French in Algiers one month earlier.

The personal intervention of Marshal Pétain may be the only reason that everyone on the train isn't executed immediately.

DETERMINATION, DIGNITY, AND LUCK are the three requirements for survival. Remarkably, those are the attributes André still has in abundance. "After three weeks of murderous drills, the survivors still hadn't given up," Gilbert Farges recalled. The fearful scene reminded him of a saying of Montaigne: "They bent their knees, but held their souls high."

The prisoners watch the smoke spewing from the chimneys of the crematoria of Auschwitz all day and all night. After a few weeks, the survivors of the first convoy are put onto a new train of cattle cars, this one destined for Buchenwald. The transfer means a

tiny improvement in André's chances for survival. Ninety-five percent of the deportees to Auschwitz died at that camp, compared to
85 percent of the inmates at Buchenwald.

The capos at Auschwitz tell them their new home will be practically a "sanitarium" compared to their present one.

Twelve

Of course the two years through which Free France had endured
had also been filled with reversals and disappointments, but then we
had to stake everything to win everything; we had felt ourselves
surrounded by a heroic atmosphere, sustained by the necessity of
gaining our ends at any price.
—Charles de Gaulle

B ACK IN PARIS, Christiane and Jacqueline have finally moved
out of their parents' home into a new secret apartment. Apparently, it doesn't occur to anyone that Jacques, or André, might have
been tortured into giving up their parents' address. In any case,
their father never considers resigning his job as the director of the
bureau of highways or going into hiding with his wife. His main
concern, Christiane believes, is to keep his country working, "for
the French."

As James L. Stokesbury observed, men like Christiane's father
"were servants of the state, sworn to defend it; the accidents of
war had made the legitimate French government a tool of the conqueror, yet it was still the official French government. It took a special kind of person to throw aside the norms of a lifetime, to make
the lonely decision that there was a higher loyalty, a higher duty,
than that he had always acknowledged, and in the name of some
abstract moral principle to work against his own government."

Robert Paxton, the preeminent American historian of Vichy France, points out that "as the state came under challenge by Resistance vigilantism, a commitment to the ongoing functioning of the state reinforced the weight of routine...Resistance was not merely personally perilous. It was also a step toward social revolution."

After André Boulloche's arrest in January 1944, de Gaulle replaces him as military delegate in Paris with André Rondenay, André's college classmate, whom he had run into in Spain a year earlier, when Boulloche was on his way to London.

Rondenay is a man of parts. His thick brown hair and horn-rim glasses give him the look of an intellectual, and he favors three-piece suits with double-breasted vests.

Three and a half years into the war, Rondenay is a famous escape artist. First taken prisoner in the Vosges region of France near the German border in June 1940, he spends time as a prisoner in Saarburg and Westphalia before being transferred to Mainz in October.

After escaping and being recaptured several times, he is taken to Colditz Castle, a prisoner-of-war camp for officers, in January 1942. In May, he is moved again, this time to Lübeck.* There he manages to manufacture the perfect papers of a German officer. On December 19, 1942, he and a comrade walk out unchallenged through the front gate of the camp.

His fake identity continues to protect him during an incredible journey through Hamburg, Frankfurt, Mayence, Ludwigshafen,

---

* Two months before Rondenay got there, on March 28, Lübeck was subjected to a horrendous attack by the RAF, when 234 British bombers dropped 400 tons of bombs, including 25,000 incendiary devices, which created a firestorm that burned one-third of the city. The intent was to demoralize the civilian population. Nazi propaganda minister Joseph Goebbels wrote in his diary: "The damage is really enormous, I have been shown a newsreel of the destruction. It is horrible. One can well imagine how such a bombardment affects the population."

André Rondenay was a master forger and a famous escape artist. When he became Christiane's boss in the Resistance in 1944, she was mesmerized by him.

and Strasbourg. After a brief stay in France, he crosses the Spanish frontier on January 23, 1943.

Arrested by the Spanish police, he is interned at Pamplona, where he runs into his old classmate André Boulloche, who had arrived in Spain four weeks before him.

Managing to fabricate the fake papers of a German officer for himself and a comrade named Noël Palaud, Rondenay escapes yet again with Palaud and a third conspirator. Within a few weeks, they reach Portugal, and Rondenay finally makes it to England on April 4, 1943.

IN THE FACE of mounting danger in the spring of 1944, Rondenay remains surprisingly cheerful. His fearlessness is lightened by an infectious sense of humor and a beguiling ability to make fun of himself. To boost Christiane's spirits, he writes a song that makes fun of her youth and the fact that she has never told her parents exactly what she is doing. And he continues to con-coct everything from a train ticket to a German officer's iden-tity card at a moment's notice. His wife, Solange, is one of his deputies.

Christiane knows Rondenay as "Jarry"—the latest of his many wartime aliases. The others are Lemniscate, Sapeur, Jean-Louis Lebel, and Francis Courtois. He gives Christiane "very large sums" of money, which arrive from London, and she distributes it to their confederates. "I was twenty," she said. "It was completely crazy. He had total confidence in me. I think he had more confidence in me than he did in himself."

Now Monsieur and Madame Rondenay are living with the Boulloche girls, plus Georges, another force of nature, who has escaped Germany three times. This motley crew is rounded out by their radio operator, Riquet, and his wife, Gaby. All of them live together in the same apartment, in total secrecy.

CHRISTIANE had become a student at Sciences Po in the fall of 1941, and André told her to continue to show up there occasionally, after she went to work for him in the fall of 1943. She also contin-ued to live with her parents. Only after André's arrest does she stop going to school and move out of her parents' apartment, to begin a completely clandestine life.

One part of Christiane's job is to take care of Riquet's radio equipment. His transmissions are in constant danger of being dis-covered by the Gestapo, which deploys "gonios"—trucks equipped with homing devices to locate the secret transmitters.

To reduce the chances of being discovered, they never transmit from the same location for very long. At one point, Christiane's aunt, Françoise Farcot, allows her niece to use her modest country house to make a few broadcasts. One day, when Christiane isn't there, the Gestapo arrives at her aunt's house.

Seeing them at the front door, one of Christiane's cousins snatches the radio and manages to hide it in the attic. If he hadn't been so quick, everyone in the house would have been arrested.

Even as a teenager, Christiane is already a person of tremendous self-control. One night in Paris, she is in a secret apartment with four confederates, waiting for an important phone call. One of her comrades, a boy who has just been parachuted in from England, soothes his nerves by downing one cognac after another. Christiane is quietly disdainful. She thinks to herself, *At least I am courageous—even though I am a girl!*

When the phone finally rings, they are all ordered outside. Christiane is carrying their radio equipment. Suddenly her suitcase bursts open, and all of the electronic contraband spills out into the street. Christiane scrambles to put everything back, then disappears into the night as quickly as possible.

Christiane is also responsible for coding and decoding the telegrams that go to and from London. It is exacting work, and her least favorite task. Sometimes she delivers weapons to assist in sabotage missions. Whenever possible, London prefers to get things blown up in France on the ground, rather than bombed from the air, because it reduces the chances of civilian casualties.*

She continues to follow all the rudimentary rules of spy craft that the British have taught her brother. She particularly loves the "Métro trick": In the first car there is a conductor who controls the doors. "You put yourself in the first car, close to the conductor. The Métro stops, and you don't move. And then when you see he is about to push the button to close the doors, you jump out. Then you can't be followed."

---

* On April 20, 1944, an Allied bombing raid on Paris leaves 651 dead and 461 wounded, provoking a mini-rebound in the popularity of General Pétain, the collaborationist chief of state. (Jackson, *France*, p. 535)

She always chooses a secret apartment with two exits, and she never waits more than ten minutes for someone to show up for a rendezvous. She trains herself to be suspicious of everyone, all the time: That is the hardest part of her job.

She has to memorize dozens of addresses and telephone numbers, because she is not allowed to write anything down. Once, when she is carrying important telegrams in her purse, she is stopped at a Wehrmacht checkpoint. The German soldier who searches her never recognizes what she is carrying, even though the telegrams don't look like normal documents, with their coded, disjointed letters. "He looked at them. He saw them. And he let me go." She rode her bicycle two hundred yards from the checkpoint—until her legs didn't work anymore. Her terror had paralyzed her. She knew she had "been incredibly lucky," and she "couldn't count on that kind of luck all the time."

AT THE BEGINNING OF 1944, the Germans are starting to feel threatened on all fronts. In January, the German siege of Leningrad is finally lifted by the Soviets, almost nine hundred days after it began. That victory comes exactly one year after the Germans lost the crucial battle of Stalingrad, where the Soviets encircled nearly all of the German 6th Army under General Friedrich Paulus. The Germans and Soviets suffered gigantic losses there: nearly two million military and civilian casualties. The historian Ian Ousby argues that the Reich's failure on the eastern front was a main impetus of the French Resistance. The other was the Reich's brutality in France.

In July 1943, more than three thousand ships had arrived off the beaches of Sicily, and almost half a million Allied soldiers invaded—a larger force than the one used in the initial stages of the assault at Normandy eleven months later. By July 22, American troops had entered Palermo, the major city of western Sicily. On

July 25, the Italian king summoned Mussolini and dismissed him as prime minister. His successor, Pietro Badoglio, announced publicly that Italy would stay in the war on the side of the Germans. Privately, he immediately opened negotiations in Portugal with the Allies to switch sides.

At the end of the third week of January 1944, the Allies launch Operation Shingle. Fifty thousand American and British troops land at Anzio, south of Rome. The Allies will finally enter Rome on June 4.

Meanwhile, the Germans occupying France are nervously awaiting the main Allied invasion, still not knowing where it will occur, as the American and British air forces continue a brutal bombardment of Germany. The Americans carry out their first raid on Germany on January 27, 1944. Three and a half weeks later, 823 British bombers attack Leipzig, and 73 British planes are lost in the raid. The next day, 200 American bombers continue that attack, as the British make a massive assault on Stuttgart.

Four days after that, bombers from the U.S. 8th Air Force attack the German cities of Augsburg, Stuttgart, Regensburg, and Braunschweig. On March 4, the Americans make their first attack on Berlin. Two days later, British bombers attack the French national railway complex at Trappes, southwest of Paris, and inflict enormous damage without losing any planes. These are the opening salvos of the Allies' Transportation Plan, designed to disrupt German reinforcement routes prior to the Normandy invasion. By the time of the final attack of this campaign on June 2—once again at Trappes—the Allies have launched 9,000 sorties in 69 attacks, with a loss of 198 planes.

At the end of the third week of March, Hitler makes one of his most accurate predictions. He tells his commanders in the west that if they are able to prevent a successful Allied landing, that will decide the outcome of the war. At almost the same moment as Hitler's prediction, the Allies decide to delay Operation Anvil, which would have meant an invasion in southern France at the same moment as the onslaught at Normandy in the north.

On April 17, the British government suspends all diplomatic pouches leaving Britain, except those going to the United States and the Soviet Union, to try to prevent a leak of the location of the forthcoming invasion at Normandy.

CHRISTIANE AND JACQUELINE are aware of the general course of the war, through the broadcasts of the BBC and the stream of new confederates who continue to arrive from England. The life of one of the sisters is about to take a dramatic turn, with the arrival of a dashing confederate, another fresh graduate of Patriotic School.

His name is Alex Katlama. He is thirty-three years old when he is parachuted into a secret reception area, northwest of Dijon, on the night of March 15, 1944. A strapping young man with elegant, delicate features, he reaches Paris two days later. His mission is to teach others how to carry out sabotage.

Born in Moscow in 1910, Alex is the third and last child of Russian-Estonian parents. His father had been a well-known owner of racehorses, an "elitist" avocation that made him conspicuously unwelcome in Russia after the success of the Bolshevik Revolution.

In 1918, the Katlamas escaped Russia through Odessa, the southern Ukrainian port on the Black Sea. Then they spent eighteen months in Constantinople, waiting for the revolution to fail. When the Bolsheviks prevail, the Katlamas move on to France in 1920. Alex is homeschooled until the age of thirteen, before attending the Lycée Russe in Paris. He is brought up by a French govern-ness, who teaches him that Alsace is part of France, and that it was a scandal when the Germans "stole" it in 1871.* He studies higher

---

* Alsace became French again at the end of World War I, reverted to Germany after the conquest of France in 1940, and then returned to being part of France in 1945.

mathematics at the Lycée Louis le Grand for two years. There he also becomes a star of the basketball team. Just shy of six feet, Alex is much taller than most of his contemporaries; before the war, the mean height for Frenchmen is closer to five foot six.

In 1933, he graduates from the Ecole Supérieure Aéronautique, with an aircraft engineer's diploma. Two years later, Alex becomes a French citizen, which makes him immediately eligible for military service. He is drafted as a corporal and sent to the air base at Rheims. After the Germans reoccupy the Rhineland in March 1936, Alex is thrilled when bombs are suddenly put on the wings of French airplanes. But the bombers never take off. He assumes the inertia of the French is due to a fear of repeating the catastrophe of World War I.

Because of his knowledge of Russian and of aeronautics, he is promoted to sergeant and transferred to the Air Force intelligence bureau in Paris. There he translates the Russian technical press on aircraft topics, until his army service ends in 1937. Upon his return to civilian life, he gets a job as a sound engineer at Metro-Goldwyn-Mayer in Paris. He remains there until war is declared in 1939, when he is mobilized again.

He is assigned to Air Force intelligence, where he alternates between studying aviation developments in the Soviet Union and choosing targets there for future bombardment, since the Soviets are still in a nonaggression pact with the Nazis when the war begins.

When he hears Pétain's surrender speech in June 1940, Alex has exactly the same reaction as André Boulloche: He is determined to find a way to continue the fight against the Germans. As a Russian immigrant who chose French citizenship, he is especially patriotic.

First he tries to commandeer a plane to fly to Britain, but his superior officers prevent him from taking off. Then he and a friend convince a captain to fly them to Oran in North Africa. But—again

Alex Katlama was a star of the French national basketball team. He is second from
the right in the back row.

like André—he discovers there is no way to fight the Germans in
Europe from the French colony, which has remained loyal to the
collaborators in Vichy.

Demobilized in August, he rejoins his family in France. At
the beginning of 1941, he redoubles his efforts to reach England.
He learns that the easiest way to escape to England is from North
Africa, but he needs an excuse to return there. Opportunity knocks
when he is invited to join the French national basketball team,
which is about to play in Algeria, Tunisia, and Morocco.

But during the basketball tour he fails to find a passage to
England, and so once again he returns to France. In November
1942, he finally decides to go over the Pyrenees to Spain.

Katlama meets three Jews in Osséja, on the eastern border with
Spain, and persuades them to accompany him to Spain. In a café,
he finds two guides, who are Spanish Republican refugees. Alex
and his Jewish companions agree to pay the Spaniards 7,500 francs
to lead them across the border.

They set off at nine P.M. on November 11, 1942.* The guides take them over the Pyrenees, and they arrive in Berga twenty-four hours later. From there, Alex takes the train to Barcelona, where he is immediately arrested.

Alex pretends that he is an American named Glen Boylen, who was born in Bedford, England. His English is excellent, thanks to his regular visits to the American church in Paris before the war— first to play basketball, and then to listen to jazz. He also happens to love being with Americans. And before the war, he had spent six weeks in England with a family he found through an ad in the *Times* of London.

Somehow, he manages to get his identity papers mailed to George Favre, a Spanish reporter who had accompanied the Catalonian basketball team to France, and to whom Katlama had confided his plan to escape.

Favre has friends at the British consulate in Barcelona, who forward Alex's papers to the British military attaché in Madrid. In January, he is imprisoned at the camp at Miranda, where foreign prisoners are mixed in with Spanish Republicans from the losing side of the Spanish Civil War. Alex is shocked that Republicans are still being executed in the camp, three years after Franco's Fascists defeated them.

The foreigners at Miranda are assigned their nationality on the basis of their birthplace, and Alex continues to insist that he was born in England. After five months, British diplomats finally convince his captors that Alex really is a British citizen. At the end of May, he is put on a train from Barcelona to Gibraltar, the ancient British colony on the Mediterranean coast. On May 30, he sets sail for England, where he arrives one week later.

After a month of vetting at Patriotic School, he is given the alias of Lieutenant Alex Daniel. In August, he begins training to

---

*Which happens to be Christiane's nineteenth birthday.

become a secret agent in France. Because he is still recovering from the harsh treatment he received in the Spanish prison camp, the initial assessment of his British handlers is mixed:

A quiet intelligent intellectual type with ideas of his own, but these are not always very practical...Conscientious and serious of purpose. His mind works slowly and he has shown a lack of self-assurance under stress. Is at present in a poor state of mind and body, which has probably spoilt his performance. He is...abnormally slow, lacking in physical assurance, nervous and worried about his shortcomings. Under these conditions the board has failed him but strongly recommends that he should receive treatment and be reconsidered at a later date.

Four months later, he has regained his strength and impressed his trainers. They have noticed that Katlama is "motivated by gratitude to the country of his adoption." He is the kind of man who works hard to succeed at every goal he sets for himself, and by now, the British understand that. His affection for the British also helps with his rapid adjustment.

His new evaluation is much more enthusiastic:

Intelligent, both practical and academic. He is quick, clearheaded, logical and has plenty of common sense and imagination. He is keen and worked hard, took great pains, and was neat and accurate. He is determined and conscientious. He has plenty of self confidence but is not conceited nor over sure of himself. His personality is pleasant but not very forceful. He is a good mixer and has a good sense of humor. He was generally popular. He should make a competent and loyal assistant.

Alex receives his final training certificate on March 3, 1944. Twelve days later, he is parachuted into France. Two weeks after that, he is in Paris. He carries with him the vital *Plan Vert*, which he will deliver to Rondenay. The plan details how the Resistance is supposed to disrupt the French railroad system when the invasion at Normandy begins.

As soon as he reaches the French capital, Alex is spared by another accident of fate—the kind that rescues so many of the Resistance members who are lucky enough to survive the war. For Alex, it is an Allied bombardment near Paris that halts the Métro train he is traveling on, for half an hour.

Sometime during those thirty minutes, the contact he is supposed to meet is arrested. Thus, when Alex reaches the location of his rendezvous, there is no longer anyone there to greet him.

If Alex had been on time, he too would certainly have been seized by the Germans.

The next day, Alex's other contact in the Resistance in Paris is arrested. After that, he loses all contact with the underground for a month. In the third week of April, he goes to an emergency address he has been given to use in case of such a catastrophe: a clothing store on rue de Flandre.

Rondenay is always worried about sending Christiane into a trap. Concealing his habitual anxiety as well as he can, he dispatches her to the clothing store, with a password to identify herself to the clerk. After Christiane says the secret word, she has a moment of panic: At first the saleswoman doesn't seem to recognize the code. When Christiane repeats the password, the clerk finally leads her into a back room, where Alex Katlama is waiting for her.

CHRISTIANE likes the handsome Alex "very much—but no more." She feels too consumed by her duties to pursue a romance with him, or anyone else. But when Alex meets Jacqueline, sparks fly quickly.

It is Jacqueline who becomes Alex's "precious collaborator, the only person in my service on whom I could count completely"—

and, soon, his lover. Even if Christiane is a bit jealous, Jacqueline's romance does nothing to diminish the sisters' extraordinary closeness.

About a month after making contact with Christiane and Jacqueline, Alex begins a secret course on sabotage for a cell of *Résistants* on rue des Entrepreneurs.

On May 19, Alex leads three confederates on a sabotage mission. Their target is a ball-bearing factory, and they are so successful, production there is never resumed. For some reason, the twenty Germans responsible for guarding the factory never engage them during the attack.

By now everyone knows the Allied invasion is imminent, but the Germans still have no clear idea of when or where it will occur. On May 8, Dwight Eisenhower secretly chooses June 5 as the tentative date for the attack at Normandy. The next day, the British bomber command makes its first attack on German coastal batteries near Pas de Calais.

CHRISTIANE AND JACQUELINE know that their brother has been shipped off to Germany. But they don't know which camp he is in, or what it really means to be in a concentration camp. They bury themselves in their clandestine duties to distract them from a debilitating terror about what could happen to him in Germany.

Meanwhile, their boss, Rondenay, is leading sabotage missions against many factories outside Paris. To prepare for the Allied invasion, he meets with Resistance members working for the national telephone company, to plan how to blow up underground long-distance telephone lines (code name: *Plan Violet*) and with railroad workers, who are supposed to blow up strategic railroad lines (*Plan Vert*).

Thirteen

Rather than just being liberated by foreigners . . . France herself would rise up to take an honorable part in her own liberation. That, really, was what resistance was all about.
—Ian Ousby

I opened the window [in London on the morning of June 6] and the noise became deafening . . . It was possible to see the aircraft flying in massed formation above the sleeping capital. They flew over in a never-ending stream. Holding my breath and looking steadily in the direction of Nazi Germany, I could see, beyond the barbed wire sealing the frontiers, beyond the prisons, the dawn that was bringing to our enslaved friends the first glimmer of their victory.
—Marie-Madeleine Fourcade

ACROSS THE CHANNEL, on the southeastern coast of England, the Allies have assembled a gigantic collection of airplanes, tanks, trucks, jeeps, and more than two million men. "All southern England was one vast military camp," Eisenhower recalled.

By the eve of the invasion, fifty-two million square feet are filled with supplies, including almost half a million tons of ammunition. Soldiers joke that if the invasion doesn't happen soon, the southern edge of England will sink into the sea beneath the weight of their preparations.

"The southernmost camps where assault troops were assembled were all surrounded by barbed-wire entanglements to prevent any soldier leaving the camp," Eisenhower remembered. "The mighty host was tense as a coiled spring, and indeed that is exactly what it was—a great human spring, coiled for the moment when its energy...would vault the English Channel in the greatest amphibious assault ever attempted."

The Germans have fifty-five divisions assigned to the defense of France, while the Allies have only thirty-five divisions assembled for the invasion. But not all the German soldiers can be used to defend the northern coast of France. Some of them must remain in the south to defend the Mediterranean coast, and the Russians have promised to begin a new offensive on the eastern front when the invasion begins, to discourage the Germans from sending any reinforcements.

In the weeks before the invasion, the Allies do their best to cripple communications in the north of France, to isolate the Normandy beaches from the rest of the country. Between May 24 and June 6, British and American bombers destroy all nine railroad crossings and a dozen highway bridges in the region. The Allies keep them closed by repeatedly bombing the boats and the temporary bridges the Germans try to put in their place. This will severely limit the Germans' ability to send in reinforcements after the invasion begins.

Meanwhile, the Allies are continually leaking false invasion plans to prevent Hitler from figuring out that Normandy is their real target. They make a special effort to convince the Germans that they will land near Boulogne, Calais, and Dunkirk, and many of Hitler's generals are taken in by the ruse.

The British even create a fictitious 4th Army headquarters at Edinburgh Castle, which pours out phony radio messages to convince the Nazis that the Allies are also about to invade Norway, where the Germans have stationed twenty-seven divisions. Again, the deception works: Those German divisions never leave Norway to defend France.

Realizing that it will be crucial for the French to participate in the liberation of their own country, Churchill makes a special appeal to Eisenhower to find enough transport to allow the 2nd French Armored Division to land in Normandy during the summer of 1944. Eisenhower agrees to his request. This will eventually make it possible for French soldiers commanded by General Jacques-Philippe Leclerc to spearhead the Liberation of Paris.

On the last day of May, 245 minesweepers begin clearing the English coast. Then they start to create paths to the landing sites on the French coast. Two days later, two British submarines leave Scotland to head for the Normandy coast. Their task is to mark the approaches for the landing craft that will arrive there four days later.

On June 3, Dwight Eisenhower gives de Gaulle his first briefing on Operation Overlord, the code name for the Normandy invasion. This is the first official information the Frenchman has received about the gigantic operation that will liberate his country—a good indication of the "warmth" between the two generals.

IN THE WEEKS before the Normandy invasion, Resistance leaders in Paris are notified how they will be alerted to the great event. The Allies apparently believe this is necessary because so much depends on the extensive sabotage of railroad tracks and other communication channels that the Resistance has been ordered to carry out just as the invasion begins.

At the moment when the French should begin to ready themselves for the invasion, the BBC will broadcast the first lines of "Chanson d'automne," one of France's best-loved poems, by Paul Verlaine, one of its most celebrated nineteenth-century poets. On June 1, the chosen French listeners who know the code are riveted when they hear these seven words traveling across the channel from the BBC:

Les sanglots longs
Des violons
De l'automne
(The long sobs of autumn violins)

Someone with a literary sensibility, a decent knowledge of French culture, and a fine sense of history has clearly made this selection. The melancholy poem comes from the "paysages tristes" (sad countrysides) section of Verlaine's first volume of poetry. When the next stanza is broadcast, the Normandy countryside will be drenched with the blood of hundreds of thousands of Allied and German soldiers, and at least fifteen thousand French civilians, most of whom will be victims of Allied bombardments.

After the first lines are broadcast, Christiane, Jacqueline, and scores of their confederates in the Resistance know that the moment they have been waiting for since the bleakest days of 1940 has finally arrived. Within days, Allied troops will return to French soil, to try to expel the Germans.

From Belgium and the Netherlands to Poland, Czechoslovakia, and Greece, millions of freedom lovers are praying for the success of the invasion, without knowing yet exactly when or where it will begin.

Churchill, Roosevelt, de Gaulle, Eisenhower, and Hitler* all agree about the importance of this moment. Each believes that this will be *the* crucial event of the war. The fate of the "Thousand-Year Reich" is about to pivot on the skill, the bravery, and the good

---

* On November 3, 1943, Hitler had written in Führer Directive No. 51, "The threat from the East remains, but an even greater danger looms in the West: the Anglo-American landing! ... It is there that the enemy has to attack, there—if we are not deceived—that the decisive landing battles will be fought." (Roberts, *The Storm of War*, p. 462, and www.britannica.com/dday/article-9400228)

fortune of 156,000 mostly British, American, and Canadian soldiers, sailors, and airmen. Additional troops will hail from Belgium, Poland, Norway, the Netherlands, Czechoslovakia, Australia, New Zealand, and, of course, France.

They will use nearly 7,000 ships, 2,395 aircraft, and 867 gliders to land in and around French beaches, which have been given the code names Utah, Omaha, Gold, Juno, and Sword. It will be the largest naval armada in the history of the world.

After eleven years of Nazi atrocities metastasizing across Europe, this is the moment of truth in a global contest between democracy and tyranny. The main thing that muddles the idea that this is simply a conflict between good and evil is the role of Stalin. Like Hitler, Stalin is responsible for genocides that have killed millions of innocent people. But now, destiny has made him *the* essential ally of the Western democracies.

No one but Stalin is willing to sacrifice so much to defeat the Nazis: a staggering twenty million men and women. World War II will kill ten million Soviet soldiers and ten million Soviet civilians.* That is nearly five times the losses sustained by the Germans—and *fifty times* the losses of the United States.

Ten million civilians is also ten million more than were killed at home in America during the entire war. The United States and Canada are the only major combatants that suffer no losses at home, apart from those killed at Pearl Harbor. In France, on the other hand, 350,000 civilians will perish between 1940 and 1945.

The worst per capita civilian losses of all are in Poland, where 5.7 million will die, including 2.8 million Jews, out of a prewar population of just under 35 million—more than one-seventh of all Polish citizens.

---

* That was the number given by the Soviets immediately after the war, but when Mikhail Gorbachev was president of the USSR, he said the total number of Soviet deaths could have been 29 million. (O'Neill, *The Oxford Essential Guide to World War II*, p. vii)

ON JUNE 4, Eisenhower's meteorological committee predicts low clouds, high winds, and formidable waves, and the American general decides to reject a June 5 invasion date, against the advice of British field marshal Montgomery. "The tension continued to mount as prospects for decent weather became worse and worse," Eisenhower remembered.

Driving to the next meeting of the meteorological committee, at three thirty on the morning of June 5, "our little camp was shaking and shuddering under a wind of almost hurricane proportions and the accompanying rain seemed to be traveling in horizontal streaks." Under those circumstances, Ike thought it wasn't even worth discussing the situation. But when the meeting began a half hour later, the weathermen had a welcome surprise.

They were now confident of thirty-six hours of relatively good weather, beginning on the morning of June 6. At four fifteen A.M. on June 5, Eisenhower tells his colleagues he has decided to proceed with the massive invasion the following day.

With the fate of the entire war weighing on his shoulders, Eisenhower pauses to write a resignation letter, to be released in the event that Operation Overlord is a failure: "If any blame or fault attaches to the attempt it is mine alone." Then he orders the gigantic operation to go forward. "I hope to God I know what I'm doing," he tells his staff.

At eleven fifteen on the evening of June 5, Christiane is sitting in her secret apartment with her confederates, listening to the "personal messages" on the BBC, when the magic words crackle out of the radio:

Blessent mon coeur
D'une langueur
Monotone.
(Wound my heart with a monotonous languor)

Everyone in the room jumps up to embrace one another. Then Christiane's boss, Rondenay, dispatches her into the blacked-out streets of Paris, to deliver the joyful tidings to their colleagues. She rides her bicycle without any lights. It is thrilling to be the bearer of such happy tidings.

Some days earlier, a leader of the Maquis, as the Resistance is known in the countryside, has been arrested—after he has learned that the invasion will be heralded by the Verlaine poem. Unbeknownst to the Allies, after being tortured by the Germans, the Maquis member has revealed the existence of the code.

As a result, when the poem's lines are read on the night of June 5, the commander of Germany's 15th Army in the Pas de Calais immediately puts his troops on alert.

But the Allies' vast disinformation campaign has a completely unpredictable—and quite miraculous—effect on the German officers at Army Group B's headquarters at La Roche–Guyon. There have been so many false reports of so many imminent invasions before, for them the truth is transformed into a mirage. And thus they decide to pay no attention at all to the secret gleaned from the tortured Maquis leader.

Why would the BBC possibly broadcast the time of the invasion in advance? these Germans ask themselves.

Obviously this is just another feint on the part of the Allies!

So the commanders of the 7th Army—the one defending Normandy—are never warned on the night of June 5 of the imminent attack. Two other factors contribute to the lackadaisical attitude of many of the German commanders. During May there have been eighteen days when the weather, the sea, and the tides have been perfect for a landing, and the Germans obviously noticed that Eisenhower has not taken advantage of them.

And on June 4, the German Air Force meteorologist in Paris has predicted that inclement weather means that no Allied action could be expected for at least a fortnight.

Field Marshal Erwin Rommel had been shifted from Italy to northern France by Hitler in January 1944, where he became commander of Army Group B, which has the main responsibility for repelling an Allied invasion. On the basis of everything he has been told, the Desert Fox writes a situation report on June 5 stating that the invasion is not imminent. Then he sets off to Germany, first to celebrate his wife's birthday and then to meet with the Führer. The second meeting will not occur.

Around one A.M. on June 6, one British and two American airborne divisions begin descending by parachute and glider right into the middle of the German 7th Army. But even this isn't enough to convince Field Marshal Gerd von Rundstedt, the German commander in chief in the west. At two forty he sends word to the chief of staff of the 7th Army that he does "not consider this a major operation."

Hitler himself has been up until three A.M. with his deputy, Heinrich Himmler, "reminiscing, and taking pleasure in the many fine days...we have had together," Himmler recorded. When three of his generals call his headquarters to beg for permission to rush two tank divisions to the front, word comes back that Hitler wants to wait and see what develops. Then he goes to bed and sleeps undisturbed until three o'clock the following afternoon.

Even after the gigantic Allied armada starts arriving later that morning, the chief German general in the west remains convinced that the main invasion is going to happen elsewhere.

At five fifty on the morning of June 6, the Allies open a massive naval bombardment on beach fortifications and nearby Normandy villages. The main American landings take place forty minutes later at Utah and Omaha beaches.

There is heavy fighting everywhere, but the Allies are particularly successful at Utah, where 23,000 men get ashore with only 210 dead and wounded on the first day. After the 101st Airborne manages to block four exits from the beach, the only regiment facing them from the German 709th division surrenders in large numbers.

At Omaha, the situation is catastrophically different. This is the site of by far the largest landing of D-day by Americans. Here, 34,250 troops face the Germans dug in on bluffs 150 feet above the beach, and the inward curvature of the coast also allows German fields of fire to overlap.

The disasters for the Allies begin at six A.M., when waves of American B-24 bombers drop thirteen hundred tons of bombs intended for German defenses at Omaha and completely miss their targets, bombing too far inland.

The official history of the 116th Infantry, 29th division, was written by S. L. A. Marshall, a World War I veteran who rejoined the army in 1942 as a combat historian. In his notebook he recorded the horrific conditions faced by the men who hit the beach at Omaha at six thirty that morning:

> ABLE Company riding the tide in seven Higgins boats is still five thousand yards from the beach when first taken under artillery fire. The shells fall short. At one thousand yards, Boat No. 5 is hit dead on and foundered. Six men drown before help arrives...
>
> At exactly 6:36 a.m....the men jump off in water anywhere from waist deep to higher than a man's head. This is the signal awaited by the Germans atop the bluff. Already pounded by mortars, the floundering line is instantly swept by crossing machine-gun fires from both ends of the beach...
>
> The first men out...are ripped apart before they can make five yards. Even the lightly wounded die by drowning, doomed by the waterlogging of their overloaded packs. From Boat No. 1, all hands jump off in water over their heads. Most of them are carried down...All order has vanished from Able Company before it has fired a shot.
>
> Already the sea runs red. Even among some of the lightly wounded who jumped into shallow water the hits prove fatal.

Knocked down by a bullet in the arm or weakened by fear and shock, they are unable to rise again and are drowned by the onrushing tide. Other wounded men drag themselves ashore and, on finding the sands, lie quiet from total exhaustion, only to be overtaken and killed by the water. A few move safely through the bullet swarm to the beach, then find that they cannot hold there. They return to the water to use it for body cover. Faces turned upward, so that their nostrils are out of water, they creep toward the land at the same rate as the tide. That is how most of the survivors make it. The less rugged or less clever seek the cover of enemy obstacles moored along the upper half of the beach and are knocked off by machine-gun fire.

. . . From the cliff above, the German gunners are shooting into the survivors as from a roof top.

In spite of the huge initial casualties, the terrible handicaps of Omaha's topography, and the almost total lack of cover, seven hours after the first troops hit the beach, General Leonard Gerow signals General Omar Bradley that "troops formerly pinned down on the beaches" are finally "advancing up heights behind the beaches."

At a cost of two thousand Americans killed at Omaha, by the end of the first day more than thirty thousand men have made it ashore. Two Ranger battalions scale the hundred-foot-high Pointe du Hoc with rope ladders, only to discover that the Germans have already dismantled their big cannon.

It isn't until four o'clock that afternoon (one hour after he was finally awake) that Hitler agrees to send two more Panzer divisions into the battle to bolster the 12th SS and 21st Panzer Divisions. "But the reinforcements dribbled into the invasion front were never enough," writes the historian Gerhard Weinberg, "and the Allied air forces as well as the sabotage efforts of the French resistance and Allied special teams slowed down whatever was sent."

Indeed, the actions of the Resistance were probably just as important to the success of the invasion as the incredible bravery of the men storming the beaches. "We were depending on considerable assistance from the insurrectionists in France," Eisenhower reported.

During the first twenty-fours of the assault, nearly one thousand acts of sabotage paralyze the French railways. Locomotives are destroyed, trains are derailed, and more bridges are blown up, reducing rail traffic by 50 percent. For a week after the invasion, every train leaving Marseille for Lyon is derailed at least once, and in the department of Indre, which includes the line from Toulouse to Paris, there are eight hundred acts of railroad sabotage in June alone.

This is vital to the success of the Allies, because 90 percent of the German Army is still transported by train or horse. The disruptions achieved by the Resistance give the troops on the beaches crucial additional hours, and then days, to prevail, before significant German reinforcements can arrive.

Across the French coast, by the end of the first day, there are 9,000 Allied casualties, of whom one-half were killed: 2,500 Americans, 1,641 Britons, 359 Canadians, 37 Norwegians, 19 Free French, 13 Australians, 2 New Zealanders, and 1 Belgian. British air chief marshal Arthur Tedder had predicted a casualty rate of 80 percent for the airborne troops, but the actual number was 15 percent.

Rommel finally makes it back to the front from his wife's birthday party at the end of the first day of the invasion, after canceling his meeting with Hitler. By the time he returns, one of his earlier predictions is well on its way to coming true. Unlike General von Rundstedt, who thought it was impossible to prevent an Allied landing and hoped to fling the invaders back into the sea with a counterattack, Rommel had been certain they had to be prevented from coming ashore at all. "The first twenty-four hours will be decisive," he said.

On the night after the invasion, Roosevelt goes on the radio to ask one hundred million Americans to pray with him:

Almighty God: Our sons, pride of our Nation, this day have set upon a mighty endeavor, a struggle to preserve our Republic, our religion, and our civilization, and to set free a suffering humanity…

They fight not for the lust of conquest. They fight to end conquest. They fight to liberate. They fight to let justice arise, and tolerance and good will among all Thy people…

With Thy blessing, we shall prevail over the unholy forces of our enemy. Help us to conquer the apostles of greed and racial arrogancies. Lead us to the saving of our country, and with our sister Nations into a world unity that will spell a sure peace, a peace invulnerable to the schemings of unworthy men. And a peace that will let all of men live in freedom, reaping the just rewards of their honest toil.

Thy will be done, Almighty God.

By the end of June 11 (D-day plus five), an astounding 326,547 troops, 54,186 vehicles, and 104,428 tons of supplies have been landed on the beaches. While there would be several more serious setbacks on the way to victory—and hundreds of thousands of additional casualties—by now the Allies have clearly turned the tide of war.

The sabotage missions carried out by the Resistance in the immediate aftermath of the invasion make a huge contribution to the success of the Allies. They also come at a tremendous cost to the French civilian population.

When the 2nd SS Das Reich Panzer Division sets out on June 8 on a 450-mile journey from the south of France, they expect to reach Normandy a few days later. Instead, the trip takes three weeks, because of the heroism of the Maquis, who attack the Germans and destroy numerous bridges and railway tracks in their path.

On the second day of the trip, in retaliation for the deaths of forty German soldiers, the Panzers seize a hundred men at random in the town of Tulle in the Corrèze and massacre all of them. "I came home from shopping on June 9 to find my husband and son hanging from the balcony of our house," recalled a woman from the town.

On the third day, Major Adolf Diekmann's unit is responsible for a much greater atrocity in the village of Oradour-sur-Glane, where 642 citizens, including 205 children, are killed. The men are shot; the women and children are burned to death in a church.

Though still shocking in France in the fourth year of the Nazi Occupation, the German war crimes committed in these villages paled in comparison to what the Nazis had been doing on a vast scale in Eastern Europe ever since 1940. Referring to the latest massacre in France, an eastern front veteran who had become one of Diekmann's officers told a colleague, "In our circles, Herr Muller, it was *nothing*."

Fourteen

Throughout France the Free French had been of inestimable value
in the campaign. They were particularly active in Brittany, but
on every portion of the front we secured help from them in a multitude
of ways. Without their great assistance the liberation of France and
the defeat of the enemy in western Europe would have consumed a much
longer time and meant greater losses to ourselves.
—General Dwight Eisenhower

ON THE DAY BEFORE the Normandy invasion, Christiane, Jacqueline, and André and Solange Rondenay are ordered by London to leave Paris, to join up with the Maquis in the Morvan, 150 miles south of Paris, near the Château de Vermot in Dun-les-Places.

The two sisters go to their parents' apartment to say goodbye. Jacques and Hélène are very unhappy that they are leaving Paris. They have had no word about their youngest son since he was shipped off to a concentration camp in Germany at the end of April, and now they won't know where their daughters are either. Only their son Robert still seems relatively safe in his government job at the Finance Ministry.

Once again, Rondenay manufactures impeccable identification cards for everyone, and they reach the Morvan without incident. They are incredibly relieved to be out of Paris. In the weeks before the invasion, the Gestapo has intensified all its activities, and the pain of seeing more and more of their friends and relatives getting arrested has become overwhelming. Now, for the first time in years, they can speak out loud without worrying about being "overheard, suspected or unmasked." They finally feel safe, although that is not necessarily the case.

In the Morvan they join up with Jean Longhi, another legendary figure of the Resistance, whose nom de guerre is Grandjean. Christiane is captivated by him. A Communist and a veteran of the Spanish Civil War, Longhi flees Paris after learning that the Germans are after him. Longhi and his friend Paul Bernard founded the Maquis de Camille in the fall of 1941.

With his sister, Longhi started a hospital at the Château de Vermot to care for the wounded of the Maquis. At the end of 1943, the Service National Maquis, which coordinated the actions of the various individual groups, made him the head of all of the Maquis in the department of Nièvre in the center of France. Even though Grandjean is a Communist, Christiane does not sense any political tension with him: "We had a common enemy, and that was enough."

Christiane and her comrades sleep in leaky tents; the weather is terrible and nothing ever gets dry. On the afternoon of June 26, four hundred Nazi soldiers arrive at Dun-les-Places in cars and trucks to search for "terrorists." Everyone's identity papers are checked, and everyone is let go. But when the Germans leave the village, they are attacked by the Maquis.

The Germans respond by attacking the château housing the hospital. The counterattack is led by Longhi, Bernard, and Rondenay. Bernard is gravely (although not fatally) wounded. Not knowing how to fire a gun, Christiane spends the battle passing ammunition to a confederate with a machine gun, and then tending to the wounded in the infirmary.

The violent attack on the château lasts for twelve hours, until the Maquis are finally forced to abandon it. When the Germans capture it, they burn it down. The Maquis suffer two dead and five wounded, but the rest are able to escape.

The Maquis regroup easily after the attack, but once again, the nearby villages suffer terrible reprisals. The hamlet of Vermot is burned to the ground, and twelve houses in Dun-les-Places are destroyed. Then all the men of Dun-les-Places are arrested, and all twenty-seven of them are killed. Among the dead are the mayor, the village priest, and the headmaster of the school.

Four days later, Rondenay gets a telegram from London ordering him back to Paris.

"I'm coming back with you," Christiane tells him. "He didn't say no, because he knew he needed me." Jacqueline decides to stay behind with the Maquis.

As the Allies slowly fight their way south toward Paris, there is fear, near famine, and growing chaos in the still blacked-out City of Light. For Christiane, her worst nightmare is yet to come.

Fifteen

ELEVEN DAYS AFTER the Normandy invasion, Hitler travels to Margival, northwest of Paris. Here the Germans have constructed the headquarters that André Boulloche had first described to London at the end of 1940. The bunker was supposed to have served as the Führer's headquarters when he invaded Britain, but of course that invasion never occurred.

Now Hitler is visiting for the first time to meet with Erwin Rommel and Field Marshal Gerd von Rundstedt, who had become the German commander in the west in the summer of 1942. The generals' purpose is to tell Hitler that the war has become hopeless.

Four months earlier, Rommel has joined the conspiracy to remove Hitler as Führer, although he is opposed to killing him, because he thinks that would make him a martyr.

To Rommel's chief of staff, General Hans Speidel, the Führer looks "pale and sleepless" and "his hypnotic powers seemed to have waned."* After a "curt and frosty greeting," Hitler speaks "bitterly of his displeasure at the success of the Allied landings, for which he tried to hold the field commanders responsible."

Emboldened "by the prospect of another stunning defeat," Rommel is remarkably frank—and accurate. He tells Hitler that

---

* A nimble fellow who was also part of the conspiracy to assassinate Hitler, Speidel became commander of NATO land forces in Central Europe from 1957 to 1963.

"the German front in Normandy would collapse and that a break-through into Germany by the allies could not be checked...He doubted whether the Russian front could be held. He pointed to Germany's complete political isolation," and "concluded with an urgent request that the war be brought to an end."

Finally, Hitler cuts Rommel off. "Don't you worry about the future course of the war," the Führer tells his general, "but rather about your own invasion front."

One month after this meeting with Hitler—and three days before the next attempt on Hitler's life—Rommel's car is strafed by a low-flying Allied Spitfire. The general barely survives the attack and then recovers slowly.* Speidel believed that the anti-Hitler conspirators "felt themselves painfully deprived of their pillar of strength."

WHEN CHRISTIANE AND RONDENAY return to Paris at the end of June, the streets are still patrolled by German soldiers, but now many of them look like they are no more than fourteen. There are also German street signs that hadn't been there at the beginning of June: ZUR NORMANDIE FRONT.

After the initial successes of the invasion, the battle in Normandy is going much slower than the planners had anticipated. But the wide incursions of the Allies in the first days of the invasion have convinced a very large number of senior German Army officers that the war is essentially over: It is now only a matter of time before the Allies will cross the Rhine and obliterate what is left of Germany.

---

* Three months after the failure of the plot to kill Hitler, the Führer sends two generals to Rommel's home to offer him the choice of committing suicide or facing the People's Court for his role in the conspiracy. Told that his family will be taken care of if he chooses the first option, Rommel goes upstairs to say goodbye to his wife. Then he gets in a car with the two generals and swallows a cyanide capsule. He is dead fifteen seconds later.

It now seems clear that right from the start most German generals knew that Hitler was psychotic. But as long as he was winning the war, almost all of them were happy to overlook that detail—as well as the massive war crimes they were committing at his behest.

By the middle of 1944, very few of them remain under the spell of the Führer's much diminished "magic powers." As a result, a remarkably large number of generals and colonels are recruited for the latest plot to assassinate their supreme leader. Many more are aware of the conspiracy without participating in it—or betraying it.*

Seven decades after the war, German opposition to Hitler is barely remembered. But there were actually some two dozen unsuccessful attempts on his life.

In the summer of 1944, Major General Hening von Tresckow is the chief of staff of the 2nd Army on the rapidly deteriorating Russian front. He is also a longtime opponent of Hitler. As the latest conspiracy against the Führer takes shape, the general is asked for his advice by some of the nervous young plotters. He provides them with the most compelling and prescient reason for carrying out the latest plot to kill Hitler—the attempt that will come closest to success, six weeks after the Normandy invasion: "The assassination must be attempted at any cost. Even should it fail, the attempt to seize power in the capital must be undertaken. We must prove to the world and to future generations that the men of the German Resistance Movement dared to take the decisive step and to hazard their lives upon it. Compared with this object, nothing else matters."†

---

* In February 1944, the Swiss minister to Vichy met with Prime Minister Pierre Laval, who predicted the annihilation of Russia and said there was no question of a breach of the Atlantic Wall. When the Swiss diplomat repeated this assessment to one of Laval's close collaborators, he was told, "What do you expect! Laval has gambled and he knows he has lost. But he wants neither to believe nor admit it." (Jackson, *France*, p. 527)

† Von Tresckow had been involved in several previous plots to kill Hitler. When the one on July 20 failed, he committed suicide the next day.

The historian William Shirer points to another reason for a growing sense of urgency among the conspirators: "The threatened collapse of the fronts in Russia, France and Italy impelled the plotters to act at once."

ON THE OTHER SIDE of the battle, the Allies are increasingly concerned by how much the Germans have delayed the Allies' progress—so much so that Eisenhower remembers late June as "a difficult period for all of us. More than one of our high-ranking visitors began to express the fear that we were stalemated and that those who had prophesied a gloomy fate for Overlord were being proved correct."

Seven weeks pass after the Normandy invasion before the Allies are finally able to launch a new offensive from the area they had hoped to reach on D-day plus five: a line of cities and towns stretching from Caen through Caumont to St. Lô.

THE LATEST PLOT to kill Hitler is led by Claus Schenk Graf von Stauffenberg, an aristocrat with many famous German generals among his ancestors. In the spring of 1943, Stauffenberg was attached to the 10th Panzer Division in Tunisia when his car drove into a minefield. It may also have been strafed by an Allied plane. Stauffenberg is gravely injured and recovers slowly—after losing one arm, one eye, and two fingers.

At end of June 1944, the anti-Hitler plotters get a boost when Stauffenberg becomes a full colonel and is appointed chief of staff to General Friedrich Fromm, commander in chief of the Home Army. This gives Stauffenberg the power to issue orders to the Home Army in his boss's name, which will be necessary to carry out the coup d'état that is supposed to take place after the assassination. It also gives him regular access to Hitler.

By July 1944, the conspiracy, code-named Valkyrie—named for the maidens in Norse-German mythology who hovered over battle-fields, choosing who would die and who would survive—includes Stauffenberg's former boss, General Friedrich Olbricht; General Hemuth Stieff; General Eduard Wagner, first quartermaster general of the army; General Erich Fellgiebel, the chief of signals of the Wehrmacht (Supreme Command of the Armed Forces); and General Fritz Lindemann, head of the Ordnance Office. General Paul von Hase, chief of the Berlin Kommandantur (High Command), is important because he can provide the troops needed to take over Berlin. Colonel Freiherr von Roenne, head of the Foreign Armies Section, and his chief of staff, Captain Count von Matuschka, as well as Count von Helldorf, the head of the Berlin police, are also part of the plot.

On July 20, Stauffenberg drives to the airport outside Berlin to board a plane provided by General Wagner. In his suitcase he carries a British-made bomb that is set off by breaking a glass capsule. The capsule contains acid that eats away a small wire, which releases a firing pin against a percussion cap. British fuses are favored by the conspirators because they do not make a telltale hissing noise. The thickness of this particular wire should make Stauffenberg's bomb explode ten minutes after he shatters the capsule.

The plane delivers Stauffenberg to Rastenburg soon after ten A.M. From there he is driven to Hitler's secret Wolfsschanze (Wolf's Lair) headquarters, named after Hitler's longtime Nazi code name, Wolf. It is located in a gloomy forest in East Prussia. General Alfred Jodl describes the atmosphere there as "somewhere between a monastery and a concentration camp."

With a staff of two thousand, the complex sits in the middle of three security zones protected by mine fields, pillboxes, and an electrified barbed-wire fence, all patrolled by fanatical SS troops. The compound includes two airfields, a railway stop, a power station, saunas, cinemas, and tearooms. Hitler's own headquarters, the Führerbunker, has six-foot-thick concrete walls, electric heating, and air-conditioning.

At twelve thirty-two in the afternoon, Stauffenberg shatters the glass capsule in the bomb he has carried in a briefcase and marches into the conference barracks where Hitler is already being briefed about the eastern front. The Führer is sitting at the center of one side of a heavy oak table, eighteen feet long and five feet wide, which stands on two massive supports instead of legs. Its unusual construction will determine his fate.

Stauffenberg sits down at the table and slides his briefcase on the side of one of the two heavy supports—the side closer to Hitler, about six feet from the dictator's legs. Then Stauffenberg tells a colleague, Colonel Heinz Brandt, that he has to leave the room to make an urgent telephone call.

After Stauffenberg leaves, Brandt stands up to examine the map that is sitting on the table before him. Finding Stauffenberg's briefcase in his way, Brandt reaches down and moves it to the far side of the barrier supporting the table—farther away from Hitler. That random act will sharply change the history of the next twelve months of the war: When the bomb explodes ten minutes later, Colonel Brandt is killed—but Hitler survives.

Stauffenberg is about two hundred yards away when the bomb goes off, and he watches as bodies and debris fly out the shattered windows. He is certain everyone inside must be dead. After bluffing his way through three checkpoints, he boards the plane waiting to take him back to Berlin.

When the head of the conspiracy finally reaches the German capital late in the afternoon, he learns that his fellow conspirators know the explosion has occurred. But because they aren't certain that Hitler has been killed, they have done nothing to put the planned coup into effect.

Hitler's hair is singed, his legs pierced by a hundred splinters, his right arm paralyzed temporarily, his eardrums punctured, and his back is hit by a falling beam, but he manages to stumble out of the demolished building. Four of his colleagues are killed. Initially, the Führer thinks his headquarters are the victim of an Allied bombardment, but gradually the clues accumulate implicating Stauffenberg.

From Berlin, Stauffenberg telephones Paris, where more senior German army officers are involved in the conspiracy than anywhere else. He speaks to his cousin, Lieutenant Colonel Caesar von Hofacker, at General Carl-Heinrich von Stuelpnagel's headquarters in Paris, and tells him that the army is proceeding with a coup.

Before darkness has fallen in Paris on July 20, General Stuelpnagel has arrested all twelve hundred SS and SD officers and men in Paris, including their commander, SS major general Karl Oberg.

But back in Berlin, the conspiracy is in total disarray. It begins to fall apart altogether when Major Otto Remer is ordered to arrest Joseph Goebbels, the propaganda minister and the highest-ranking Nazi official in Berlin at this moment. When Remer confronts Goebbels in his office, the minister manages to get Hitler on the telephone and puts the major on the line with him. Realizing the Führer is still alive, the major reverses his loyalties on the spot.

At six thirty in the evening, Goebbels manages to get the Deutschlandsender, a radio station powerful enough to be heard all over Europe, to broadcast a brief announcement that an attempt to kill Hitler has failed. (The conspirators' failure to secure the radio station earlier in the afternoon is one of their many elementary blunders.) Goebbels initially blames the Allies for the bombing. Hearing the bulletin that Hitler is still alive, German Army generals in Prague and Vienna who have already started to arrest SS and Nazi party leaders begin to backtrack.

Stauffenberg's boss, General Friedrich Fromm, who has tolerated the conspiracy against Hitler for months without actively participating it, now turns decisively against the plotters, in the hope of saving his own skin. He pretends to carry out an instant court-martial of Stauffenberg, as well as two generals and a lieutenant who were among his collaborators. Then he orders all of them shot immediately by a firing squad in the courtyard—to make sure they can't implicate him in the conspiracy.

By one A.M., Hitler is on the airwaves himself, describing a plot by "a very small clique of ambitious, irresponsible, and at the same time, senseless and stupid officers... It is a gang of criminal elements which will be destroyed without mercy."

By now the twelve hundred SS and SD officers and men who had been arrested in Paris have been released.

"Seized by a titanic fury and an unquenchable thirst for revenge," William Shirer wrote, Hitler "whipped Himmler and [Ernst] Kaltenbrunner to ever greater efforts to lay their hands on every last person who had dared to plot against him." During the next nine months, at least two thousand and perhaps as many as five thousand Germans are executed for their alleged roles in the plot, some of them in concentration camps, just days before the war is over.

One of the worst effects of the assassination's failure is the rekindling of Hitler's belief that he is protected by divine providence. Churchill believed that these were Hitler's first words after the attack: "Who says I am not under the divine protection of god?"

The other terrible effect was to convince Hitler that since so many of his enemies in the army had now been unmasked—men he decided must have been undermining him all along—Germany's success in the war was now assured. Minutes after the bombing, this is what he tells his private secretary: "Believe me, this is the turning point for Germany. From now on things will look up again. I'm glad the *Schweinehunde* [bastards] have unmasked themselves."

Sixteen

*Although the smell of retreat wafted on the summer air, the business
of Nazi horror continued as usual.*
—Matthew Cobb

*A great tide of popular enthusiasm and emotion seized me on my entry
into Cherbourg, and bore me onward as far as Rennes, passing through
Coutances, Avranches and Fougères. In the ruins of demolished cities
and burned-out villages, the population gathered along the roads and
burst out in jubilant demonstrations... The contrast was remarkable
between the ardor of their spirit and the ravages endured by their
persons and property. Certainly France would live, for she was equal
to her suffering.*
—Charles de Gaulle, describing his triumphant journey through
the countryside toward Paris, days before its liberation

IN PARIS, the Nazi establishment reacts with horror to the slow
but steady progress of the Allied invasion. The surge of hope
Parisians feel after Normandy is miserably balanced by a huge new
anxiety. After the failure to assassinate Hitler, the Germans in the
occupied French capital become completely unhinged: Their vin-
dictive sadism knows no bounds.

"We had our hands at their throats," Christiane remembered,
"and they were scared that our specialty—sabotage—might hinder

their retreat. It wasn't funny before, but now it was horrible. Everything that they had already done was multiplied many times over." Sensing their imminent exile from the French capital, the Nazis lash out at the local population more viciously than ever, arresting, shooting, and deporting scores of Parisians who had never felt threatened before.

At the same time, the broader population of Paris is displaying growing public disdain for their Nazi oppressors. On July 14, a huge illegal demonstration of one hundred thousand people marches through the city to celebrate Bastille Day. German troops fire shots in the air to try to contain the crowds, but French policemen stand by and do nothing. The Occupation apparatus is plainly breaking down.

In the second half of July, Christiane lives through another catastrophe; at the same moment, she dodges another extremely close call. Then, unexpectedly, her parents get their first hopeful news about the fate of their younger son, André.

Jacqueline has stayed behind with Alex Katlama and the Maquis in the countryside, while Christiane is leading a clandestine life in Paris. She lives with the Rondenays and three other confederates in a secret apartment on avenue Mozart.

Nevertheless, Christiane continues to visit her parents, without ever giving any details about her secret life. The summer of 1944 is extremely difficult for Jacques and Hélène Boulloche: "They had a deported son," Christiane remembered, "and two daughters working in the Resistance at a time when the Gestapo seemed especially dangerous. It was hard for them to bear, even though they were in complete agreement with what we were doing. We never talked about it but in a sense, our involvement was a direct result of everything they had taught us."

On July 27, Rondenay tells Christiane she will accompany him to a meeting with Alain de Beaufort, who has just arrived in Paris from the Morvan. But as the temperature inches toward eighty-four degrees on another sweltering Paris day, something makes Rondenay change his mind. At the last minute, he decides to send Christiane to a different rendezvous.

During June and July alone, de Beaufort has distributed more than 150 tons of arms and supplies for the Maquis in the departments of Aube, Yonne, and Nièvre. He and Rondenay have escaped numerous assassination attempts, including one just ten days earlier, organized by Henri Dupré, a double agent for the Abwehr, the German military intelligence service.

Rondenay has escaped from half a dozen German and Spanish prisons since the beginning of the war. He has carried out dozens of successful sabotage missions, crafted countless fake identity cards, and fought bravely with the Maquis in the French countryside. But on this steamy Thursday, just four weeks before the Liberation of Paris, the luck of these two remarkable *Résistants* finally runs out.

Disaster strikes as soon as Rondenay greets de Beaufort at the Passy Métro station in the 16th arrondissement—and Gestapo agents with guns drawn swarm around them. De Beaufort tries to escape, and he is shot in the foot. For the next two weeks, both men are brutally tortured, but neither of them ever talks.

The news about her hero reaches Christiane very quickly. Immediately she goes into her standard routine after every arrest: "There was no question of giving in to panic; we had to act as quickly as possible. We spent the night burning all the incriminating documents in our possession. It was that night when I realized how *slowly* things could burn!"

She still has a clandestine apartment on rue de Lille, but she is afraid it won't be safe there anymore. So she goes to her parents' apartment for a couple of days instead.

"Despite everything," Christiane recalled, "there was no time to be discouraged. I didn't have time to be miserable because of Jarry's arrest. There was so much I had to do, as there always was after every arrest: change the contact places, change the mailboxes.

At times like this, you feel incredibly useful, because you believe in what you're doing.

"At the same time I felt a trap was being set around us. After you've survived so many disasters, you say to yourself, 'I can't always be so lucky!' It was exhausting, especially because the atmosphere in Paris was so electric. The Allies were advancing, the Germans were standing their ground. We were truly in a waiting game. On top of everything else, it was incredibly hot!"

Now Christiane always thinks she is being followed. One day, she is waiting outdoors at a bistro in Saint-Germain-des-Prés to meet a contact, when a strange-looking man begins to stare at her. Gripped with terror, she jumps on her bicycle—and the man follows her. Finally he runs straight into her. But it turns out he isn't trying to arrest her; he only wants to flirt!

"At times like this, we felt really odd," Christiane remembered. "We were living on another planet, but we had to act as naturally as we could. It was a completely different world of extraordinary intensity." Christiane won't really understand how she feels right now until after the Liberation. Then she will enter "a terrible void: one that was almost impossible to fill."

AFTER SHE IS BACK in Paris, her parents receive the first hopeful news they've had all year: a two-page letter from André. It is sent from Flossenbürg, a German concentration camp in Bavaria. This is the third camp he has been sent to in three months, after Auschwitz and Buchenwald.

Official German policy allows prisoners of the camps to write one letter a month,* as long as it is written in German, but for some

---

* The notation on a 1942 letter from Auschwitz stated, "Each prisoner in protective custody may receive from and send to his relatives two letters or two cards per month...Packages may not be sent, because the prisoners in the camp can purchase everything." (www.historyinink.com/935308_WWII_Auschwitz_letter.htm)

reason, André has been forced to wait three months before he is permitted to send his first message:

Dear Father: Finally I am allowed to write you a letter. My health is good, my wound is better and my morale is excellent. I hope to get letters from you soon. I will write you once a month.

André explains that he is allowed to receive packages, as long as they weigh "less than 5 or 6 kilos." Among other necessities, he asks for a pullover sweater.

His sister Jacqueline writes back immediately, describing the family's joy at receiving his letter and promising that Christiane will send him the requested package. "The conditions of our daily lives are more and more difficult, but they are bearable," Jacqueline writes. "Of course, there is no possibility of leaving Paris this summer...We embrace you from the bottom of our hearts."

A few days later, on August 2, 1944, Hélène writes to her imprisoned son: "We are happy to know you are healthy. We hope to see you again soon. The whole family kisses you very tenderly."

TWO DAYS AFER mailing her letter to André, Hélène gets another pleasant surprise: a forty-eight-hour visit from her older son, Robert. Now thirty-one, Robert has never joined the Resistance, although he has provided important information to the Free French from time to time. Like his father, he has kept his government job throughout the war, after being demobilized following the armistice in 1940. Now he is an inspector with the Finance Ministry, posted to Toulouse. A bachelor and a dutiful son, he has traveled to Paris for the weekend to visit his beleaguered parents.

It is now Saturday, August 5, 1944. In the south, the Allies have begun a massive aerial bombardment to prepare for Operation Dragoon, the second Allied invasion of France, which will start in just ten days on the Mediterranean coast between Cannes and Toulon.*

In exactly twenty days, the tanks of the 2nd French Armored Division, commanded by General Jacques-Philippe Leclerc, will finally roll into the exhausted capital, to the most rapturous welcome for any reconquering army of modern times.

But today, the Germans are still in control, food supplies are dwindling, and Parisians are increasingly nervous about the sluggish progress of the Allies toward their capital, two long and stifling months after their spectacular assault on Normandy.

On Saturday night, Christiane's aunt and uncle host a small dinner for all the Boulloches who are in Paris this weekend—Christiane and Robert, and fifty-six-year-old Jacques and Hélène. For Christiane, the dinner feels like a parenthesis in the middle of her life of permanent stress. Nothing important is discussed, and among the guests, only Christiane's parents know about her secret life as a *Résistante*. Christiane excuses herself around ten thirty and bicycles back to her clandestine apartment on avenue Mozart.

Her parents and her brother return to the family's large apartment on avenue d'Eylau. The Boulloches' servants, Marie and Simone, are asleep in the maids' rooms nearby when the family retires for the night. The apartment is a short walk from the Palais de Chaillot, the concert hall where Jacqueline had miraculously snatched Christiane from the Nazis' clutches eight months earlier.

At three A.M., the deep Sunday morning silence of the pitch-black 16th arrondissement explodes into terror, when the Gestapo storms the third-floor apartment. The Nazis rouse the horrified sleepers from their beds, then bellow the reason for their nocturnal invasion: "We are here to arrest Christiane Boulloche."

---

* Eight hundred eighty-five ships will disgorge 151,00 Allied troops in another huge operation, barely remembered because it was overshadowed by Normandy. Seven of the eleven divisions under American general Alexander Patch are actually Free French soldiers commanded by General Jean de Lattre de Tassigny. (Ousby, *Occupation*, p. 279)

But Christiane is not here. She is sound asleep in her secret apartment on avenue Mozart.

So the Nazis seize her father, her mother, and her brother in her place.

JUST AS THEY HAD after André Boulloche's arrest, the Gestapo leaves the apartment unguarded for an hour or two, with the servants all alone. Marie seizes the moment to telephone Christiane's aunt Ginette to tell her the terrible news—and to implore her to prevent Christiane's next visit to her parents, which she is planning to make that very morning.

But Ginette doesn't know where Christiane is or how to reach her on the telephone. There is only one thing she can do: At the crack of dawn she dispatches her maid, Odette, to the rond-point de Longchamps, and Christiane's cousin, Louis, to place du Trocadéro, to try to intercept her niece before she reaches 28 avenue d'Eylau. There the second wave of the Gestapo has camped out in the concierge's apartment and tacked Christiane's photograph to the wall.

For Christiane there will be one more miracle. She sets out on her bicycle for her parents' house around eight thirty on Sunday morning. After a few minutes, to her great annoyance, she gets a flat tire. When she can't pedal anymore, she changes her route. Normally she would cycle up from Trocadéro to her parents' apartment. But today, because she is forced to walk her bicycle, she takes the route through the rond-point de Longchamps. Because Christiane is pushing her bicycle down the street, Odette easily intercepts her—seventy yards from her parents' front door. Christiane knows what Odette has done: "She saved my life."

FOR THE NEXT WEEK, the Germans, and then the Milice, the Vichy paramilitary force, terrorize her parents' apartment building. An elderly woman who tries to visit Hélène Boulloche is detained for three hours; a young girl who comes to visit someone else in the building is stripped and searched.

As soon as Odette tells Christiane about the arrests, her only concern is to alert the rest of her unit, and then to disappear as quickly as she can. Alone in Paris, without Jacqueline, or any other member of her immediate family, this twenty-one-year-old secret agent must summon all of her inner strength to escape confusion and despair.

Later that morning, Christiane runs into a close family friend, Dr. René Cler. When she tells him she is on the run from the Gestapo, the thirty-four-year-old doctor immediately invites her back to his apartment on avenue Sully-Prud'homme. What strikes him most about this brave young woman is her "sense of immediate spontaneity."*

Eight months earlier, Cler had already collaborated with the movement, after Jacqueline Boulloche had arrived "very agitated" at his house for lunch.

"Our unit has just been arrested," she declared. "Can we hide our radio transmitter with you?"

"I had no choice," the doctor remembered. "So then I passed several unpleasant nights." He recognized "a remarkable simplicity" in the Boulloche sisters: "For us, it is our duty."

A year earlier, the doctor had had his own close call, when he answered a summons from the Gestapo, after they became suspicious of the activities at his apartment. "It was not pleasant. An

---

*"It was obvious," Christiane said many years later. "I never thought I was doing anything extraordinary. Never. *Never!*" (author's interview with Christiane Boulloche-Audibert, March 11, 1999)

attractive French girl interrogated me for two or three hours. And there was a sexual current between us. When she went next door to make her report in German, she said, 'This man came voluntarily to see us, and we should let him go.'" And they did.

Cler decides that it's too dangerous to lodge Christiane in his fourth-floor apartment. But there is an empty apartment on the sixth floor that belongs to an absent Swedish diplomat, and the concierge allows him to put Christiane in there. Now, not even the members of her own unit know where she is living.

The apartment building next door is filled with Germans. During the final days before the Liberation, there are German snipers on the roof—and a Senegalese sniper fighting with the Free French in an apartment across the way. Christiane spends most of her days in the doctor's apartment and her nights in the apartment of the Swedish diplomat. One night when she goes back upstairs, she discovers bullet holes from stray shots lodged in the wall exactly where she had been sleeping.

The next eighteen days will determine the fate of the City of Light. But Christiane will never leave her secret hiding place—until de Gaulle finally makes his triumphant return to the capital.

Seventeen

*Even when motionless, which he often was, others could feel
the volcano inside.*
— Gregor Dallas describing Charles de Gaulle

ONE DAY AFTER Jacques, Hélène, and Robert Boulloche are
arrested, Adolf Hitler summons General Dietrich von Choltitz to meet with him at Wolfsschanze. At the first of the three
security rings, all of the general's luggage is removed from his
car—a new precaution inaugurated after Stauffenberg's failed assassination attempt.

A fourth-generation Prussian soldier, Choltitz had led the
Nazi assault on Rotterdam in 1939. Three years later, he captured
Sebastopol in the Russian Ukraine. When the siege there began,
Choltitz was leading a regiment of 4,800 men. When it ended, only
347 of his soldiers were still alive. But the Germans had won the
battle.

Shortly, Choltitz will tell a Swedish diplomat, "Since Sebastopol, it has been my fate to cover the retreat of our armies and to
destroy the cities behind them."

His flair for destruction and his fierce loyalty to the Führer
are the reasons he is meeting with Hitler on August 7. Hitler has
been told Choltitz is a man who never wavers in the execution of
an order. Coming from France, where his corps has failed to halt

the breakout of American forces into Brittany, the general hopes to be rejuvenated by his leader after his recent setback on the battlefield.

But when the general reaches Hitler's lair, he finds the same hollow man Erwin Rommel and Field Marshal Gerd von Rundstedt had encountered in France a few weeks earlier. "I went into the room and there he stood, a fat, broken-down old man with festering hands," Choltitz remembered two months later. "I was really almost sorry for him because he looked horrible."

Then Hitler "began reeling off a gramophone record like a man stung by a tarantula and spoke for three-quarters of an hour!" The Führer told him that "dozens of generals" had already "bounced at the end of a rope" since the assassination attempt, because they had tried to prevent him from fulfilling his destiny of leading the German people.*

Today Hitler is making Choltitz his new commander in Paris. The Führer has chosen the Prussian to make sure that he has someone who will turn Paris into ashes if the Germans are forced to abandon their greatest prize. He is making Choltitz a Befehlshaber, a title that gives him the widest possible powers for a commander of a German garrison. Hitler orders him to "stamp out without pity" any act of terrorism against the German armed forces in Paris.

But Choltitz leaves the meeting more pessimistic than ever

---

* The Führer is not exaggerating. The day after this meeting with Choltitz, at least nine people are executed for their role in the assassination plot, including one field marshal, four generals, two captains, and Berthold von Stauffenberg, the brother of the ringleader. Four months later, Choltitz told his fellow generals, "This 'Putsch' of 20 July will be regarded as an event of historic significance. Those 1,500 men, hanged by these criminals, will all get a memorial dedicated to them, for they were the only patriotic, resolute and 'ready to act' men that we had." (Neitzel, *Tapping Hitler's Generals*) In fact, the widows of most of the anti-Hitler conspirators were initially denied pensions by the West German government, on the grounds that their husbands had been traitors. (www.dw.de/germany-remembers-operation-valkyrie-the-plot-to-kill-hitler/a-1271174)

about the future of the Third Reich. When the Allies reach the outskirts of Paris, he knows exactly what the next order will be from the mad dictator: *Blow it all up.*

THE URGENCY to liberate Paris felt by the Resistance fighters in the capital and the Free French Forces under de Gaulle is not shared at all by Eisenhower and the rest of the generals leading the Allied invasion. While they obviously understand the power of the capital's symbolism, they don't think it has much importance as a military objective.

De Gaulle is worried that Communists will try to seize control of the capital if there is a premature insurrection there. But the Allies believe that the liberation of the French capital will require the diversion of tremendous resources from the effort to defeat the Germans. Right now they are determined to save every ounce of fuel and food and ammunition for combat operations that will "carry our lines forward the maximum distance" to wipe out the Nazi armies.

A planning document that lands on Eisenhower's desk after the Normandy invasion warns that "Paris food and medical requirements alone are 75,000 tons for the first two months, and an additional 1,500 tons of coal daily are likely to be needed for the public utilities."

For all of these reasons, Eisenhower hopes to put off the "actual capture of the city" as long as possible—unless he receives "evidence of starvation or distress among its citizens."*

---

* In fact, Patton's 3rd Army does run out of gasoline, one hundred miles from the Rhine, on August 30—five days after Paris is liberated. (Collins and Lapierre, *Is Paris Burning?* p. 219)

ALTHOUGH CHRISTIANE is confined to Dr. Cler's apartment building, she still manages to learn the fate of her newly arrested family members, because the doctor is in touch with some of her comrades. Her parents and Robert are going to be shipped off to Germany on a train that is scheduled to leave the Gare de l'Est in Paris on August 12.

But with the Allies pushing steadily forward, and the Liberation achingly near, the Resistance redoubles its efforts to prevent any more deportations. On August 10, national railroad workers in the Paris region declare a general strike. Their leaflet exhorts, "To make the Hun retreat, strike! For the complete and definitive liberation of our country, strike!" Within two days, half of the eighty thousand railroad workers have walked off the job, and the train that is supposed to deport Christiane's parents and brother is stranded at the station.

On the night of August 12, the Resistance launches another sabotage mission, which cripples the Gare de l'Est. But nothing will halt the demonic momentum of the Nazis.

Instead of bringing them to the Gare de l'Est, on August 15, General Choltitz orders more than two thousand prisoners assembled on the *"quai au bestiaux"* (the animal platform) of the Pantin station.

Among those boarding the train are Jacques, Hélène, and Robert Boulloche, André Rondenay, and Alain de Beaufort—while Christiane remains cut off from all of them in her secret hiding place.

This will be the final train of French prisoners to depart Paris for Germany, the infamous *dernier convoi.**

---

* Although this is the last such prisoner train from Paris to reach Germany, there are several later ones from other parts of France. (http://dora-ellrich.fr/les-hommes-du-convoi-du-15-aout-1944/)

Unusually, the train carries 168 Allied airmen—Americans, Britons, and Canadians—who have been rescued by the Resistance only to be captured by the Nazis afterward.

The Red Cross arrives at the station before the train leaves and manages to distribute some food rations to the prisoners. Somehow, the Red Cross agents also convince the Germans to release thirty-six prisoners who are sick or pregnant. Then the train rumbles out of the station.

Half an hour after it leaves Paris, the long line of wooden cattle cars suddenly shudders to a halt. At the last minute, the Nazis have figured out the identity of two of their most important prisoners. A Gestapo officer gives the order to unlock the doors on one of the cars, and Rondenay and de Beaufort tumble off the train, along with a handful of others. Minutes later, they are driven to the Domont forest, where they are executed by a German firing squad. Christiane imagined the horror of their final moments: "They must have thought they were being taken off the train so that they could return to Paris."

The three Boulloches remain in their fetid cars to continue their wretched journey.

A survivor of the convoy remembered hearing railroad workers yelling at the train, "You won't go any further, the war is over! The Allies have landed at Saint-Tropez"—as indeed they had. But despite more attempts by the Resistance to halt the convoy—several prisoners try to escape and are immediately shot, and another insurrection forces the Germans to transfer all the prisoners to a new train at Nanteuil-Saâcy—the convoy continues its relentless progress.

On August 19, the train arrives at Weimar, Germany. The following day, the men are dispatched to Buchenwald and the women to Ravensbrück.

Much later, Christiane learns that her mother has been waterboarded by the Gestapo after her arrest and before her final train ride. But Hélène Boulloche never tells the Germans anything.

BACK IN PARIS, German demolition teams are planting the charges necessary to blow up every bridge, every factory, and every telephone exchange, as well as every famous Paris landmark, from the Palais du Luxembourg to Napoleon's tomb and the Quai d'Orsay, home of the French Foreign Ministry. The chief German engineer promises General Choltitz that the Allies won't find a single working factory when they reach the capital—the industry of Paris will be paralyzed for at least six months.

Since Allied bombers are continuing their obliteration of German cities every day, German generals see nothing unusual about their plan to level Paris. They have just finished demolishing Warsaw, after the uprising there.

After receiving an anonymous phone call, warning of the Germans' plans to blow up every bridge crossing the Seine, the capital's Vichy mayor, Pierre-Charles Taittinger, decides to pay a call on the German commander. Choltitz recites his plan to blow the whole city up "as indifferently as if it were a crossroads village in the Ukraine."

Taittinger decides there is nothing he can do except to try to convey his love for the city. "Often it is given to a general to destroy, rarely to preserve," Taittinger begins. "Imagine that one day it may be given to you to stand on this balcony as a tourist, to look once more on these monuments to our joys, our sufferings, and to be able to say, 'One day I could have destroyed all this, and I preserved it as a gift for humanity.' General, is not that worth all a conqueror's glory?"

"You are a good advocate for Paris," Choltitz replied. "You have done your duty well. And likewise I, as a German general, must do mine."

The general's response is disheartening. But the Frenchman has planted a powerful seed.

WHEN DE GAULLE returns to France from his headquarters in Algiers, he reaches General Eisenhower's headquarters on August 20. Once again, Eisenhower declares his intention to bypass Paris when his troops cross the Seine. De Gaulle says this strategy might be acceptable, if the Resistance had not already begun an uprising there.* Eisenhower replies that the uprising has begun too soon, and against the Allies' wishes.

"Why too soon?" the French general replies. "Since at this very moment your forces are on the Seine?" Ultimately, Eisenhower commits himself to liberating the capital with General Leclerc's French troops, but he still refuses to specify a date. De Gaulle believes it is "intolerable that the enemy should occupy Paris even a day longer than it was necessary, from the moment we had the means to drive him out of it."

De Gaulle also suggests to Ike that if the Allied command delays too long, he will ignore the Allied chain of command and give the order to General Leclerc's armored division to take Paris himself.

The next day, Roger Gallois, an emissary of the Resistance in Paris, sneaks through German lines to make another appeal to the Americans to get to Paris as soon as possible. When he reaches the tent of George S. Patton, the famously gruff general tells the Frenchman that the Americans are in the business of "destroying Germans, not capturing capitals." The insurrection in the city has begun without permission from the Allies, and now the Resistance will have to accept the consequences; the Allies cannot accept "the moral responsibility of feeding the city."

But Eisenhower's gratitude to the Resistance for everything it has done to make the Normandy invasion successful will soon make it impossible for him to ignore the demands of the Free French.

---

* De Gaulle doesn't know the exact numbers, but French casualties are mounting in Paris: 125 killed and 479 wounded on August 19, and another 106 killed and 357 wounded the following day.

BY NOW General Choltitz has received the order for the "neutralizations and destructions envisaged for Paris," but he does nothing to carry it out except to blow up a single telephone exchange. Eventually his troops will also set fire to the Grand Palais.

In the final week of the Occupation, the troops under Choltitz's command are increasingly skittish; now you can put your life in the Nazis' hands just by walking down the sidewalk.

One morning in the third week of August, Simone de Beauvoir leans out the window of her Left Bank apartment. This is what she remembers:

> The swastika was still flying over the Sénat... Two cyclists rode past shouting, "The Préfecture* has fallen." At the same moment a German detachment emerged from the Sénat, and marched off toward the Boulevard St-Germain. Before turning the corner of the street the soldiers let loose a volley of machine gun-fire. Passersby... scattered, taking cover as best they could in doorways. But every door was shut; one man crumpled and fell in the very act of knocking... while others collapsed along the sidewalk.

By now the walls of Paris are plastered with posters reading À CHACUN SON BOCHE! — meaning, roughly, that each Parisian should choose his or her own German to shoot.

THE NIGHT AFTER Roger Gallois's pleas are rejected by General George Patton, the Frenchman gets one more chance to make his case that the Allies must advance on Paris immediately. On August 22, he reaches the headquarters of General Omar Bradley, commander of the 12th Army Group, where Gallois is given an audience with Brigadier General Edwin Silbert, Bradley's intelligence chief.

---

* Paris Police Headquarters.

As soon as the meeting ends, Silbert and Bradley are scheduled to leave to meet with Eisenhower.

Albert Lebel, a French colonel who is a liaison officer to the U.S. Army, has already made his own written plea to General Bradley: "If the American Army, seeing Paris in a state of insurrection, does not come to its aid, it will be an omission the people of France will never be able to forget."

Now Silbert is accompanying the haggard envoy of the Paris Resistance, as Gallois begins to pour his heart out: "You must come to our help, or there is going to be terrible slaughter. Hundreds of thousands of Frenchmen are going to be killed."

By the time Silbert climbs into a Piper Cub to fly to Eisenhower's headquarters, he has already begun to reconsider his opposition to an immediate move on Paris.

When Silbert and Bradley give their report to Eisenhower, the supreme commander realizes that his hand has finally been "forced by the action of the Free French forces inside Paris." Because they had begun their uprising, "it was necessary to move rapidly to their support." Eisenhower also recognizes that de Gaulle "was always determined to get where he wanted to go, and he wasn't about to let anybody stop him."

When Silbert and Bradley fly back to their headquarters a few hours later, General Jacques-Philippe Leclerc, commander of the 2nd French Armored Division, is waiting for them on the tarmac. He rushes up to their airplane before the propeller has stopped turning. "You win," General Silbert tells him. "They've decided to send you straight to Paris."

ON THE SAME DAY that Eisenhower finally decides to move on the capital, General Choltitz has summoned Swedish consul general Raoul Nordling to a remarkable meeting. Nordling has already convinced the general to release 3,893 prisoners, including 1,482

Jews held at Drancy, although he has failed to halt the train that has carried the three Boulloches to concentration camps in Germany.

By now the German general has decided that he has nothing to gain by following Hitler's orders to blow up the City of Light. So Choltitz makes an extraordinary request of the Swedish diplomat: He asks him to cross German lines, so that he can tell the Allies they must advance on Paris immediately. If they don't, they will enter a city that is already in ruins.

Choltitz then hands the Swede a laissez-passer: "The Commanding General of Gross Paris authorizes the Consul General of Sweden R. Nordling to leave Paris and its line of defense." But before Nordling can leave Paris that night, he is stricken with a heart attack. In his place, he sends his brother, Rolf, accompanied by two Allied intelligence agents and two Gaullists the consul has selected, to improve the chances that the improbable story of the defecting German general will be believed by the Allies.

When the motley crew finally reaches General Bradley's headquarters the next day with their bizarre message, the American commander reacts immediately: "Have the French division hurry the hell in there," he declares. He also orders the American 4th Division to get ready to "get in there too. We can't take any chances on that general [Choltitz] changing his mind."

De Gaulle has tried hard to convince the Allies that there is a danger of a Communist takeover of the capital if his forces don't get there quickly enough. French Communists are indeed "the driving force" behind the on-again, off-again insurrection in Paris, but the historian Julian Jackson and others argue that this did not mean they were trying to seize power. If there was a strategy for that, it came from the Gaullists: They were the ones who decided to occupy the Préfecture on August 19 and the Hôtel de Ville (City Hall) the next day.

After fierce fighting with the German troops dug in on the outskirts of Paris, most of General Leclerc's 2nd Armored Division has reached the "immediate proximity" of the capital on the evening of August 24. When the spectral outline of the Eiffel Tower finally appears on the horizon, the troops are "galvanized by an electric current" that propels them forward.

SHORTLY AFTER NINE P.M., a tiny French detachment of three tanks and four half-tracks form a steel ring around the Hôtel de Ville. At last, Free French troops are back in Paris—four years and seventy-one days after the first German troops passed through the Porte de la Vilette to begin their odious Occupation.

A Paris radio station has been seized by the Resistance five days earlier. Pierre Schaeffer grabs the microphone and begins to shout:

Parisians rejoice! We have come on the air to give you the news of our deliverance. The Leclerc Division has entered Paris. We are crazy with happiness!

To mark the glorious moment, the station broadcasts the mystic chords of "The Marseillaise," the rousing anthem that had been banished in Paris ever since the Germans arrived here. Spontaneously, thousands of residents turn their radios up full blast and fling open their windows to make the still-darkened streets explode with the joyful sound of freedom.

Then Schaeffer returns to the microphone to command every Paris parish to start ringing its bells. Within minutes, every block is reverberating with the clanging noise, from the south tower of Notre-Dame to Sacré-Coeur high up on the hill.

IT WAS PARTICULARLY APPROPRIATE that this was all happening on the radio, because this was the medium that had done the most to stoke the fires of Resistance since the Occupation began. It was also the radio that transformed Charles de Gaulle from an unknown officer into the larger-than-life figure who was now being embraced as the nation's savior—practically a Joan of Arc for his time.

His celebrity was almost entirely the product of the regular broadcasts the British had allowed him to make on the BBC. Between 1940 and 1944, he delivered sixty-eight speeches. Gradually, his broadcasts became as beloved among his countrymen as Churchill's in Britain and Edward R. Murrow's and Roosevelt's in the United States. The Vichy government estimated that three hundred thousand French people were listening to de Gaulle at the beginning of 1941—and *three million* just one year later.

As Ian Ousby observes, de Gaulle used the radio to accomplish "precisely what Pétain had hoped but miserably failed to do as leader of Vichy: he had become France. Actually, the claim to be France in some indefinable but potent way had been implicit in de Gaulle's wartime utterances right from the moment of his arrival in Britain."

The six-foot-five general is mobbed by grateful Frenchmen in every town and city he travels through after the Normandy invasion. Yet no one is more aware of the deep canyons of division in France, where some have fought the Germans, some have collaborated—and the vast majority have simply kept their heads down and tried desperately to get enough to eat.

De Gaulle knows exactly how he will smooth these divisions. He understands that France has been infected by a terrible disease, and denial is a necessary part of the cure, an indispensable part of the healing. On the eve of his return to Paris, this is how he envisions his task: He will "mold all minds into a single national impulse, but also cause the figure and the authority of the state to appear at once."

DINING WITH HIS FELLOW OFFICERS at his headquarters at the opulent Hôtel Meurice hotel, facing the Tuileries, General Choltitz hears the clanging bells, and he knows exactly what they mean. "Gentlemen," he tells his guests, "I can tell you something that's escaped you here in your nice life in Paris. Germany's lost this war, and we have lost it with her." Later that evening, Choltitz's aide, Count Dankwart von Arnim, writes in his diary, "I have just heard the bells of my own funeral."

Shortly after midnight, Captain Werner Ebernach pays a visit to Choltitz. This is the German officer who has placed several hundred oxygen bottles, at a pressure of 180 atmospheres, to magnify the effect of the dynamite planted in the cellars of Les Invalides, two tons of explosives behind the pillars of the Chamber of Deputies, five tons of explosives under the Ministry of the Marine on the Place de la Concorde, mines on the southeast leg of the Eiffel Tower, and dynamite under more than forty Paris bridges spanning the Seine.

Ebernach has also heard the bells, and he understands what they mean just as well as the general does. Declaring his mission accomplished, Ebernach asks Choltitz if he has any further orders. The general does not. Then the captain asks for permission to withdraw, to avoid being captured by the advancing Allies. He explains that he will leave behind enough men to detonate all the bridges and monuments he has readied for destruction.

But Choltitz has another idea: "Take *all your men* and leave us," he tells the colonel. Three hours later, all of the demolition experts of the 813th Pionierkompanie (combat engineers) have left the city, taking with them the principal menace to its most magnificent structures. From now on, the increasingly urgent query from Hitler and his minions—"Is Paris burning?"—will be greeted by nothing but silence.

Choltitz explained later that he had no fear of death, but he had begun to have nightmares in which he saw his own corpse suspended over the ruins of the City of Light.

FRENCH AND AMERICAN TROOPS roar into the city under a perfect summer sky on Friday, August 25, the Feast of St. Louis, which honors an unusually benevolent French king of the Middle Ages who had made his officials swear to give justice to all.

Choltitz is eager to surrender, but his sense of military honor compels him to put up a token defense. There is a brief but brutal battle outside his headquarters at the Hôtel Meurice and some heavy fighting near the Ecole Militaire and Les Invalides. German snipers increase Allied casualties, especially near the Tuileries.

French officers conduct the German general to the Préfecture, where General Leclerc has just started a celebratory lunch. Henri Rol-Tanguy, the Communist commander of the Forces Françaises de l'Intérieur, barges in to demand that his name appear next to Leclerc's on the document of surrender. Then the generals proceed to the Gare Montparnasse for the formal signing.*

---

* Choltitz was taken prisoner by the British, who sent him, along with many other captured German officers, to the Combined Services Detailed Interrogation Centre at Trent Park, near Enfield in Middlesex, where all of their conversations were secretly bugged. In October 1944, Choltitz declared, "We are also to blame. We have cooperated and have almost taken the Nazis seriously...We've let those stupid cattle talk and chatter to us...I feel thoroughly ashamed. Maybe we are far more to blame than those uneducated cattle who in any case never hear anything else at all. It wouldn't be so bad if we Generals, or the generation before us, for that matter, hadn't taken part. The trouble is that we participated without a murmur." The general also said, "The worst job I ever carried out—which however I carried out with great consistency —was the liquidation of the Jews. I carried out this order down to the very last detail." Choltitz was probably referring to actions he took in Crimea. (Neitzel, *Tapping Hitler's Generals*) From Britain, Choltitz was sent to Camp Clinton, Mississippi. He was released by the Allies in 1947. In 1950, he published a memoir, *Brennt Paris?* (Is Paris Burning?). He wrote that he had refused to blow up Paris because he thought Hitler was crazy and the destruction of the French capital would make any future friendship between France and Germany impossible. His memoir was a principal source for *Is Paris Burning?* by Larry Collins and Dominique Lapierre. He received a German general's pension of $675 a month. He died in Baden-Baden in 1966 at the age of seventy-one.

German prisoners being marched down the rue de Rivoli on August 25, 1944.

At seven o'clock that evening, de Gaulle finally enters the capital. From the Hôtel de Ville, he delivers a radio address to the nation. In a speech that lasts less than five minutes, he sets the tone for all of his future efforts to bind up the wounds of his tortured nation.

Why should we hide the emotion which seizes us all, men and women, who are here, at home, in Paris that stood up to liberate itself and that succeeded in doing this with its own hands?

No! We will not hide this deep and sacred emotion. These are minutes which go beyond each of our poor lives. Paris! Paris outraged! Paris broken! Paris martyred! But Paris liberated! Liberated by itself, liberated by its people with the help of the French armies, with the support and the help of all France, of the France that fights, of the only France, of the real France, of the eternal France!

With those words, de Gaulle immortalizes all those who had fought the Germans as the only "real" Frenchmen of "eternal France."

Well! Since the enemy which held Paris has capitulated into our hands, France returned to Paris. She has returned bleeding but resolute. She has returned, enlightened by this immense lesson, but more certain than ever of her responsibilities and her rights . . .

It would not even be enough, after what has happened, if with the help of our dear and admirable allies we chased him out of our country. We want to go to his country as we should, as conquerors.

This is why the French advance guard has entered Paris with guns blazing. This is why the great French army from Italy has landed in the south and is advancing rapidly up the Rhône valley. This is why our brave and dear Forces of the Interior are going to arm themselves with modern weapons. It is for this revenge, this vengeance and justice, that we will keep fighting until the last day, until the day of total and complete victory.

This duty of war, all the men who are here and all those who hear us in France know that it demands national unity. We, who have lived the greatest hours of our History, we have nothing else to wish than to show ourselves, up to the end, worthy of France.

Long live France!

Immediately after his speech, he reinforces his message of the one "real France" when he is asked to "proclaim the Republic before the people who have gathered here." De Gaulle refuses to do so: "The Republic has never ceased. Free France, Fighting France, the French Committee of National Liberation have successively incorporated it. Vichy always was and still remains null and void. I myself am the President of the government of the Republic. Why should I proclaim it now?" (Two days earlier, he had said, "France is a country which continues, not a country which begins.")

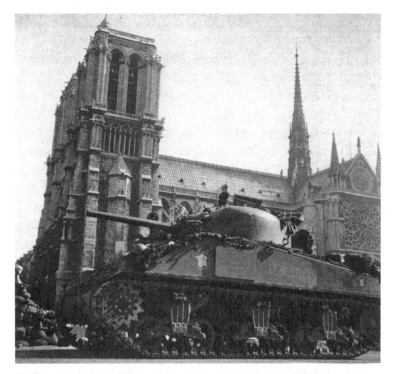

Shots were fired as de Gaulle approached Notre Dame, and continued as he strode down the aisle inside, but the general never flinched at the sounds of gunfire.

The next day, de Gaulle defies American commanders who want to use General Leclerc's troops to guard the northeast approaches to the city. The French general concedes that militarily, the Americans are correct, but he insists, "We must have this parade," and he needs Leclerc's troops to provide security for the huge festivity, "Today we were to revive, by the spectacle of its joy and the evidence of its liberty, the self-awareness of a people who yesterday were crushed by defeat and scattered in servitude."

At three o'clock in the afternoon, de Gaulle lays a huge wreath on the tomb of the unknown solider under the Arc de Triomphe and relights the eternal flame, the first Frenchman to do so without German minders watching since the Occupation had begun four years earlier. De Gaulle thinks Parisians are watching him "as though I were the materialization of a dream."

Shots ring out as de Gaulle leaves the Champs-Élysées to turn into the place de la Concorde, and thousands dive to the sidewalks, although de Gaulle thinks most of the fire is pointed up into the air. The same thing happens again when he arrives in front of Notre-Dame, and it even continues inside the cathedral. But no one has ever been more certain that he is a man of destiny than he is. He wrote about himself on this day, "Since each of all of those here had chosen Charles de Gaulle in his heart as the refuge against his agony and the symbol of his hopes, we must permit the man to be seen…so that the national unity should shine forth at this sight."

And so de Gaulle walks straight down the nave of the cathedral, never flinching at the sounds of gunfire.*

CHRISTIANE is among the millions of Parisians who descend upon the Champs-Élysées to celebrate their liberator. But she never really experiences "the euphoria of the liberation."

"Everyone seemed happy and relieved," she remembered. "There were many who greeted de Gaulle with acclaim, after they had supported Pétain. I viewed all of this from a certain distance. It was true that the war was almost over, but my parents and my brothers had been deported, my sister had stayed with the Maquis in the countryside, and I was completely alone in Paris."

---

* None of the snipers was ever caught alive, or identified. De Gaulle believed they were agents provocateurs, who had fired "a few bullets into the air" to "create the impression that certain threats were still lurking in the shadows" and "that the resistance organizations must remain armed and vigilant." (de Gaulle, *Complete War Memoirs*, p. 658)

At midnight on August 26, hours after de Gaulle's triumphant march through the city, the Nazis return one more time to terrorize the French capital. Ignoring the surrender, which had been signed by General Choltitz, German planes bomb Paris, destroying five hundred houses, setting fire to the wine market, and killing or wounding a thousand citizens.

Eighteen

We must not forget that we owe a great debt to the blunders—
the extraordinary blunders—of the Germans.
—Winston Churchill, addressing Parliament, September 1944

TWO DAYS AFTER the Liberation, Christiane goes to a police
station to request a gendarme to accompany her to her parents' apartment. When she walks through the front door, she
discovers a hovel: the Germans have looted everything, from her
mother's jewelry to her father's rare books.*

When she is alone in the ravaged apartment, a neighbor appears,
the father of a young girl who is Christiane's age. He says he is
there to comfort her, but when she lets him in, he tries to rape her.
"I was shocked and quite undone. After everything else I had been
through, this was really too much."

To escape her brutal neighbor, her loneliness, and her parents'
decimated home, Christiane leaves Paris at the end of August by
car to rejoin the Maquis and Jacqueline in the Morvan: "She was

---

* During the time General Choltitz was a prisoner of the Allies, he declared, "I'm
saying that we steal! We collect the stuff up into stores, like proper robbers...that's
the frightful part of it. This revolting business of engaging in organized robbery
of private property...Throughout the whole of France...Whole train-loads of
the most beautiful antique furniture from private houses! It's frightful; it's an
indescribable disgrace!" (Neitzel, *Tapping Hitler's Generals*)

all I had left." At the end of September, the region is liberated. On October 21, Jean Longhi (Grandjean) presents Christiane with the Croix de Guerre. The self-effacing *Résistante* is annoyed by this recognition of her bravery: "I considered all of my clandestine activity to be a matter of course, and now a decoration! After so many dramas and so many deaths, it seemed like a ridiculous gesture."

Christiane and Jacqueline return to Paris and their parents' apartment. Their lives are brightened by their new tenant, Lieutenant Henry Kaiser, the charismatic Brooklynite who is a labor lawyer and the labor adviser to the occupying American Army.

Then Christiane suffers one more serious scare. Jacqueline becomes ill, and the doctor telephones Christiane and asks to see her alone. He tells her Jacqueline has only a few months to live. After all the other catastrophes she has already endured, Christiane feels completely overwhelmed—until she takes the X-rays to her friend Dr. Cler for a second opinion.

After examining them, Cler explains that they actually show only a few benign traces of an old case of pleurisy. He promises Christiane her sister will recover before long—and she does.

THE SISTERS' GREATEST PREOCCUPATION is the fate of their parents and their brothers, about whom they have heard nothing since André's letter from Flossenbürg the previous summer. At first they don't even know that their father has been sent to Buchenwald, their mother to Ravensbrück, a women's concentration camp about ninety miles north of Berlin, and Robert to Ellrich, a subcamp of Dora-Mittelbau, about twelve miles away.

By November, they have learned their father's whereabouts. A family friend, Pierre Lefaucheux, miraculously returns from Buchenwald, and Christiane immediately goes to see him. When she arrives at his house, he is at the dinner table with friends. She hears laughter from the dining room while she waits for them to finish. When dinner ends, he finally tells Christiane that despite the dire conditions at Buchenwald, her father is fine. But the friend is obviously uncomfortable, and she wonders if he is telling the truth or just doesn't want to alarm her.

The daughters know nothing about their mother's fate. But her husband, Jacques, actually hears from Hélène shortly after he arrives at Buchenwald. She is permitted to write one letter a month, and he receives her first one toward the end of September. Jacques's college classmate Etienne Audibert, who was with him in the camp, recorded what happened next.

> Although letter writing from one camp to another continued to be authorized, after that [Jacques] never received another letter [from his wife]. He could not fail to understand what that meant. This was the greatest blow that could have struck him, and it crushed his indomitable energy. Once his moral resolve had been broken, there was nothing left for him but death; that is the law of the camp. He succumbed on February 18, 1945.

Jacques's deduction had been correct: Hélène had died at Ravensbrück on October 25, 1944, just two months after she had been waterboarded by the Nazis.

Etienne Audibert's remembrance continued:

> It is something entirely different to die in a concentration camp. Death from action or during combat, consensual death accepted with one's full strength, has nothing in common with gradual physical and moral erosion, a progressive degradation, when the victim sees his faculties slowly disappear, his personality silently breaking up. Those who knew Jacques Boulloche, his wife, and their children could not fail to appreciate the extreme refinement of their milieu. Everything breathed elegance; everything carried the luster of high culture and good taste. Could they recognize

these tattered people when they were dressed in rags, deprived of everything, famished, shivering from the cold, treated worse than any beast has ever been, struck by blows for no reason, weakened daily by humiliations that could only be conceived by the deranged imaginations of monstrous perverts? Can others imagine their agony, alone, far from the sky of France and everyone they loved, these spectral beings with a feverish glow, their eyes like concave sockets, with protruding ears and parched skin ready to crack, living their final weeks in a ghastly atmosphere polluted by the foul smell of the smoke of the crematorium? And added to their own pain, the desperate anxiety each of them felt about the other three? When they are finally dead, no friendly hand comes to close their eyes. And then the cinders of their flesh are dispersed to the wind.

AT THE BEGINNING OF 1945, the sisters still don't know any of this. Jacqueline decides to go to Switzerland, to see if there might be a way to ransom the freedom of the rest of the family. Her trip is a failure: She learns nothing about her parents or her brothers. When she returns to Paris, she tells her sister there is only an infinitesimal chance that any of them will survive.

Christiane briefly gets a job as the secretary for the Canadian ambassador to Paris, but the position is a poor fit. Christiane doesn't even know how to type, and she doesn't last there very long. Jacqueline goes to work for the Bureau Central de Renseignements et d'Action, the same organization André had been assigned to when he was de Gaulle's military delegate in occupied Paris.

The sisters enjoy going out with the American and Canadian troops who are now crowding the city. They take them to dinner at their mess, which has much better food than what is available to most Parisian civilians. The Occupation is over, but most store shelves remain empty.

At the same time, the sisters are very much aware of the Battle of the Bulge, the last major German counteroffensive, and the greatest surprise attack on American forces after Pearl Harbor. It begins in the middle of December 1944 in the Ardennes region of Belgium, France, and Luxembourg.

On December 16, two hundred thousand soldiers from three German armies suddenly launch themselves against the Allies. There has been a serious Allied intelligence failure—the day before the attack, British field marshal Montgomery promised Eisenhower that the Germans cannot "stage major offensive operations." Just as the Germans had partly ignored the explicit BBC warning of the impending invasion at Normandy, Allied intelligence officers had discounted the information from four captured German POWs, who had warned of a pre-Christmas offensive.

The German thrust is forty miles wide and fifty-five miles deep into the Allied line, creating a shape on the map that gave the battle its enduring name. On December 19, the 5th Panzer Army surrounds the American 106th Division in the center of the offensive at St. Vith, and forces eight thousand American soldiers to surrender—the largest defeat of American troops since the Civil War.

As the weather slowly improves, the Allies' overwhelming air superiority gradually reasserts itself, the Germans begin to run out of gasoline, and the systematic destruction of railroad lines makes it impossible to bring a single German train across the Rhine. When the battle finally ends in the fourth week of January, the Germans have lost 120,000 men killed, wounded, captured, or missing, while the Americans have suffered 19,000 killed, 48,000 wounded, and 21,000 captured or missing. "The great difference," wrote Andrew Roberts, "was that in material the Allies could make up these large losses, whereas the Germans no longer could."

In the end, the Ardennes offensive weakens the remaining German troops so much that its biggest effect is to hasten the progress of the Russian advance from the east.

IT IS APRIL 1945 before Jacqueline and Christiane receive confirmation of the first of three catastrophes. They are at lunch at the home of their aunt Ginette—the same aunt who had sent her maid into the street to intercept Christiane and save her life, hours after her parents had been arrested. The telephone rings, and they learn officially that their mother is dead. A short time later, they are notified of their father's death. But they still have no news of either of their brothers.

Two weeks later, Adolf Hitler, the father of all of Europe's agony, summons his longtime mistress, Eva Braun, to his underground bunker in Berlin. He marries her on April 29. At three thirty the following afternoon, Hitler shoots himself in the mouth with a revolver, and Braun—his wife of forty hours—swallows poison. Hitler's propaganda minister, Joseph Goebbels, is the last of his top collaborators to remain in the bunker with the Führer as the Russians swarm over Berlin. The day after Hitler dies, Goebbels and his wife poison their six children inside the bunker. Then they both commit suicide.

Mussolini and his mistress are caught by Italian partisans on April 26 while trying to escape into Switzerland. They are executed two days later and then strung up by their feet from lampposts in Milan. On April 29, the Germans sign an unconditional surrender of Italy and southern Austria; it takes effect on May 2, removing one million German troops from the conflict.

In Nuremberg, the site of gigantic Nazi rallies in the 1930s, American troops replace "Adolf-Hitler-Str." signs with new ones reading "Roosevelt Blvd." Then they blow up the huge stone swastika atop the Nuremberg stadium.

On May 5, Admiral Hans-Georg von Friedeburg, the new commander in chief of the German Navy, arrives in Reims, in northeastern France, where Eisenhower has established his headquarters. Two days later, at three forty-one in the morning, Germany surrenders unconditionally. At midnight on May 8, the guns stop firing and the bombs stop falling all across Europe. The "Thousand-Year Reich" is finally extinguished, after twelve years, four months, and eight days of mayhem, perversity, destruction, and death.

A FEW DAYS BEFORE the surrender is signed ending the war in Europe, Christiane and Jacqueline get a terrible scare. The doorbell rings at their parents' apartment. It is Gilbert Farges, one of the men who had shielded André on the train when he was deported to Auschwitz. When he introduces himself—"I was deported with your brother André"—the sisters are sure he is there to announce André's death. But Farges immediately adds that their brother is still alive—the first genuinely good news they have had in 1945.

Unlike the other members of his family sent to the camps, André has a vital cadre of friends at Flossenbürg. Somehow, everyone who survives with him is equipped with "the intimate conviction that we would still be alive after the war," remembered his friend Michel Bommelaer. "Among us, there was always a faithfully burning pocket of joy and hope."

André's most extraordinary morale booster for Michel, his fellow piano player, is to teach him "the Schumann piano concerto, certain Beethoven sonatas, and the Brandenburg Concertos"—all without a piano, of course. "In this way he shared a small piece of his very tender heart, his determination to fight," and his belief—remarkable, under the circumstances—in the "intellectual quest of a humanity that, no matter what, had a chance to better itself."

Gilbert Farges said, "Survival was a constant act of will and dignity. André applied himself with discipline, determination, and a ferocious courage at all moments. The influence of his example surely saved the lives of a number of his companions. This period of his existence tempered his character—tempered it the way one used to temper a sword in an earlier era."

AROSA

POSTKARTE CARTE POSTALE CARTOLINA POSTALE

Exp: Jacqueline Boulloche
Chez Madame Gaulis
Avenue de Rumine
Genève

BOULLOCHE André

7 eptembre 1945 No. 9.460/5

d Bei Weiden.

FLOSSENBURG

Postant II. (13.A.)

2586

Allemagne

Genf den 28.2.1945

Lieber Bruder,

Ich benützte einen kleinen Aufenthalt in
der Schweiz, um Dir zu schreiben. Es ist dies eine grosse
Freude für mich. Die ganze Familie ist gesund und er-
wartet ungeduldig Deine Rückkehr. Christiane und ich
arbeiten jetzt und sind froh, uns nützlich zu machen.

Wir denken immer an Dich. Viele Gedanken
an Ernest. Alle zusammen küssen Dich innigst. Guten Mut.

Jacqueline Boulloche

A postcard Jacqueline wrote to André in German at the beginning of 1945, when he
was still a prisoner at Flossenbürg.

André Boulloche in the summer of 1945, immediately after his return to Paris from three German concentration camps.

IT WILL REQUIRE one more miracle for André to return to his sisters' arms alive. At dawn on April 16, 1945, at an altitude of twenty-five hundred feet, the camp at Flossenbürg is bathed in "a pure and wonderfully soft light," Georges d'Argenlieu remembered. The sounds of American guns can be heard in the distance. And suddenly all the SS guards leave the camp.

"We had been saved!" d'Argenlieu exulted. "There will be no evacuation! Fourteen thousand deportees with no strength lay extended, offering their bodies to the rays of this first sun of resurrection." The sounds of American guns grow closer: ten miles, then seven miles away. But when the sun goes down that night, the SS returns, heaving everyone "back into the void."

"On April 20th, the sinister evacuation—the one we had so rejoiced at escaping—begins," d'Argenlieu continued. "Fourteen thousand leave the camp in five hours. Their rescue by the Americans is three days and eighty miles away. The six thousand who succumb on the road will never know that minute."

Through a final stroke of good fortune, André Boulloche, Charles Gimpel, Henri Lerognon, another alumnus of the Ecole polytechnique, and Georges d'Argenlieu manage to slip into the typhoid ward of the camp at the moment of the evacuation. That is the only way they can avoid the death march. Three days later, on April 23, a unit of George Patton's army finally arrives to liberate the camp.

IN THE CHAOS following the liberation, it takes André nearly four weeks to make his way back to Paris, a fearfully gaunt figure with the bulging eyes of a camp survivor. On May 19, he finally enters the lobby of his parents' apartment building on avenue d'Eylau. The concierge recognizes the ravaged twenty-nine-year-old as he walks in the front door. As André gets on the elevator, the concierge sprints up the stairs to warn his sisters that their brother is finally home.

"Of course he was extremely thin," Christiane remembered. "But what was worse was the horrible look in his eyes." The sisters have agreed that Christiane will deliver the terrible news about their parents when André gets there. "But, when he was finally standing there before us," Christiane remembered, "with that ghastly appearance that all the deportees had, I could not utter a word."

When she finally gathers her strength to tell him what has happened, this is his immediate reply: "If I'd known that, I would not have come back. I would have died in the camps." When they tell him which camp Robert has been sent to, André says there is very little chance that he has survived there.

Two weeks after André's return, they are officially notified that Robert had died at Ellrich, on January 20, 1945.

Part II

Nineteen

My deportation to the camps is very largely what made me what
I am today. And it was the war that led me to socialism. I am a man
who engages in life—who feels the necessity to engage.
—André Boulloche

André Boulloche had the longest service in the Resistance,
the most audacious, the most important and the most challenging.
—André Postel-Vinay

"Did your father André ever talk about the war?"
"Once, perhaps. But he didn't have to talk about it. It was always
there. It's as if you said we're going to talk about the fact that the
walls are white. Obviously they're white! You're not going to talk about
them, because they're there, all the time."
—Agnès Boulloche

THE THREE SURVIVORS chose very different paths to salvation
when the war was over. Christiane and Jacqueline "turned
the page" by getting married* and having children—and by never
discussing the war with each other, or almost anyone else, for fifty

---

* My uncle gave Jacqueline a bottle of expensive perfume as a wedding present,
probably from the Army PX. It was dropped, and shattered—a small tragedy he
still remembered decades later.

Jacqueline and Alex Katlama. They became wife and husband shortly after André
Boulloche returned to Paris in 1945.

years. Jacqueline and Alex Katlama were the first to marry, in the
summer of 1945, shortly after André's return from the camps.

André took a very different approach. Although he also married
quite quickly and started a family, unlike his sisters he blamed himself explicitly for everything that had happened. Beyond his austere

Jacqueline and Christiane after the war. By the middle of 1947 both of them had gotten married.

personality—a mournful contrast to the cheerful young man he had been before the war—two things made his attitude clear to everyone: For the rest of his life, he kept his hair shorn to a crew cut, and he put on a black tie every day, in memory of his dead.

In the months after the Liberation, there was an orgy of retribution against those who had collaborated with the Nazis. Women who had slept with the Germans had their heads shaved in the streets, while ten thousand Frenchmen were the victims of summary executions. Another one hundred thousand were tried in civilian and military courts, and about fifteen hundred of them were executed.

When he got back to Paris, André had an operation to repair the badly tended gunshot wound to his stomach. But he quickly discovered that nearly giving his life for the liberty of France was not enough to guarantee him a warm welcome when he returned. Several of his relatives made it clear that they blamed him and his sisters for the deaths of their parents and their brother. That was something I learned from two of his nephews. Christiane never mentioned it to me. This was another taboo subject, within the larger taboo of silence the three of them embraced.

The hostility they faced from their family was probably one of the reasons he and Christiane decided to go to America for a year. André returned to his roots as a highway engineer and proposed a study of American traffic lights. He arranged for Christiane to accompany him as part of his team. "Being former *Résistants* opened a lot of doors" in 1946, Christiane explained.

Before they left on their trip, they organized a funeral mass for their parents and Robert at Saint-Honoré d'Eylau, a church eight hundred yards from their parents' apartment. It was rare for half of a non-Jewish French family to have died in the German camps. Christiane remembered the service as a horrible event, an overflowing church with an endless parade of hands to shake afterward.

Because of heavy winter seas in the North Atlantic, their trip to America on a cargo ship took twenty-two days and included plenty of seasickness. When they arrived in New York in December, they were astonished by the vitality of the city, especially after the drab postwar Paris they had left behind. But New York was freezing and covered in snow, and Christiane did not have anything to wear to cope with the weather.

"I went to Macy's to buy a coat, and I couldn't buy anything. Because there was too much! I was used to the stores in France, where there was three times nothing. So going to Macy's was horrible! My head was spinning. It really had a strange effect on me. The next day was better. I had to buy something, because I was cold!"

Their American base was Washington, D.C. Their apartment was in a black neighborhood, which shocked their American friends. Christiane was oblivious of her neighbors, except for the annoying owner of the liquor store below them, who seemed

Vous êtes prié d'assister au Service qui sera célébré le Jeudi **25** Octobre **1945**,
à *Midi*, en l'Eglise Saint-Honoré d'Eylau, à la mémoire de

Monsieur Jacques BOULLOCHE

Inspecteur Général des Ponts et Chaussées
Directeur des Routes au Ministère des Travaux Publics
Officier de la Légion d'Honneur
Croix de Guerre 1914-18

mort pour la France à Buchenwald, le **19** Février **1945**, dans sa 57ᵉ année.

Madame Jacques BOULLOCHE

née Hélène CHAPERON

morte pour la France à Ravensbrück, le **25** Octobre **1944**, dans sa 57ᵉ année.

Monsieur Robert BOULLOCHE

Inspecteur des Finances
Croix de Guerre 1939-45

mort pour la France à Ellrich, en Janvier **1945** dans sa 32ᵉ année.

PRIEZ DIEU POUR EUX

De la part de :

Monsieur André BOULLOCHE, Monsieur et Madame Alexandre KATLAMA,

Mademoiselle Christiane BOULLOCHE,

Monsieur et Madame François BOULLOCHE et leurs enfants, le Docteur et

Madame Louis FUNCK-BRENTANO et leurs enfants, Monsieur et Madame Roger

CHAPERON et leurs enfants,

Madame Raymond PÉRINNE.

Administration spéciale des Funérailles, 3, Rue Mesnil, Paris XVIᵉ (Place Victor-Hugo), Maison Henri de BORNIOL, Tél. Passy 43-61

The invitation for the memorial service for the family members who died in Germany.
Christiane remembered it as a horrible event. Soon afterward she and her brother left for
a trip to America.

determined to sleep with her. They reconnected with Henry Kaiser in Washington, and met his wife, Paula. They also met my parents there for the first time. Christiane thought New York was much more interesting than Washington, and whenever she had a little money, she would jump on the train to Manhattan.

When she got to the United States, Christiane realized she had a new duty: to educate Americans about what the Resistance had done in France. She traveled across the country, from New York to San Francisco, giving lectures about the Resistance to American college students.

Once again Christiane felt she was performing her duty. When she spoke about her experiences at a club in Washington, she got her picture in the *Washington Post*. "Fear of the Gestapo was transmitted to the children," the *Post* reported her saying. "Nevertheless, the young people are eager to shake off that haunting fear, and eager to rebuild their lives." One of the young people she was talking about, of course, was herself.

Christiane also learned that Americans generally knew absolutely nothing about how the Resistance had operated in France during the war—something that has barely changed seventy years later.

The brother-and-sister team stayed in America through the summer. André continued to suffer terrible guilt about the fate of half his family. On August 5, 1946, he revealed his feelings in his diary:

> *Why did my life have to be spared, when I was offering it so willingly, even cheerfully? And why did those three who wanted to live, and who loved life so passionately—why were their lives taken from them in the vilest, most brutal way imaginable? Why did I have to be left behind, I who had pushed the barge so far from the shore? Left behind without faith, without hope, but chained to life by my passionate love for my two sisters...*

When this unlikely and idiotic thing happened, my nature was awakened beneath a kind of false shell of wisdom. When the war came, I had, with great effort, offered the complete sacrifice of my life—mine and mine alone. When I left France [at the end of 1942], I was the only one in danger. With the near certainty of my imminent death, I felt the compensations that only a profound determination can provide.

Why didn't I have the courage to remain absolutely alone when I returned to Paris? Why did I have to add the possibility of the sacrifice of my own family members to the near certainty of my own sacrifice?

AFTER CHRISTIANE spoke at Smith College, the school offered her a full scholarship if she would live in the Maison Française. But by the end of 1946, both she and André were eager to get back to France. When they returned, Christiane decided to take advantage of the new vogue for plastic surgery. Ignoring the objections of her friends, she got a nose job: "I've always done pretty much whatever I wanted to."

André had become a Socialist because of his experience as an inmate in three concentration camps, where, in addition to the millions who perished in the gas chambers, thousands had died from forced labor. "It was when I was deported that I realized what life was like for a worker who is completely stupefied by his job, and whose only perspective is to keep working until he dies," he explained. For the rest of his life, he continued to believe that society was unjust to the average worker, barely allowing him to subsist and making it "very, very difficult" to improve his station in life.*

---

* André's second wife, Odile, added another reason for his conversion to socialism: "It was the feeling that if there is no solidarity, life is absolutely not possible." (author's interview with Odile Boulloche, March 20, 1999)

"We bourgeois learned some things during the war," Christiane explained. "We discovered that poverty existed, and injustice existed. We were young, you know."

In January 1947, there were two big events in the Boulloche family. That month another former Resistance member, Paul Ramadier, became the first prime minister of France's Fourth Republic. André Boulloche knew Ramadier through mutual friends in the Resistance, and he was tapped for Ramadier's cabinet, to handle economic issues. By the end of the year, André had become the prime minister's chief of staff, an accomplishment that even impressed André—"I was very young for that job: I was 32."

It was also in January that Jacques Boulloche's college classmate from the Ecole polytechnique, Etienne Audibert, wrote an article about their time together at Buchenwald. Composed for the school's alumni magazine, the article described how Jacques Boulloche had given up after he deduced that his wife had died in another camp. The piece included a harsh attack on their alma mater, because it had expelled anti-Nazi students from the class of 1941. Its tone was fiercely anticollaborator. It made the editor of the alumni magazine nervous because of the criticism of the school, and he initially refused to publish it.

Etienne Audibert telephoned Christiane and asked if he could meet with her to show her the piece. When he came over and she opened the door to greet him, she saw that he was accompanied by his dashing twenty-five-year-old son, Jean.

Another former student from Polytechnique, Jean Audibert had been able to get to England during the war and joined the Free French Navy. His ship engaged in antisubmarine warfare, and he had been offshore during the Normandy invasion. His mother had died in France while his father was imprisoned at Buchenwald.

Jean was taken with Christiane's strength and wit, and she was charmed by his intelligence and his roaring laugh. By the end of lunch it was obvious they had hit it off.

Both of them agreed with Etienne that nothing in the twenty-five-hundred-word article should be altered. Eventually, the editor of the alumni magazine backed down and agreed to publish all of it.

Christiane and Jean had a whirlwind romance that winter. When they met, they already shared the tragedy of the loss of their mothers during the war. And almost immediately they shared another one. Jean's brother Pierre was a former *Résistant* who had gone into the army after the war and got shipped off to Indochina. At the beginning of 1947, he was killed there in an ambush. So now they also shared the loss of a brother.

Their common grief deepened their bond. Just six months after they met, Christiane was pregnant with their first child. Soon after that, they were married, on June 18, 1947. "Obviously, we chose the date for a reason," said Christiane. It was the seventh anniversary of de Gaulle's famous appeal from England after France's collapse in 1940: the speech in which he declared "the flame of French Resistance must not, and shall not, die!"

The first member of the new generation arrived "two weeks early," but Christiane never bothered to pretend that she wasn't already pregnant when she got married. Catherine Hélène Julienne Jacqueline Audibert was born on February 3, 1948. (Naturally, just twenty-three years later, Catherine would become a judge.) Christiane considered her daughter's birth a big event for the whole family: her first step in "turning the page." Jacqueline's first child, Eric Katlama, quickly followed seven months later.

On September 24, 1949, André married Anne Richard, whom he had met shortly after returning from the concentration camp. She had played a big role in getting him readjusted to society when he first returned to Paris. Eight months after their wedding, Anne gave birth to Robert Boulloche, named for André's dead brother.

Then there was a torrent of natal activity. Noëlle Audibert joined Jean and Christiane's hearth in 1949, and Pierre followed

Jacqueline and her firstborn, Eric Katlama, in 1949.

in 1951; and the following year Jacqueline had her second son, Michel Katlama.

Just five years after Catherine's birth, there were nine members of the new Boulloche-Audibert-Katlama generation. Jean and Christiane had their fourth and last, François, four years later.

FROM THE VERY BEGINNING, all of the children were marked by their parents' silence about the war. Most of them remember seeing books lying around the house with terrifying pictures of the inmates of the German camps, but if something about World War II suddenly came on television, their parents usually left the room.

Like their own father, who had never talked to them about World War I, André, Jacqueline, and Christiane almost never spoke to their own children about World War II. And just as Christiane had complained that her parents were so close that there was no room in between them for anyone else, the children of Christiane, Jacqueline, and André saw the three siblings as an equally tight unit, almost impenetrable to everyone else, including their own offspring.

"You've never seen two sisters who were so close," said Eric Katlama, Jacqueline's older son. "I've never seen it. They were sisters of incredible proximity and complicity." They talked on the phone every single day. "I think André and Jacqueline built a wall around Christiane," Eric continued. "My mother would not allow anyone to question what Christiane had done" during the war — or its effects on the rest of her family. "Jacqueline always defended Christiane — even when there wasn't even an attack, but just a hint of anything. That was instantaneous. I can't put myself in Christiane's place, but if I were Christiane, I would have completely put it out of my mind, without ever looking back at it again."

Eric remembered his uncle André as a "very very big personality. He was very impressive. There weren't a huge number of people who came out of Auschwitz. André was like the statue of the commander in the opera *Don Giovanni*. The commander is the one who is killed at the beginning of the opera, and he comes back as the statue. So it's true we had something of that picture.

"Of course we were proud that they had all been in the Resistance," Eric continued. "But it was a pride that we kept to ourselves. We never externalized it. Never."

When I asked André's oldest son, Robert, if he agreed with his cousins that the war had been a taboo subject, he replied, "It's true. We were always scared to ask any questions. And we were always scared that we wouldn't ask them the right way, that was tragic — or else, not tragic enough." We both laughed. "It was difficult."

Beginning in 1958, the family did deal with the war directly, once a year, with a ceremony that struck the children like a grim exclamation point. The young ones "camouflaged their unhappiness with fake laughs that were a little nervous," while the two sisters stood next to their brother and cried uncontrollably. Often André cried as well. Eric Katlama thought "it was clear that André was suffering even more than Christiane and Jacqueline. My mother made us understand that André had suffered even more than she had."

The ceremony occurred every year on October 25, the date the Germans had inscribed in their meticulous records for the death of Hélène at Ravensbrück. It took place at the family plot at Père-Lachaise, Paris's largest and most celebrated cemetery, built in 1804 by Napoleon on more than one hundred acres on a sloping hillside at the north end of the 20th arrondissement. In its first years, the cemetery was a bit of a flop, because the Catholic Church hadn't blessed its land, and the fashionable people thought it was too far from the center of the city. In a brilliant marketing maneuver, the proprietors transferred the remains of Jean de La Fontaine and Molière to the new burial ground. After that it became a huge success. Balzac, Oscar Wilde, Sarah Bernhardt, Chopin, Bizet, Proust, Yves Montand, Simone Signoret, Maria Callas, and Jim Morrison eventually joined them there.

And the Boulloches. At their plot, the names of their dead parents and their dead brother had been etched on a huge polished granite sarcophagus, which was actually empty. Attendance at the annual ceremony was mandatory for all sixteen family members— ten children and six parents.

"I remember there was a feeling of meditation that began in the car on the way to the cemetery," said Eric Katlama. "They prepared us psychologically. They made us understand that it was something terribly painful for those who had lived through it—perhaps more for André than for the others, because he had been deported, so he had seen what it was like."

The black granite sarcophagus on which the family engraved the names of their dead.

André always presided. And he spoke only two sentences: "We are reunited in memory of your grandparents and your uncle, who were killed by the Nazis." ("He didn't say 'the Germans,'" his nephew, Michel Katlama, recalled. "He said 'the Nazis.'")

"Remember that they died for the liberty and the liberation of France." Then the patriarch called every grandchild forward—Catherine, the oldest, was always first—handing each of them one red rose to be placed on top of the granite box with a giant cross carved in the middle.

"This was the Boulloches," said Christiane's older son, Pierre Audibert. "There was an aspect of this ceremony which excluded: it was the pure solidarity of the Boulloche family. A pact with their dead."

As one of Christiane's children put it, "Just as there is original sin, the Boulloches had the opposite: original virtue. They had

The family reunited one last time at Père Lachaise in 2004 at my request. Christiane is second from left in the front row. On her left is her niece Véronique Katlama; on her right, her daughter Noëlle. Behind Véronique is her brother-in-law Eric Katlama.

chosen the right side. They had done everything the way you were supposed to. This feeling of belonging to some kind of martyr's elite is quite heavy. I realized later that I had made many Jewish friends in school who had lost a lot of people in their families during the war. I didn't realize they were Jewish at the time. It was unconscious. The first value transmitted by my mother was, you must not accept—you must act."

Christiane's youngest, François, echoed his sibling: "It showed that you can do good things in life. But it's also a little crushing: It sets the bar very high. Christiane was lucky to make the right choice. Lucky—with the time to pay for it."

WHEN THE WAR ENDED, de Gaulle and the Boulloches felt much the same way: The only chance they had to survive was to avoid dwelling on the past. De Gaulle's task was more complicated, because he had to paper over the mixed record of his countrymen. Stanley Hoffmann, the great historian of modern France, explained de Gaulle's postwar attitude this way: "If one wants people to win victories over their very worst flaws, one must appeal to what is noble in them. If one wants to bring out the best in them, it is the best that one must celebrate." The general adopted a kind of therapeutic optimism, which he considered essential to France's recovery. De Gaulle told the novelist André Malraux, who became his minister of culture, that "man was not made to be guilty, sin is not interesting, the only ethics are those which lead man toward the greater things he carries in himself."

DE GAULLE never literally said that "all the French were *Résistants*," explained Claire Andrieu, an associate professor of history at the Sorbonne, who is the author of a shelf of books about the war and an expert on the Occupation and the Liberation. She also happens to be André Postel-Vinay's daughter.

"Contrary to what some people say, no one has ever written that all of the French were in the Resistance," the professor continued. "On August 25, [1944], in liberated Paris, de Gaulle spoke of the 'only France [a clever adjective], the France who is fighting, the eternal France.' De Gaulle never said that all the French were *Résistants*. In fact, he often said the opposite, but not in public. For example, when he received the National Council of the Resistance on September 6, 1944, he said, 'You are the Resistance, but the Resistance is not the nation.' He knew well. He wasn't crazy."

"But obviously," I interjected, "most people were neither collaborators nor resisters."

"I don't think it's that either," she said. "The problem is that we had a quasi-totalitarian dictatorship. Because you had Vichy plus the Nazis—that was a lot. And a radical system of economic exploitation. So objectively, whatever the wishes of the French were, they collaborated. That is to say, we let freight cars full of cows and metal leave for Germany. We let six hundred thousand young Frenchmen leave to work in Germany. This is a collaboration. We allowed more than fifty thousand members of the Resistance to be deported to Germany. So objectively, it was a collaboration—without even speaking of seventy-six thousand Jews who were deported.

"The country functioned in the midst of the Vichy-Nazi system. Everyone, including the baker, was forced to do so. But elsewhere—outside of working hours—they listened to the BBC. And if a British or American aviator knocked at the door of a house, 99 percent of them were hidden. That is the figure the American Military Intelligence Service gave in 1943. Therefore, there are certain counterweights to this objective collaboration. It's why I look at things from this perspective.

"It's complicated, because it can be the same people who organized the convoys of looted goods—people who worked for the SNCF [the French national railroad]—and who also hid an Allied pilot at home. It can be the same person. So that's why I am personally not very satisfied with the existing theses on the behavior of the population. I think people forget everything that could be done outside of institutions."

While de Gaulle felt he had to disguise the history of France in public, the Boulloches merely remained mute about their own. At the beginning, this had seemed odd to me, since all three of them had been decorated for their bravery, and André was part of an elite of just a few hundred *compagnons de la Libération*, the most revered Resistance fighters of all. But that was the cost of their courage: Because half of their family had been killed by the Nazis, they needed their own silence as much as France needed its myths.

FRANCE'S SEARCH for its own truth was reignited by the strikes and riots led by students and workers against de Gaulle's government in May 1968. Among the many issues pushed by the students who barricaded the streets of Paris was a demand that their parents reconsider the official version of how most Frenchmen had behaved during the German Occupation.

André's only daughter, Agnès, was arrested after getting into a fight with a policeman during one of the demonstrations. André told her that if she "wanted to fight, there were a couple of things you should pay attention to. If you're getting hit on the head, never put your hands there, because your fingers are much more fragile than your skull, and you'll just get your fingers broken. If you carry a weapon, it is always to kill. Do not think it is to defend yourself. If you draw your weapon, never get closer than three meters to the person you want to kill, because otherwise he can take your weapon from you. All of us also learned how to strangle someone, even if you weren't strong, by taking him from behind. So we did talk about stuff, and sometimes we played with him, pretending that we were trying to strangle him."

THE UPRISINGS also had a direct effect on three journalists working for the Office de Radiodiffusion-Télévision Française, the state-owned television network. These three men would make the movie that did more to change France's self-image than any other event in the postwar period.

Marcel Ophuls, André Harris, and Alain de Sedouy all worked together for the French TV network, and when de Gaulle called for a media blackout of the barricades in the streets, the three of them joined the strike. Ophuls had written part of the strike manifesto for the TV journalists. By the late '60s de Gaulle had moved sharply to the right, and Ophuls told me that he thought de Gaulle's conception of what television should be was "very much like Franco's." When the strike failed, he and his two colleagues were dismissed, which meant they needed a new way to make a living. So at the moment when dozens of national institutions were under attack, the three of them decided to make a film about France under the Occupation.

With $160,000—raised, ironically, in Germany and Switzerland—Ophuls became the director of the documentary, and he started filming in Clermont-Ferrand, the capital of the Auvergne province in the center of France, 242 miles from Paris. He chose Clermont-Ferrand partly because of its proximity to Vichy, the capital of the unoccupied zone during the war. The region was also the birthplace of the Maquis, the guerrilla army of the Resistance that fought in the countryside.

Ophuls thought de Gaulle's myth of an almost-universally resistant France had contaminated everyone who had lived through the war. "There's something unhealthy about asking all these millions of individuals to lie to each other, to lie to themselves," he told me. "I don't think this can possibly be good politics—now or then."* So he set out to correct the record.

The result was one of the greatest documentaries of the twentieth century. After it was—predictably—banned from French television, *The Sorrow and the Pity* became a huge hit with the younger generation at the movie theaters on the Left Bank in the spring of 1971. Its honesty fit the revolutionary spirit of the '60s. The film featured interviews with everyone from the local butcher of Clermont-Ferrand to a Paris aristocrat who had served with the French division of the Waffen SS, as well as two former prime ministers of France and Great Britain: Pierre Mendès-France and Sir Anthony Eden.

---

* Jacqueline's older son, Eric Katlama, felt the same way as Ophuls: "I think what de Gaulle did is fairly unforgivable, having sustained this kind of myth about a France united against its invaders, without really wanting to make the necessary effort of memory."

The two-part, four-hour film filled a twenty-six-year vacuum of information with a brutal portrait of the stark divisions inside wartime France. Recalling a split reminiscent of the one in the Boulloche family, teachers from the lycée in Clermont-Ferrand described how their students were more active in the Resistance than their instructors, because "young people are generally much more sincere, and…more alive." It also included a searing section on the decision of the French gendarmerie to arrest 4,051 Jewish children in Paris in the summer of 1942—even though the Germans had never asked them to arrest anyone younger than sixteen. After four days of indecision, all the children were shipped off to Germany—and every one of them was gassed as soon as they arrived at the camps.

All of the Boulloche children of my generation saw *The Sorrow and the Pity*, and we all agreed it was a pivotal event.* A year later, the debate about France's wartime behavior intensified with the publication of *Vichy France* by Robert O. Paxton, a young American historian who used German archives to document the extent of French collaboration during the war. Most of the Boulloches also read Paxton's book. But neither the film nor the book lifted the veil shrouding the family's wartime experiences.

IN THE LATE 1950S AND EARLY '60S, André, Christiane, her husband, Jean Audibert, and Jacqueline all embraced France's most progressive cause, by joining the Club Jean Moulin to battle the OAS (Organisation de l'armée secrète), a paramilitary terrorist group that used bombings and assassinations to try to prevent France from allowing Algeria to become independent.

---

* It was brought to America by Woody Allen and shown at the New York Film Festival in September 1971. It opened at the Beekman Theatre in Manhattan the following March.

Christiane around 1960, just before
I met her for the first time in Paris.

France's withdrawal from its North African colony was a long, bloody process for Algeria and France alike. Once de Gaulle became convinced that it was necessary to leave Algeria, he was the main enemy of the OAS. After an OAS uprising failed in Algiers in April 1961, the organization turned to terror on both sides of the Mediterranean, including several unsuccessful attempts to murder de Gaulle.

André shared the widespread view that the Algerian quagmire posed a serious threat to French democracy. He decided very quickly that de Gaulle was the only politician powerful enough to bring about France's exit and prevent the return of a right-wing dictatorship in France. Indeed, that was the main reason he and his sisters supported de Gaulle's return to power at the head of a new Fifth Republic in 1958. After that, André lobbied the general to leave Algeria whenever he saw him.

André believed the war in Algeria was "eating the national tissue away like an acid. Civilians are scared of the military, and the military doesn't trust the government."

Meanwhile, Christiane remained as fearless as ever. She had become the treasurer of the Association for the Defense of Djamila Boupacha. The young Algerian woman was a famous and beautiful member of the FLN (Front de libération nationale algérien) who was tortured by the French into confessing terrorist activities. She was only twenty-three when she was condemned to death on June 28, 1961. Part of Christiane probably identified with the undaunted young activist.

"It was a period when there were terrorist attacks in Paris," Christiane told me. "The OAS was carrying out terrorist attacks. And when I was the treasurer of the association, my name and address was on our literature. Which was a risk—there's no question about that. When they were still very small, I tried to make [my] children understand that if they saw a suspicious package, they had to tell me right away. They thought this was very exciting! They didn't realize that it was also very dangerous."

Fortunately, Christiane's apartment was never blown up, and she celebrated when Boupacha was granted amnesty, after France signed the Évian Accords, which gave Algeria independence, in Évian-les-Bains, on March 18, 1962. Boupacha was freed one month later—the same month that 90 percent of France voted to approve the accords in a referendum.

Jacqueline, who had worked for her brother when he was a minister, later became secretary-general of the UNESCO Clubs, which gave her a forum to lobby for the interests of the developing nations of Africa, Asia, and South America.

In the 1960s, Christiane turned her attention to women's issues. Since 1920, French law had banned abortion and all information about contraception. Under the banner of *"Si je veux, quand je veux"* (If I want, when I want), Christiane campaigned for the legalization of both. In 1967, the Neuwirth Act finally legalized the sale of contraceptive devices, but abortion wasn't legalized until 1975, and advertisements for contraceptives remained banned until 2001, four decades after the pill was introduced in America.

Christiane also became a sought-after family therapist, who continued to see patients well into her seventies. "As you can see," she said, "we never lost the spirit of the Resistance."

IN 1978, André Boulloche was approaching the pinnacle of his political career. Twenty years earlier, he had shown his independence by accepting an appointment as de Gaulle's minister of education, even though the Socialist Party had voted against participating in de Gaulle's new government. But less than a year later, André had quit over a dispute about government aid to parochial schools. André was against it, while de Gaulle and his prime minister, Michel Debré, were for it. After André voiced his objection, the president beseeched him to stay on, but his minister resigned anyway.

His tenure was marred by harsh publicity when his marriage blew up while he was minister. It led to an ugly divorce and a trial to determine the custody of his three children. This was especially difficult, because divorce was still very much a scandal in Catholic France in the late 1950s (as indeed it was for any American politician in this period).

Less than four months after his divorce, he married the beautiful Odile Pathé, the daughter of Charles Pathé, a founder of Pathé pictures, the legendary French film company. Odile had first met André immediately after the war, and she had her own book-publishing company. When all the left-wing publishers in Paris ignored George Orwell's *Animal Farm* because it was a barely veiled attack on Stalinism, Odile rushed to London and secured the book for her publishing house, after two memorable lunches with the author. *Les Animaux Partout* was published by Éditions Odile Pathé in 1947.

President Charles de Gaulle at a ceremony commemorating the Resistance. André Boulloche, his education minister, is at the far right.

Following his resignation as de Gaulle's minister and his new marriage, André gradually rebuilt his career with the hyperactivity that was his trademark. His children ended up living most of the time with their mother and saw their father only on alternate weekends. The children sometimes found their father terrifying. His experiences in three concentration camps were not without their consequences.

"He had a terrible violence in him which he contained," said Jacques Boulloche, his youngest son—named, of course, for André's dead father. "But sometimes it got out of hand. And when he was driving, he was a tyrant. I was terrified. It was quite something. He raced with everyone—he would not allow himself to be passed. It was crazy. And then, when he got to [his constituency in] Montbéliard, it was the opposite. As soon as someone was trying to cross the street, he stopped. It was unbelievable. Because, you know, he would say, 'That's a voter!' It was very funny. He was the sort of person who could not allow any car to go faster than he was going."

He could also be a violent disciplinarian with his children—and his dog. He was "very rough" with Jacques, who had been a poor student when his father was minister of education—a record his father considered a personal embarrassment. "I got terrible, heavy spankings," Jacques said.

"On the other hand, when I was bigger, I had a lot in common with him through science. I have very lovely memories of when I was at his house in Montigny-sur-Loing. I had a little chemistry lab in the basement, and I did chemistry experiments. And every weekend, he would ask me, 'What do you need?' Then during the week there was a store next to the National Assembly which sold stuff for chemistry labs, and he would go there and buy me whatever I needed. That was really nice. That's how he encouraged my scientific spirit." So despite the beatings he had suffered as a child, Jacques [*fils*] admired his father enough to sustain another ancient family tradition—he named his son André.

"My father was above all scientific," Jacques told me. "I don't know why he went into politics, because he wasn't someone who knew how to communicate at all. He was a very hard worker. He was a technician, and he was very methodical. When he had a file, he analyzed it. He was, first and foremost, a *polytechnicien*."

But with hard work, André Boulloche methodically overcame his lack of the common touch. In 1965, he was elected mayor of Montbéliard, a small city on the eastern border of France next to Switzerland and Germany. In 1967, he added the position of deputy in the National Assembly. With two full-time jobs, he was constantly in motion between Paris and Montbéliard; he told a national news magazine that the secret to his success was a "good airplane." Two years later, he was a member of the directors' committee of the Socialist Party and vice president of the Socialist group in the National Assembly.

By 1978, André was mayor of Montbéliard, a deputy in the National Assembly, and a rising star in the Socialist Party.

These were remarkable achievements, especially because there had never been any warmth between him and François Mitterrand, the leader of the Socialist Party. Boulloche had been much closer to Mitterrand's earthier predecessor, Gaston Defferre, the celebrated mayor of Marseille. Raymond Forni, a young friend and colleague in the National Assembly, remembered his mentor's attitude toward Mitterrand this way: "Boulloche was certain that he was working for France—and Mitterrand was working for himself." But despite the coolness between them, Mitterrand recognized that Boulloche was a man to be reckoned with. By 1978, André had become his party's chief spokesman on economic affairs, and most people expected Mitterrand to make him the first Socialist finance minister since the war, if Mitterrand was elected president in 1981.

But a fateful plane trip during the 1978 parliamentary campaign would change all that.

FRANÇOIS MITTERRAND was invited to participate in a debate at Saint-Dié-des-Vosges by Christian Pierret, a thirty-two-year-old Socialist candidate for the National Assembly there.* Pierret's district adjoined André's. When the party leader was too busy to participate in the debate, André Boulloche stepped in for him at the midday gathering in the provincial city in the Vosges Mountains.

André's noontime appointment was less than a hundred miles from his own city of Montbéliard. But if he took a regularly scheduled airline, he wouldn't be able to get back in time for his own campaign meeting that evening. So he asked his secretary to arrange another way to get there. Christian Pierret offered him an air taxi. "I don't like to take those little planes," André told his secretary. "But if I have to, I will."

The weather was calm, with ten miles of visibility, when André took off at two thirty in the afternoon of March 16 from the airstrip outside Saint-Dié-des-Vosges. He was alone with the twenty-three-year-old pilot, Renaud Mary, who was the son of the president of the commuter line they were traveling on.† Now André was returning to his own adopted city of Montbéliard, which was only a half an hour away by plane. He expected to address a thousand constituents at his own political meeting that night.

As he had all his life, the sixty-two-year-old politician was pushing himself as hard as he could. The first round of the election had gone badly for the Socialists, and this was no time to let up. The second, decisive round of the election was only four days away.

Montbéliard was the city that Boulloche had "parachuted" into in 1962 to create a new political base for himself. He had chosen it partly because it was a region of liberal Catholics and devout Protestants. Boulloche was a very liberal Catholic himself (none of his

---

* Pierret was elected to the National Assembly that year and remained there for fifteen years.

† Although he was only twenty-three, the pilot had been flying since he was sixteen.

children had even been baptized) and his new constituents quickly embraced him. Three years after his arrival in Montbéliard, he was elected mayor.

His political accomplishments were the result of pure determination. A technocrat who had been an engineer of bridges and highways before the war, Boulloche didn't start out with any aptitude for politics. He certainly didn't fit the profile of a typical politician: One reporter wrote that the man with the gray crew cut and a somber countenance looked like a "secular monk." He once described politics as "an infernal life." But this was also someone who brought an unbreakable will to bear on everything he did.

"Are you ever discouraged?" a radio reporter asked him in 1976.

"Yes, but not very often."

"What do you do when that happens?"

"I wait for it to pass."

When he first arrived in Montbéliard, Boulloche had bonded with the workers of Peugeot, whose factories employed thirty-seven thousand workers in the region. His constituents recognized him as a gifted administrator. After thirteen years at City Hall, his adopted city boasted an improved public transportation system, a bustling cultural life, a new sanitation system, and a rebuilt city center.

After his first decade as mayor, André declared, "I think I can say without exaggeration that my team has completely transformed the place. People who come back after being away for fifteen years don't even recognize it." Now, whenever there was an election, the popular Socialist had the luxury of being able to spend much of his time assisting the campaigns of his less-well-established friends and allies.

AS THE LITTLE AIRPLANE headed south, it followed a flight path parallel with the Rhine. Suddenly, Boulloche's preoccupation with the election was replaced by a lethal danger. Half an hour into the flight, cruising at 150 miles an hour, the small aircraft started bouncing in high winds. Without warning, they were at the center of a violent winter storm. As they approached Montbéliard, snow and sleet blanketed the windscreen and hail rattled the cockpit, cutting their visibility to less than three hundred yards. The provincial airstrip at Montbéliard had no radar, and it waved them away. A policeman on the ground spotted them circling overhead; later he remembered that it had looked as if they were searching for the proper path.

From there they headed for Belfort-Fontaine, which was ten miles away. Raymond Forni, who represented a neighboring constituency, spotted the red-and-white plane when it was trying to land at the second airport. But the storm was fierce there too, so they decided to make for Basel-Mulhouse, an international airport equipped with radar for all-weather landings. It serves Basel, Switzerland, and Mulhouse, France. By now they had been flying for nearly two hours. Boulloche had been trained as a pilot in Morocco after the war, but he never got to fly because of a shortage of planes. Now he climbed into the copilot's seat to try to help guide the plane to safety.

It was four twenty-three in the afternoon. The weather had cleared up at Montbéliard, but the pilot and his passenger didn't know that, and the storm had followed them to Basel-Mulhouse.

"I can't come down—I'll manage by myself."

Those were the last words the tower at Basel-Mulhouse heard from the plane's young pilot. As he headed east toward Frankfurt, air traffic controllers watched the plane disappear from their radar screens. The Piper started losing altitude because of the weight of the ice on its wings. At the same moment, its radio stopped working, because the antenna had been torn off by the storm.

A MOMENT LATER, buffeted by severe winds, or disoriented by the storm, the pilot changed direction by forty-five degrees—and slammed into the side of the Hochblauen, twenty-three hundred feet up the side of the thirty-eight-hundred-foot mountain.

This unconquerable man—the one who had survived three German concentration camps—had crashed in the Black Forest of Germany.

The little Piper was demolished, its shattered shell suspended upside down from the branches of a tree. Boulloche and the pilot were ejected from the plane at the moment of impact. They tumbled out of the cockpit into a foot-deep cushion of snow. The pilot's face was smashed in, and André had a punctured lung. They were dazed and bleeding and suffering enormous pain. And yet, somehow, they were still alive.

When they realized they were able to walk, they began to limp down a path leading into the valley. They were assaulted by sheets of wet, white snow dropping out of the black sky. After struggling toward the valley a few hundred yards, they reached a shed built of logs, which had been erected to shelter summer tourists.

There they stopped to rest. Two miles away in the distance, they could hear a faint church bell, chiming five o'clock in a nearby village.

BACK IN PARIS, it was Boulloche's secretary, Andrée Vauban, who was the first to raise the alarm. André had told her that he would be back in his office in Montbéliard by four thirty in the afternoon, and he would call her when he arrived. When she hadn't heard from him by five o'clock, she called Montbéliard to check up on him.

"The plane must have left late," Boulloche's aide in Montbéliard told her. The aide seemed unperturbed, but Vauban was immediately suspicious. Her next call was to Christian Pierret, the candidate in Saint-Dié-des-Vosges for whom Boulloche had been campaigning earlier that afternoon. Pierret told her that Boulloche had taken off on time. Then his secretary made another call to Montbéliard to inquire about the weather there.

"Snow! Terrible wind! Hail!"

Andrée Vauban immediately sensed that her boss was in danger. *Something is happening*, she said to herself. *He should have arrived by now.* Her next call was to the Ministry of the Interior. Then she contacted Odile. Mme. Boulloche rushed off to Le Bourget to catch the last plane of the night to Belfort-Fontaine, one of the airports where André's plane had been unable to land a few hours earlier. As soon as she arrived, this formidable spouse started phoning civil and military officials to get them to expand the search.

André's younger son, Jacques, was now a twenty-four-year-old medical student in Paris. He was driving across the city when he heard a radio report that his father's airplane had disappeared. His first thought was that his father might have been the victim of a terrorist attack.

When André's sister Christiane returned home to her Paris apartment on square Alboni, in the 16th arrondissement, it was her husband, Jean, who greeted her with the disquieting news: "André's plane hasn't arrived back in Montbéliard."

That was all they knew.

That night, François Mitterrand, the leader of the Socialist Party, issued a statement:

> This is a very remarkable man—remarkable among the remarkables—greatly loved by all who know him. I feel great pain and great concern. When one says those two words, "André Boulloche," they are a salute to someone quite exceptional, on every level. He is an exemplary man.

German and French helicopters swarmed above the Black Forest in search of the plane on Thursday night, but darkness and the snowstorm prevented them from finding anything. It was the following afternoon when a search party found the bodies of André and Renaud Mary, a hundred yards apart, down the hill from their fallen plane. Apparently the young pilot had kept searching for help after André could go no farther.

Their bodies were found by French troops of the 12th Regiment stationed in Mulheim, Germany. Years later, Jacqueline's daughter, Claudine Lefer, had a clear memory of her mother's reaction to the news: "And on top of everything else, the plane crashed in Germany."

FOUR DAYS AFER HIS DEATH, André's body lay in state in the Montbéliard City Hall, surrounded by a silent honor guard of local council members and city officials. "Men and women of every class and every age passed his coffin, sometimes depositing a small bouquet of flowers," the local newspaper, *L'Est Républicain*, reported. "One had the impression of the entire city parading by, like a river flowing slowly and majestically. There was an extraordinary impression of grave sadness, but above all, of dignity, which was symbolic of the particular influence of André Boulloche, who had attracted such affection and respect." Seven special airplanes flew dignitaries in for the funeral on March 21, plus an eighth for François Mitterrand.

At 9 o'clock in the morning, André's wooden coffin was taken from City Hall by six white-gloved firemen, followed by an army officer holding a pillow displaying the dead man's four most important decorations—Commandeur de la Légion d'Honneur, Compagnon de la Libération, Croix de Guerre, and Médaille de la Résistance. Outside, the firemen wrapped the coffin in the French Tricolor, then placed it in the center of a fire truck and covered it with a glass enclosure. As rain began to drench the slow procession, umbrellas of every color bobbed up and down above the huge crowd that followed the peculiar red funeral coach. The mourners included four delegations of deportees who had survived the German camps.

The funeral itself took place at the Fairgrounds Hall of Montbé-liard. Because it could accommodate only three thousand people, an outdoor sound system was installed for thousands more who came to listen outside.

There were half a dozen speakers, including Mitterrand, André Postel-Vinay and, remarkably, two Germans: Volker Hauff, a prominent Social Democrat who was minister of science and technology, and Otfried Ulshöfer, the mayor of Ludwigsburg, the German twin city of Montbéliard.

Every speaker described the main postwar preoccupation of this survivor of three German concentration camps: André's unstinting efforts to foster friendship and reconciliation between France and Germany. In a remarkable act of intellectual jiu-jitsu, André had taken all of the ghastly energy from his wartime incarceration and turned it around to make sure that nothing like what had happened to him would ever happen to another Frenchman or German again.

In his funeral oration, Mitterrand, the future president of France, declared that André had wanted to "sublimate his sufferings, to give them meaning beyond this moment in history. It was as if he had found the capacity within Europe to construct peace and harmony among all peoples...He considered reconciliation with Germany a necessity. When he turned toward the Germans, he was the first among us who knew how to say, 'My friends.'"

Otfried Ulshöfer quoted André's speech from three years earlier, when the two mayors had celebrated the twenty-fifth anniversary of the twinning of their two cities. "Today the two of us maintain the flame of friendship between us. Tomorrow, others will have this duty, and I am convinced that they shall not fail."

Then the German mayor spoke for himself: "Today we consider that sentence as the duty he has left us. Now we must endeavor to carry it out."

Twenty

Courage is more exhilarating than fear and in the long run it is easier.
We do not have to become heroes overnight. Just a step at a time.
—Eleanor Roosevelt

Don't make it too sad.
—parting words from André's son Jacques,
   after I interviewed him about his father

AFTER THE SHOCK of his death, Christiane and Odile went to work right away to assure André's legacy. Odile drew on her experience as a book publisher to produce two beautiful volumes, one illustrated, one not, with extraordinary stories from André's closest friends about every phase of his remarkable life, from his time at the lycée, to his life as de Gaulle's secret agent in Paris, to his survival at three concentration camps. Then there were his three interlocking postwar careers: the brilliant mayor of a provincial town on France's eastern border, a force to be reckoned with for more than four decades in the capital's corridors of power, and an indefatigable advocate of reconciliation between France and Germany, and the unity of Europe. One book was privately published; the other was a special issue of the municipal review of Montbéliard.

This book would not have been possible without dozens of contributions from those two volumes. André Postel-Vinay's memoir,

Un fou s'évade (A Fool Escapes), published in 1996, was another crucial resource for me. But I still needed one more actor's full cooperation before I could write my own account.

Ever since I became a reporter for the *New York Times* at the age of twenty-four, and probably even before that, I knew that the Boulloche saga could be the most extraordinary story I would ever tell. I had been mesmerized at eleven when I first heard it recounted by my uncle Henry, and I have never been less than mesmerized ever since. Meeting the main actors when I was eleven—and falling in love with one of them—only made me more eager to write about them.

During many visits to France over the next three decades, I often shared my ambition to write this book with Christiane's children, especially François and Noëlle. But we agreed it would be impossible for me to do so as long as Jacqueline and Christiane maintained their silence.

Two more tragedies were necessary before the floodgates could open, even a little bit. In 1989, Jean Audibert, an exceptionally vigorous sixty-eight-year-old, died suddenly of a massive stroke, making Christiane a widow. Four years later, Jacqueline received a fatal diagnosis, and this time it was not a false alarm. She had leukemia, she was too old for a bone-marrow transplant, and she died one year later at the age of seventy-six.

Now Christiane was the unmistakable head of her family, the indomitable matriarch. The death of her sister acted as a release mechanism for her. For fifty years, she had considered her secrets too fraught to share with her children, because of the horrors suffered by her parents and her brothers.

Suddenly, she felt just as compelled to tell the story as she had felt required to remain silent about it. Realizing that it would disappear if she failed to record it, she forced herself to write a forty-five-page memoir—"for my grandchildren." Once again, Christiane acted out of a sense of obligation.

"It was obvious," she told me, using the same words she had used to describe her decision to join the Resistance. She had never wanted to write this book, but, at the age of seventy-one, she had to. "It was extremely painful for me to relive these black years. But it was also my duty."

With the help of Mathilde Damoisel, a brilliant young history student at the Sorbonne whose specialty was women in the Resistance, Christiane produced an amazing narrative. Mathilde considered it an "homage to the spirit of her family."

When Christiane was writing her book, her older daughter, Catherine, visited her every Monday evening. "She would read me what she had written the previous week," Catherine remembered. "And she cried, and she cried and she cried."

At the end there was still a great deal missing: Christiane's emotions were almost completely absent from her pages. The essential facts were all that she could manage. But when Catherine told her it was "too dry," Christiane refused to change her approach. "No," Christiane told her daughter. "I don't want to. It's enough this way. And there are things that I won't say. That I don't want to say and that I will not say. So I'm putting in what I want to put in, and that's all."

When I visited Paris again at the end of the 1990s, Christiane's younger son, François Audibert, met me at the Gare du Nord. He greeted me with the startling news of Christiane's book. When I reached his house, I devoured it all in a single sitting. Then I embarked upon my own, relying heavily on Christiane's for guidance.

I SPENT TWO AND HALF YEARS living in France, interviewing all of the surviving Boulloches, as well as many others who had worked with them or hidden them during the Occupation. An oral history of the Resistance in the French National Archives included the accounts of many others who had known the Boulloches during the war. At my request, the Public Record Office in London declassified all the files MI5 had compiled on André Boulloche, Alex Katlama, and Charles Gimpel when they were in Britain during the war.

Remarkably, everything I learned in the British and French archives confirmed and elaborated upon everything Christiane had told me.

Neither Christiane nor I enjoyed my efforts to force her to reveal as much as possible. But she never refused any request. She also urged everyone in her family to cooperate with me, and everyone did. One thing in particular surprised me. I hadn't expected to share any of Christiane's ambivalence about unearthing her secrets. But very gradually, I realized that it was also painful for me to part with the black-and-white version of her family's heroism that I had grown up with.

ALTHOUGH THE COST of their courage was gigantic, there are more triumphs than tragedies in this story. It is true that the *Résistants* in the family conveyed a certain malaise to many of their children by never talking about war. But I don't believe they could have made any better choices about how to deal with their history. And despite their private agony, they managed to transmit all of the finest values of the Boulloches, the Audiberts, and the Katlamas.

Christiane had four fabulous children, twelve grandchildren, and seven great-grandchildren. All of them became righteous, rigorously informed, and deeply committed citizens of France, as did their cousins, and their offspring.

"We did not talk about the Resistance in terms of what each of them had done," said Michel Katlama, Alex and Jacqueline's younger son. "But I think the whole generation that followed was enormously marked by that. The whole family was extremely conscious of its political choices. Never Communist. But it was a family that always voted for the left. Almost everyone. The Audiberts and the Katlamas all voted for the left. And it wasn't just an accident. I can't imagine any member of our generation being anti-Semitic. Or a Fascist. Or not a democrat—and very attached to democracy."

WHEN CHRISTIANE had finished her book, she summoned all her children and grandchildren and nephews and nieces to her grand apartment in Passy.

"Christiane said she had done what she had to do," her niece, Claudine Lefer, remembered. "Because she was the last person who could tell this story. She didn't give a speech, she said it in tête-à-têtes with small groups of us."

Christiane's granddaughter, Hélène Dujardin, believed that "she had done her duty. And in the end—I'm going to say something terrible—she could leave now, knowing that she had done what she had to do. That touched me enormously."

I repeated those words to Christiane.

"Yes," she said. "That's true. Absolutely true."

From time to time, I suggested that Christiane's survival had been her destiny, rather than just the product of good fortune. A woman with no taste for superstition, she mostly turned away the idea that fate had played any role in her longevity. But in our final interview before I moved back to New York, she hedged a bit. "I was born on November 11, 1923, in Paris in the seventh arrondissement, during the minute of silence—at 11 a.m. on November 11th. That's what they always told me."

Then she laughed at the idea, but warmly: "So perhaps I was a little predestined."*

---

* World War I had ended at the 11th hour of the 11th day of the 11th month of 1918; the minute of silence is in memory of its dead.

Christiane receives the galley of this book from the author. Square Alboni,
December 23, 2014.

As I write these words, she is still flourishing in the elegant
apartment she moved into with Jean Audibert and their children in
1958, the one where I first met her in 1962. She is on her own, but a
steady stream of children, grandchildren, and great-grandchildren
come to bask in her warmth and her wisdom. She and I remain in
constant touch, by e-mail and on the telephone.

She still remembers everything.

Afterword

MOST AMERICANS are smugly dismissive of the way the French behaved during the Nazi Occupation. "Was there one?" That was the question I was asked most often—even by intelligent people—whenever I mentioned that I was writing about the French Resistance.

That reflexive condescension is coupled with a popular amnesia about the German sympathies of famous American appeasers, from Charles Lindbergh to Joseph P. Kennedy. Equally forgotten are the anti-Semitic organizations that flourished in the United States in the 1930s. The pro-Nazi German-American Bund counted eight thousand storm troopers among its members, and filled New York City's Madison Square Garden at the beginning of 1939 with twenty thousand supporters shouting, "*Heil Hitler.*"

The bund worked closely with the Reverend Charles Coughlin's Christian Front. In the 1930s, Coughlin was one of the nation's most influential broadcasters, and his supporters organized Buy Christian rallies across the country. After the Nazis looted Jewish stores and burned down synagogues all across Germany in November 1938, Coughlin even defended the horrors of Kristallnacht on his national radio show, describing them as appropriate retaliation for Jewish persecution of Christians.

THE TRUTH IS, there were hundreds of thousands of French men and women like the Boulloches who risked everything to liberate their country from the Nazis, while Americans at home never had to risk anything the way the French did during World War II. American servicemen and women made gigantic sacrifices, from Normandy to Iwo Jima, to free the world from the tyranny of Germany and Japan. But American civilians, living thousands of miles from the battlefields, never faced anything remotely resembling the choices that confronted everyone who lived in Nazi-occupied Europe.

However, these facts are not the main reason I cannot judge France harshly for its behavior during World War II. To me what is most persuasive is the attitude of the two men who did more than anyone else in the 1960s and the 1970s to bring about a more balanced view of France's record: Robert Paxton and Marcel Ophuls.

Both men understood that if you have never actually faced life-and-death decisions, it is easy to assume that you would have done the right thing if the Nazis had occupied your country. It is also a great mistake to do so.

In his brilliant book *Vichy France*, Paxton wrote that "an American reader who honestly recreates the way the world looked from France [in 1940] cannot assume that he or she would easily have found the path to a 1944 hero's role." And Ophuls told me that former British prime minister Anthony Eden was also speaking for the filmmaker when the statesman made this crucial observation at the end of *The Sorrow and the Pity*: "If one hasn't been through—as our people mercifully did not go through—the horror of an occupation by a foreign power, you have no right to pronounce upon what a country does which has been through all that."

That is one of the most important and least understood lessons of World War II.

Envoi

ONE NIGHT, a few months after Christiane and her children had read this book, I was in Paris, sitting outside with Christiane and her elder daughter, Catherine. "We are lucky that you fell in love with our story," said Catherine.

"Oh no," I said. "I am the lucky one."

And Christiane exclaimed, "It's reciprocal." The closure I had contributed was my proudest achievement. It had taken me so long to finish writing her story, I wondered whether Christiane might even have waited for it.

Six months later my husband, Joe, and I said good-bye to Christiane for the last time, on January 28, 2016, two months, three weeks, and one day after her ninety-second birthday. We weren't certain that this was adieu, but we knew that it might be. Christiane took us to lunch at Café Le Passy, a hundred and fifty yards from her apartment on square Alboni. The brisk walk up the little hill above the Passy Métro station was an effort, but there were blue skies, and we were all in high spirits. Then, once more, we talked about our families, and the movies, and politics—and about the new threats to our countries from Donald Trump and Marine Le Pen.

Christiane still remembered everything.

Then she repeated something I had heard her say before: "I don't want to live forever." When her time came, she wanted a quick exit. "But the problem is, you can't choose that." When lunch was over, we walked back down the hill to her apartment. We accompanied her upstairs, in the narrow wooden elevator I had traveled up and down in since 1962. Then, as we said au revoir, she reminded us, very gently: "It's possible I won't be here the next time you return."

Three months later, she sent me a final e-mail. "Congratulations on Joe's show. I'm sorry I won't be able to see his paintings in person. Politics goes really badly, for you and for us." And then, two words she had never used before: *je viellis* ("I am getting older.")

"Je vous embrasse tout les deux."

Two months later she had a massive stroke in her kitchen. As the Seine burst its banks, after the worst flooding in France in more than a century, Christiane lingered a few days longer. Then she died peacefully in a Paris hospital, surrounded by her family. It was Sunday, June 12, 2016.

I jumped on a plane in New York to reach Paris one day before Christiane's funeral. Her sons were both waiting for me when I arrived at square Alboni. They were huddled over a computer, writing her eulogy. That night I slept alone in Christiane's apartment. The next morning, at 10 A.M., two hundred of her friends and family members arrived at the crematorium at Père Lachaise.

This, of course, was the same Paris cemetery where the Boulloches had gathered every October 25, so that each member of the postwar generation could place a red rose on top of an empty granite sarcophagus, to remember their grandparents and their uncle—the ones who had "died for the liberty of France," as André Boulloche always put it.

Christiane's children, Catherine, Pierre, and François, composed a beautiful eulogy, which was read by François, the youngest. (Their sister Noëlle had died of lung cancer at fifty-five in 2004. That had been the family's worst tragedy, after the war's calamities.) Her children recalled the pride that came from watching their mother conduct her whole life with resolution and courage. "A life open to the world and open to others, a life of combat, and a life of affection." They spoke of her unbreakable bond with her sister, Jacqueline, and her brother André, of their common struggle for the liberation of Algeria "and against the fanatics of the OAS,"* and of Christiane's fight for the rights to contraception and abortion, and, finally, for the right to die with dignity.

They remembered her "painful act of memory, which she accomplished with conviction, but also with pleasure, despite her fatigue." Together, her book and my own had made it possible to "close the quotation marks completely." But her life had not only been about "duty and tragedy." She also loved reading and music and plays and movies and museums, and most of all, her children, her grandchildren, and her great-grandchildren.

Ever prudent, she had written a little "texte d'adieu" back in 1994:

> This is not a last testament nor my "final wishes," but just a simple good-bye. I love all of you passionately. You have made me very happy. Thank you. What I ask of you is that you remain united, and that you help one another. Family is really a fundamental thing. One realizes this especially in old age. For my burial, something like [my husband] Jean's, but less elaborate, will suit me very well.

When the eulogy was over, her family members and I stepped forward. Each of us picked up a red rose. I smiled, I kissed my rose, I placed it on her coffin. *Adieu, Christiane.*

The next day I drove out to the little cemetery in Fontainebleau where the ashes of her husband, Jean Audibert, had been interred in 1989. His grave had been opened to receive Christiane's remains.

---

* *Organisation de l'armée secrète*

Their granddaughter Camille placed a drawing inside the crypt, showing Jean waiting to greet his wife in heaven—a reunion a skeptical Christiane was most certainly not expecting.

Inside the modest cemetery, encircled by the tall trees of the Fontainebleau forest, we were close to La Cruche, the family's longtime home in the country.

Several of us spoke at graveside.

By chance—or was it?—we had gathered on the morning of June 18, the sixty-ninth anniversary of Christiane's wedding, and the seventy-sixth anniversary of de Gaulle's original call to arms: "No matter what happens, the flame of French Resistance must not and shall not die!" I quoted those words, then bowed to the seven decades our families have been united, in extraordinary friendship. "The most successful Franco-American alliance since Lafayette came to America in 1777! May we do everything in our power to make sure that this bond goes on forever."

FIVE DAYS after Christiane's burial, the United Kingdom voted to leave the European Union, whose creation had been a sacred project for André Boulloche. François Mitterrand remembered that André had been "the first among us to say 'my friends,' when he turned toward the Germans" after World War II. The Boulloches, who had suffered so much because of that war, understood better than anyone the need to build a united Europe in the ashes of that conflict, to make sure that such a catastrophe would never happen again. Christiane was one of the last surviving members of her generation to cherish that dream of unity and peace.

Five months after she died, the world suffered an even greater calamity than Brexit: the election of Donald Trump as president of the United States. His success immediately pushed us closer to the abyss than any other event since the end of World War II. Not only had Trump made direct appeals to all of America's worst impulses toward racism, sexism, and xenophobia, he had even declared that the united Europe which had kept the peace on most of that continent for seventy years was now "obsolete."

Our new president has given each of us an urgent call to duty. We must fight against the echoes of fascism that are already rumbling so ominously as I write these words, less than one full week into his presidency. All of us must search for ways to emulate Christiane's courage, to fight against a twenty-first-century variant of the terrible totalitarians she and her fellow *Résistants* somehow, miraculously, managed to vanquish. To preserve our freedoms, we must prove that we can still act upon the lessons of World War II, long after the last of its heroes have left us.

Above all, we must never forget the first value Christiane instilled in each of her children.

"You must not accept—you must act."

New York City, January 26, 2017

ACKNOWLEDGMENTS

THE COST OF COURAGE would never have been written without the help of dozens of enthusiastic collaborators.

Although she was extremely reluctant at the beginning, Christiane has been unfailingly helpful at every stage of my research, and my life. Her children, grandchildren, nephews, and nieces all followed her lead. François Audibert, Noëlle Audibert, Catherine Dujardin, Pierre Audibert, Eric Katlama, Michel Katlama, Claudine Lerer, Robert Boulloche, Jacques Boulloche, Hélène Katlama, Hélène Dujardin, Laurence Dujardin, and Stephane Dujardin all shared their knowledge and their memories. Catherine Dujardin also provided dozens of news stories about her uncle André's untimely death.

Agnès Boulloche and Odile Boulloche shared hundreds of photographs, news clippings, and diary entries, some of them more than a hundred years old. Like Christiane, Odile offered her friendship, her affection, and her intelligence, and she did everything she could to make sure I got the story right. But any errors that crept into the manuscript are mine alone.

When we lived in Paris, Joe and I formed cherished bonds with Vincent Demongeot, Mark Trilling, Meredith Artley and Naka Nathaniel, Robert and Barbara McCartney, Jeffrey and Casey O'Brien Blondes, Alan Riding, Pascale Belzacq, David Tanis and Randal Breski. Laure de Gramont is the best friend anyone has ever had in Paris: she opened her home and shared her friends, and all of her passions. Laure and her sisters, Claire Shea and Isabelle de Lastours, also loaned me their amazing country house so that I could begin to write in solitary splendor. Andrew Jacobs, Dan Levin, Tom Donaghy, and Shaffiq Essajee were equally generous with their Napanoch paradise.

Bob Paxton and Marcel Ophuls freely offered their time and their wisdom. Paxton's extraordinary books and Ophuls's brilliant movies remain the essential touchstones for anyone writing about this period. Claire Andrieu is one of the great French historians of her generation. She became my good friend and my essential guide through the French National Archives and dozens of other mysteries of wartime and postwar France. She also gave her blessing for me to borrow long sections from her father's extraordinary memoir, *Un fou s'évade.*

Early readers of the manuscript who spurred me on and offered dozens of corrections included my great friend Rick Whitaker, Janet Suzman, Victor Gurewich, Eugene Gregan, Frank Rich, Rick Hertzberg, Michael and Laura Kaiser, Peter Duchin, Judy Barnett, Walter Isaacson, Nick Rostow, Lisa Chase, Sarah Burke, Russell T. Davies, and Rebecca Kaiser Gibson. Since I first started writing books thirty years ago, Sal Matera, Stephanie Lane, Mark Polizzotti, and Renata Adler have been my essential readers and magnificent supporters.

Mathilde Damoisel was Claire Andrieu's student when she became Christiane's assistant on her memoir, and her interviews with Christiane were a source of dozens of insights. Now a brilliant documentarian, she made more contributions to this effort than I could possibly enumerate.

Steve and Nancy Shapiro, Sal Matera and Ann Jensen, Rich Meislin and Hendrik Uyttendaele, Beverly and Eugene Gregan, Katie Hustead, Rick Whitaker and Javier Molina, Michael Finnegan, Judy Knipe, Alice McGillion, Michelle Clunie, Jean Graham,

Paul Goldberger and Susan Solomon, Bryan Lowder and Cam McDonald know that their importance in my life defies definition. The empathy and insights of Gerald Dabbs have sustained me for almost two decades.

I am especially grateful for constant encouragement from Eric Gelman, Maralee Schwartz, Steve Weisman, Mary Stouter, Linda Amster, David Korzenik, Syd Schanberg, Steve Marcus, Henry Bloomstein, Jackie Green, Hope Kostmayer, Craig Zadan, Heyden White Rostow, Will Parker and Stephen Schwalen, Lynn Goldberg, Gordon Wheeler, Peter Wittig and Huberta von Voss-Wittig, Ben Wheeler and Kate Cortesi, Nick and Judgie Graham, David Whitaker, Sam and Andi Shapiro, Roger and Kay Greeley, Steve Kay, Cyd Savage, Martha Fay, David Dunlap, Tom Stoelker, Mary Murphy, Thatcher Barton, Judy Hottensen, Virginia Cannon, Wolf Hertzberg, François Fortin, Michael Butler, Tomas van Houtryve, Tree Adams, Ben Golberger, Mel Rothberg, Alex Goldberger, Anna Wainwright, Kirk Semple, Frank Clines, Alison Mitchell, Shelley Wanger, Steve Rattner, Steve Adler, Bill Carey, Jimmy Hayes, Peter Goldman, Margo and Garth Johnston, Juliet and Simon Oliver, Arabella Kurtz and Nick Everett, Lucy Howard, and Zarrina and Antony Kurtz.

Arthur Gelb was my first newspaper editor and my lifelong friend. It is a great sadness that he did not live to see this book published, but we continue to cherish our friendship with his wonderful wife, Barbara.

It has been my great good fortune to have been born into a family of brilliant writers and voracious readers, starting with my magnificent parents, Hannah and Phil Kaiser. My thanks and love go to Charlotte, Emily, Dan, Tom, Josh Thelin, Nick Peterson, Lauren Langlois, Linus Peterson, David and Bob, Hannah and Patti, Tema, Mark, Abe, Ezra and Isaac Silk, Moss and Adelaide Kaiser, Tamara Kaiser, and Sarah Hyams.

This book would never have come about if I hadn't fallen in

love with the story through its telling by my uncle Henry, known to most as Husky. He and my uncle Jerry Kaiser were two of the greatest men I have ever known.

Everyone at Other Press has been a pleasure to work with, especially Keenan McCracken, Yvonne Cárdenas, Bill Foo, Jessica Greer, Terrie Akers, Charlotte Kelly, and Iisha Stevens. Kathleen DiGrado found a brilliant image and designed a beautiful cover; Julie Fry worked the same sort of magic on the interior of the book.

All my life I have been looking for the perfect professional collaborator. When Judith Gurewich sat down next to me at a lunch she was hosting three years ago, I finally found her. She transformed my life. In short order she became my editor, my publisher, and my very close friend. Her warmth, her brilliance, and her passion are the greatest gifts an author could aspire to.

After thirty-six years my husband, Joe Stouter, continues to astonish me every day with his love, his imagination, and his art. It is hard to imagine feeling even closer to each other after nearly four decades, but we do. I have never done anything important without him.

PRINCIPAL ACTORS

The parents

Jacques Boulloche (b. 1888)   Director, French Bureau of Highways

Hélène Boulloche (b. 1888)   Wife of Jacques Boulloche

The children

Robert Boulloche (b. 1913)   Inspector, Minister of Finance

André Boulloche (b. 1915)   *Résistant*; Charles de Gaulle's personal
                                  representative in Paris, 1943–1944;
                                  arrested by the Gestapo January 12, 1944

Jacqueline Boulloche (b. 1918)   *Résistante*

Christiane Boulloche (b. 1923)   *Résistante*

The spouses

Alex Katlama (m. 1946)   *Résistant*, Jacqueline's husband

Jean Audibert (m. 1947)   Christiane's husband, member of the
                               Free French Navy

Anne Richard (m. 1949)   André's first wife, mother of his three
                              children

Odile Boulloche (m. 1959)   André's second wife, George Orwell's
                                 French publisher (*Animal Farm*, 1947)

The postwar generations

Eric Katlama (b. 1948)   Children of Jacqueline and Alex
Michel Katlama (b. 1950)
Claudine Lefer (b. 1953)

Catherine Dujardin (b. 1948)   Children of Christiane and Jean
Noëlle Audibert (b. 1949)
Pierre Audibert (b. 1951)
François Audibert (b. 1957)

Robert Boulloche (b. 1949)   Children of André and Anne
Agnès Boulloche (b. 1951)
Jacques Boulloche (b. 1953)

Hélène Dujardin (b. 1979)   Daughter of Catherine
                                   and Hubert Dujardin

OTHERS

Etienne Audibert   Fellow prisoner of Jacques Boulloche at
                                   Buchenwald, father of Jean Audibert

Harold Cole (b. 1906),   Resistance member who became a
code name "Paul"   notorious double agent for the Gestapo
                                   after he was arrested on December 6,
                                   1941. Betrayed André Postel-Vinay
                                   on December 14, 1941; killed by a
                                   French police inspector in January 1946

Albert-Marie Edmond Guérisse   *Résistant*, colleague of Postel-Vinay;
(b. 1911), code name   father of the "O'Leary line," which
"Patrick O'Leary"   rescued 600 allied pilots

André Postel-Vinay

Inspector, Finance Ministry; recruited André Boulloche for the Resistance in 1940; arrested by the Gestapo on December 14, 1941; escaped September 3, 1942

André Rondenay (b. 1913)

Résistant; classmate of André Boulloche who succeeded him as de Gaulle's military delegate in Paris in January 1944; arrested by the Nazis on July 27, 1944; executed on August 15, 1944

Henry and Suzanne Rollet

Résistants who assisted André Postel-Vinay in his escape from France.

Bernard Vernier-Palliez (b. 1918)

Résistant; later CEO of Renault; French Ambassador to the USA, 1982–1984

GOVERNMENT/MILITARY

Winston Churchill

British Prime Minister, 1940–1945 and 1951–1955
First honorary citizen of the United States, 1963

Charles de Gaulle

Leader of the Free French
President of France, 1959–1969

Dwight Eisenhower

Supreme Commander,
Allied Forces in Europe
President of the United States, 1953–1961

Adolf Hitler

Führer of German Third Reich, 1934–1945

François Mitterrand

Elected first secretary of the
Socialist Party, 1971
President of France, 1981–1995

Henri-Philippe Pétain

French hero of World War I
Chief of state of Vichy France,
1940–1944

Franklin Roosevelt

President of the United States,
1933–1945

Dietrich von Choltitz

Final German commander (*Befehls-
haber*) of German forces in occupied
Paris, who refuses to carry out
Hitler's order to blow the city up

Claus Schenk Graf
von Stauffenberg

Leader of the plot to kill Hitler
in July 1944

NOTES

vii "If mankind lasts": Ophuls, *The Sorrow and the Pity*, introduction by Stanley Hoffmann, pp. viii–ix.

vii "This is such": Author's interview with Eric Katlama March 13, 1999.

4 "it was necessary to turn the page": Boulloche-Audibert, *Souvenirs.*

8 "If an old pair of shoes": Ophuls, *The Sorrow and the Pity*, p. 71.

9 They are called *gazogènes*: Collins and Lapierre, *Is Paris Burning?*, p. 15.

9 a good bicycle can cost: Eparvier, *À Paris sous la botte des Nazis.*

9 "taxis hippomobiles": Ophuls, *The Sorrow and the Pity*, p. 71.

9 The fastest pedicab: Collins and Lapierre, *Is Paris Burning?*, p. 16.

9 four men pedaling: Ibid., p. 18.

9 Huge yellow posters: Permanent exhibit, Paris Museum of World War II.

9 After four years of war: Churchill, *Second World War*, V:ix.

10 Deeply religious: Interview with Raymond Jovignot, conducted by Melle Patrimonio, February 1, 1946, French National Archives, box 72AJ42.

10 Christiane's clandestine duties: Boulloche-Audibert, *Souvenirs.*

10 "We wouldn't just resist them": Author's interview with Christiane Boulloche-Audibert, Fontainebleau, March 19, 1999.

11 hypnotized and horrified: Mathilde Damoisel's interview with Christiane Boulloche-Audibert, February 3, 1997.

11 There is no heat: Ibid.

11 Four months earlier: Madame Grenlet's interview with André Boulloche, February 1, 1950, French National Archives, box 72AJ68.

12 In the fall of 1942: Cobb, *Resistance*, p. 160.

13 The STO requires *and* Faced with the prospect: Ibid., p. 162.

13   As one historian put it: H. R. Kedward, *In Search of the Maquis: Rural Resistance in Southern France, 1942–1944*, quoted ibid., p. 161.

13   "I never felt": Christiane Boulloche-Audibert interviewed by a French television reporter, March 22, 1999, on the occasion of the unveiling of a bust of André Boulloche.

13   During his brief time: British Intelligence file on Eric Katlama.

15   "Strangle me": Author's interview with Dr. René Cler, Paris, March 17, 1999. Cler told me he had heard this story from Jacques's cell mate. He no longer remembered his name.

16   Instinct propels the Frenchman: His son Jacques said, "I was told that one of them had a submachine gun, and he threw himself on it." Author's interview with Jacques Boulloche at this home in Le Havre, February 1, 2004.

17   Jacqueline performs the secret knock *and the rest of this section*: Boulloche-Audibert, *Souvenirs*.

21   "Dignity is incompatible with submission": Letter from André Boulloche to C. Hettier de Boislambert, Grand Chancelier de L'Ordre de la Libération, June 13, 1969, French National Archives, box 72AJ2056.

22   "*When will I see them again?*": Boulloche-Audibert, *Souvenirs*.

23   "In general," Christiane recalled: Author's interview with Christiane Boulloche-Audibert, March 19, 1999.

23   Her parents don't consider themselves: Author's interview with Christiane Boulloche-Audibert, March 11, 1999.

25   Those casualties transform: Paxton, *Vichy France*, p. 12.

25   "To continue an enforcement": Cooper, *Old Men Forget*, p. 199.

26   "Politically Czecho-Slovakia": *Manchester Guardian*, October 1, 1938.

27   After "immense exertions": www.winstonchurchill.org/learn/speeches/speeches-of-winston-churchill/101-the-munich-agreement.

28   At one o' clock: *Argus de la Presse*, Paris, August 15, 1900.

28   As early as 1937: Author's interview with Christiane Boulloche-Audibert, March 19, 1999.

29   "A Hun alive": Martin Gilbert, *Churchill: A Life*, p. 680.

29   "The great day has finally arrived": Letter from Jacques Boulloche, November 1, 1918, collection of Agnes Boulloche.

29   He regards them as "imbeciles": Mathilde Damoisel's interview with Christiane Boulloche-Audibert, Paris, February 10, 1997; author's interview with Christiane Boulloche-Audibert, March 25, 1999.

30   "We triumph," declares the chief judge: This quote was famous among
     his grandchildren. Some thought his words referred to the inferior
     social class of their fellow *Dreyfusards*, but Christiane Boulloche
     believed his comments were just about politics. "He was a republican,
     and most of Dreyfus's supporters were leftists," she explained. She
     thought her ancestors had abandoned the conventional wisdom of
     their social milieu because they were magistrates. "When you're a
     magistrate, you do have a particular point of view—you're in favor of
     justice." And to these magistrates, it had always been obvious that
     Dreyfus was innocent.

30   A young friend: Author's interview with Dr. René Cler, March 17, 1999.

30   Their parents encourage: Letter from Dr. Robert Desmond, collection
     of Agnès Boulloche.

31   Trains, planes, and automobiles: Dr. Robert Desmond, Témoignage,
     p. 17.

31   As a teenager: *André Boulloche, 1915–1978*, p. 12, Maurice
     Bourgès-Maunoury.

31   No priest ever joins them: Mathilde Damoisel's interview with
     Christiane Boulloche-Audibert, Paris, February 3, 1997.

31   Christiane is certain: Author's interview with Christiane Boulloche-
     Audibert, March 19, 1999.

31   Their parents' favorite writers: Author's telephone interview with
     Christiane Boulloche-Audibert, November 21, 2003.

31   Jacques plays the piano: Mathilde Damoisel's interview with Christiane
     Boulloche-Audibert, February 3, 1997.

33   who are suddenly forbidden: Author's interview with Christiane
     Boulloche-Audibert, March 19, 1999.

33   In a letter home: Letter from Hélène Boulloche to André Boulloche,
     March 12, 1926, collection of Agnès Boulloche.

33   When the parents finally return: Author's interview with Christiane
     Boulloche-Audibert, March 19, 1999.

33   "It was implicit": Ibid.

33   "It was as if the plague": *New York Times*, September 1, 1989.

33   "Either he could ally": Stokesbury, *Short History of World War II*, p. 65.

34   "Germans Rush Gayly": *New York Times*, September 3, 1939, p. 11.

35   "Throughout the 30's": *New York Times*, September 1, 1989.

35   gape "at each other": Churchill, *Second World War*, I:434.

36 most French officers still believe in: Ibid., II:32.

36 "new and exciting adventure": Mathilde Damoisel's interview with Christiane Boulloche-Audibert, February 10, 1997.

37 "an imperialist and capitalist crime": Churchill, *Second World War*, I:511–12.

37 undermined by shortages: Jackson, *France*, p. 116.

37 "raring to go": Quoted ibid., p. 117.

37 "scores of towns": Churchill, *Second World War*, II:53.

38 At the end of the emergency: Ousby, *Occupation*, p. 43.

38 Across the channel: *New York Times*, June 1 and 2, 1940.

38 mobs of refugees: Quoted in Jackson, *France*, p. 120.

39 "This is what we dreaded": *New York Times*, June 4, 1940.

40 "I can't describe": Letter from Jacques Boulloche, collection of Agnès Boulloche.

40 There are twenty thousand people: Ousby, *Occupation*, p. 46.

40 "The German guns": *New York Times*, June 12, 1940.

41 "My Beloved": Letter from Jacques Boulloche, collection of Agnès Boulloche.

43 "Had all of us in France": Commandant le Baron de Vomécourt, who served with both the British Army and the French Resistance during the war, replies with an emphatic yes to Captain Liddell Hart's article, "Was the Maquis Worthwhile?" Peter [aka Pierre] de Vomécourt, [London] *Daily Mail*, February 4, 1947.

43 There are ninety thousand: Ousby, *Occupation*, p. 33.

43 Meanwhile, French prime minister Paul Reynaud: Churchill, *Second World War*, II:176.

44 A French minister of state: Ibid., pp. 180, 184, 187. The minister was Jean Ybarnégaray.

44 A prescient Reynaud: Jackson, *France*, p. 389.

44 At nine A.M.: de Gaulle, *Complete War Memoirs*, p. 80.

44 "carried with him": Churchill, *Second World War*, II:192.

46 André distinguishes himself: Biography of Jean-Pierre Berger, www.ordredelaliberation.fr/fr_compagnon/82.html. André gave different dates in different places for this departure date. In 1943, he told British intelligence officers that the ship had left France on June 22 and reached Algeria on the day of the Armistice. Seven years later, he thought he had left on June 24 and arrived two days later.

46 He thinks "that we [will] win": Letter from André Boulloche to C. Hettier de Boislambert, Grand Chancelier de L'Ordre de la Liberation, June 13, 1969, French National Archives, box 72AJ2056.

47 On June 21: Churchill says 21 deputies; Ousby says 19. In a speech before the National Assembly, its president, Raymond Fourni, said there had been 26 deputies and 1 senator aboard.

47 "I embarked on the *Massilia*": Ophuls, *The Sorrow and the Pity*, pp. 59–60.

47 Churchill noted with disgust: Churchill, *Second World War*, II:193–94.

48 One and a half million French prisoners: Jackson, *France*, p. 127.

49 At the end of the opera tour: Albert Speer, *Inside the Third Reich*, pp. 171–72.

50 "My Dear Father": Letter from André Boulloche, collection of Agnès Boulloche.

52 "And they sang well": Author's interview with Christiane Boulloche-Audibert, March 19, 1999.

52 She sees it as: Author's interview with Christiane Boulloche-Audibert, March 19, 1999.

52 "It was a succession of shocks": Mathilde Damoisel's interview with Christiane Boulloche-Audibert, February 10, 1997.

52 "You should have been here": Eparvier, *À Paris sous la botte des Nazis*.

53 This is when Christiane: Mathilde Damoisel's interview with Christiane Boulloche-Audibert, February 3, 1997.

53 Three months later: Ousby, *Occupation*, p. 99.

53 By the start of 1941: Jackson, *France*, p. 356.

53 Adding insult to the humiliation: Ousby, *Occupation*, p. 182.

55 As the British historian: Jackson, *France*, p. 243.

55 Like his father: Author's interview with Christiane Boulloche-Audibert, March 19, 1999.

56 But he has a terrific sense of humor: Author's interview with Agnès Boulloche, December 8, 2001.

56 At the end of 1940: "Hommage à André Boulloche," p. 13.

57 He is appalled by the savage sight: Author's interview with André Postel-Vinay, Paris, February 2, 2004.

58 "war is the only way": Author's interview with Claire Andrieu (Postel-Vinay's daughter), January 31, 2004.

58   In December 1940: Jackson, *France*, p. 403; *Ordre de la liberation* website, biography of André Postel-Vinay, www.ordredelaliberation.fr/ fr_compagnon/801.html.

59   "I know someone": Author's interview with André Postel-Vinay, February 2, 2004.

60   "Andre was very passionate": Ibid.

60   "For the two of us": Ibid.

61   "Then whose bombers are those": Stokesbury, *Short History of World War II*, p. 150.

61   visit it for the first time: Shirer, *Rise and Fall of the Third Reich*, p. 1039.

61   he believes that they are reaching London: When Pierre Pène is arrested, he sees in the Gestapo's dossier the plan for the works at Margival, which was supposed to have arrived in London.

61   never discusses his clandestine: Author's interview with Dr. René Cler, March 17, 1999.

62   Churchill hopes that he will attract: Jackson, *France*, p. 389.

62   "Their idea was to get out": Ophuls, *The Sorrow and the Pity*, pp. 56, 58.

62   Only one deputy: Paxton, *Vichy France*, p. 42.

62   de Gaulle notices: Jackson, *France*, p. 398.

63   felt like a man who had been skinned alive: Ibid., pp. 392–93.

63   There was one other thing: Ibid., p. 396.

63   But the general sees: Ibid., p. 397.

63   Not until November: Ibid., pp. 397–98.

63   At the same time, French-language: Ibid., p. 398.

64   Almost anyone who volunteers: Ibid., p. 399.

64   "The island of Sein stands watch": Ousby, *Occupation*, p. 44.

64   Nearly all of what Dewavrin knows: Jackson, *France*, p. 399.

65   an almost inevitable invasion: *New York Times*, June 1 and 6, 1940.

67   "Everywhere a feeling": Orwell, *Diaries*, p. 299.

68   Three years later: Nicholas Lemann, "The Murrow Doctrine," *New Yorker*, January 23 and 30, 2006.

69   "could not agree to forcing De Gaulle": Eisenhower, *Crusade in Europe*, p. 248.

69   "The familiar slur": Ousby, *Occupation*, p. 236.

69   "a very, very explicit act": Author's telephone interview with Robert Paxton, January 29, 2004. In 2014, Paxton told me he had recently seen an interview on the Internet with Pétain's chauffeur saying the Cadillac

had been left on the dock in Bordeaux by someone fleeing in June 1940, and Pétain had purchased it then, so Paxton was no longer certain that the automobile was a gift of the American ambassador. However, most other sources agree that it came from Admiral Leahy.

69   American public opinion begins to rally: Ibid.

69   "vitally interested statement": *New York Times*, June 22, 1941.

71   "This was our obsessive fear": Boulloche Audibert, *Souvenirs*.

71   Thanks to their complicity: Postel-Vinay, *Un fou s'évade*, p. 8, used by permission of the author's estate.

71   At that moment: Ibid., pp. 8–9.

72   And yet he still doesn't want: Ibid., p. 9. Most of the rest of this chapter is taken from *Un fou s'évade*.

78   Probably to avoid: www.rafinfo.org.uk/rafescape/guerisse.htm.

79   Postel-Vinay considers: Remarks of Postel-Vinay honoring André Boulloche, January 26, 1986.

80   His ultimate nightmare: This and most of chapter 9 is from Postel-Vinay, *Un fou s'évade*.

86   And when a downed British or American: Author's interview with Claire Andrieu, January 31, 2004.

92   Patriotic School has been created: Andrew, *Defend the Realm*, p. 250.

93   Those identified as "goats": Ibid., p. 251.

95   The big question is: Stokesbury, *Short History of World War II*, p. 224.

95   As Operation Torch begins: www.ibiblio.org/pha/policy/1942/421107b.html.

95   De Gaulle observed that by not firing: de Gaulle, *Complete War Memoirs*, p. 358.

96   It would be a huge prize: Ibid., p. 359.

96   Just one destroyer: Ibid.

97   There is an immediate uproar: Stokesbury, *Short History of World War II*, pp. 228–29.

97   "There was a tremendous outcry": Author's telephone interview with Robert Paxton, January 29, 2004.

97   "If the tragic character": De Gaulle, *Complete War Memoirs*, p. 379. This is the other key paragraph about Darlan's assassination in de Gaulle's book: *The man who had killed him, Fernand Bonnier de la Chapelle, had made himself the instrument of the aggravated passions that had fired the souls around him to the boiling point but behind which, perhaps,*

*moved a policy determined to liquidate a "temporary expedient" after
having made use of him. This young man, this child overwhelmed by the
spectacle of odious events, thought his action would be a service to his
lacerated country, would remove from the road to French reconciliation
an obstacle shameful in his eyes. He believed, moreover, as he repeatedly
said until the moment of his execution, that an intervention would
be made in his behalf by some outside source so high and powerful that
the North African authorities could not refuse to obey it. Of course
no individual has the right to kill save on the field of battle. Moreover,
Darlan's behavior as a governor and as a leader was answerable to
national justice, not, certainly, to that of a group or an individual.
Yet how could we fail to recognize the nature of the intentions that
inspired his juvenile fury? That is why the strange, brutal and summary
way the investigation was conducted in Algiers, the hasty and abbreviated
trial before a military tribunal convened at night and in private session,
the immediate and secret execution of Fernand Bonnier de la Chapelle,
the orders given to the censors that not even his name should be known—
all these led to the suspicion that someone wanted to conceal at any price
the origin of his decision and constituted a kind of defiance of those
circumstances which, without justifying the drama, explained and, to
a certain degree, excused it.*

97   Darlan's disappearance from the scene: Stokesbury, *Short History of
World War II*, p. 229.

98   "Everything is ruined anyway": Perrault, *La Longue Traque*, p. 120.

99   At seven o'clock in the evening: Témoignage de M. André Boulloche.

101   impeccable identity card: André never actually uses this fake identity
card, and by the time he reaches England he can no longer remember
the name in which it was issued.

101   "deep satisfaction": British Public Record Office HS 9/190/6 114106.

102   the intelligence section of BCRA: Rossiter, *Women in the Resistance*,
pp. 13–14.

102   a "capable type": Public Record Office HS 9/190/6 114106. SECRET.
Y box 3558.

103   For a long time afterward: Témoignage de M. André Boulloche.

105   "I was recruited": Boulloche-Audibert, *Souvenirs*. Raymond Jovignot,
a member of the Resistance who knew André Boulloche after his arrest
in 1944, told an interviewer in 1946 that Jacques (code name: Crassus)

was in fact tortured by the Germans. Jovignot described him as "a very good boy, deeply religious, who loved his boss," André.

106 "Perhaps I was wrong": Postel-Vinay, *Un fou s'évade*, p. 172n.

106 By dawn, Farges: Remarks of Gilbert Farges honoring André Boulloche, January 26, 1986.

107 As Gimpel's British handlers have noted: British Intelligence file on Charles Gimpel.

108 "Because it meant": Author's interview with Christiane Boulloche-Audibert, March 19, 1999.

108 Seventeen hundred *through* Porte will survive deportation: All details about the prisoners on the train are from the catalog for an exhibit at the Musée Jean Moulin mounted in 2002, www.french-art.com/ musees/jean_moulin/auschwitz.htm.

109 "The crazy people": Remarks of Gilbert Farges honoring André Boulloche.

109 Just once, the Germans offer: Farges quoted in *André Boulloche*, p. 27.

110 As he climbs out of the train: Remarks of Gilbert Farges honoring André Boulloche.

110 given their first drink: Montbéliard, p. 24.

110 "precarious survivors": Remarks of Gilbert Farges honoring André Boulloche.

110 The personal intervention of Marshal Pétain: Author's interview with Odile Boulloche, March 20, 1999.

111 Ninety-five percent of the deportees: Gilbert Farges, "Hommage à André Boulloche," p. 25.

112 As James L. Stokesbury: *Short History of World War II*, pp. 225–26.

113 "as the state came under challenge": Paxton, *Vichy France*, p. 286.

113 His fake identity continues: www.ordredelaliberation.fr/fr_ compagnon/855.html.

114 To boost Christiane's spirits: Boulloche-Audibert, *Souvenirs*.

115 The others are Lemniscate: www.ordredelaliberation.fr/fr_ compagnon/855.html.

115 "I was twenty": Author's interview with Christiane Boulloche-Audibert, March 19, 1999.

116 Seeing them at the front door: Boulloche-Audibert, *Souvenirs*.

116 *At least I am courageous*: Ibid.

117   That is the hardest part: Mathilde Damoisel's interview with Christiane
      Boulloche-Audibert, February 10, 1997.

117   "been incredibly lucky": Author's interview with Christiane Boulloche-
      Audibert, March 25, 1999; *Souvenirs.*

117   The historian Ian Ousby: *Occupation*, p. 245.

117   In July 1943: Stokesbury, *Short History of World War II*, p. 293.

118   His successor, Pietro Badoglio: Ibid., p. 296.

119   Then they spent eighteen months: Author's interview with Eric
      Katlama, Hotel Des Deux Continents, March 23, 1999 (for the fact
      they were waiting for the revolution to fail). Most of this account
      of Katlama's early years comes from Alex Katlama's interviews with
      the British during the war, which were declassified at my request:
      Public Record Office HS 9/823/1.

119   He is brought up: Author's interview with Michel Katlama,
      March 14, 1999.

120   the mean height for Frenchmen: Timothy J. Hatton and Bernice E.
      Bray, "Long Run Trends in the Heights of European Men, 19th–20th
      Centuries," privatewww.essex.ac.uk/~hatton/Tim_height_paper.pdf.

120   He assumes the inertia: Author's interview with Eric Katlama,
      March 23, 1999.

120   As a Russian immigrant: Author's interview with Michel Katlama,
      March 14, 1999.

122   He also happens to love: Ibid.

123   "A quiet intelligent" *through* "a competent and loyal assistant":
      British Intelligence file on Eric Katlama.

124   In the third week of April: Christiane's memoirs place this event in
      January, but Alex remembers it clearly as April.

124   Christiane likes the handsome Alex: Author's interview with Christiane
      Boulloche-Audibert, March 19, 1999.

125   he meets with Resistance members: www.ordredelaliberation.fr/fr_
      compagnon/855.html.

126   "All southern England": Eisenhower, *Crusade in Europe,*
      p. 248.

126   By the eve of the invasion: Roberts, *Storm of War*, p. 466.

126   Soldiers joke that if the invasion: Stokesbury, *Short History of World
      War II*, p. 311.

127   "The southernmost camps": Eisenhower, *Crusade in Europe*, p. 249.

127 This will severely limit: O'Neill, *Oxford Essential Guide to World War II*, pp. 86–87.

127 They make a special effort: Shirer, *Rise and Fall of the Third Reich*, p. 1037. Rundstedt and Rommel were certain it would be in the Pas-de-Calais area, where the channel was at its narrowest.

127 Again, the deception works: Stokesbury, *Short History of World War II*, p. 211; O'Neill, *Oxford Essential Guide to World War II*, p. 87.

128 Knowing that it's crucial: Churchill, *Second World War*, V:544–46.

131 "The tension continued to mount": Eisenhower, *Crusade in Europe*, p. 249.

131 At four fifteen A.M.: Ibid., p. 250.

131 "I hope to God": Roberts, *Storm of War*, pp. 469–70.

132 It is thrilling: Boulloche-Audibert, *Souvenirs*.

132 So the commanders: Jane Penrose, ed., *The D-Day Companion*, quoted in Roberts, *Storm of War*, p. 471.

132 And on June 4: Shirer, *Rise and Fall of the Third Reich*, p. 1036.

133 On the basis of everything: Ibid., pp. 1036–37.

133 Around one A.M.: Ibid., p. 1038.

133 Hitler himself has been up: Roberts, *Storm of War*, p. 472.

133 Then he goes to bed: Shirer, *Rise and Fall of the Third Reich*, p. 1038.

133 At five fifty on the morning: Roberts, *Storm of War*, p. 473.

133 After the 101st Airborne: Ibid., p. 473.

134 "ABLE company riding through from a rooftop": *The Atlantic*, November 1960. www.theatlantic.com/magazine/archive/1960/11/first-wave-at-omaha-beach/303365/.

135 At a cost of two thousand Americans: Roberts, *Storm of War*, p. 476.

136 "We were depending": Eisenhower, *Crusade in Europe*, p. 248.

136 For a week after the invasion: Cobb, *Resistance*, p. 245; Jackson, *France*, pp. 544–45 (for Marseille and Toulouse).

136 This is vital: Cobb, *Resistance*, p. 245.

136 British air chief marshal Arthur Tedder: Roberts, *Storm of War*, p. 477.

136 "The first twenty-four hours": Quoted ibid., p. 459.

137 By the end of June 11: www.ddaymuseum.co.uk/d-day/d-day-and-the-battle-of-normandy-your-questions-answered. By July 2, those numbers had swelled to about 1,000,000 men, 171,532 vehicles, and 566,648 tons of supplies.

138 "In our circles": Roberts, *Storm of War*, pp. 479–80.

139   "Throughout France the Free French": Eisenhower, *Crusade in Europe*.

140   Now, for the first time in years: Boulloche-Audibert, *Souvenirs*.

140   Christiane is captivated: Ibid.

140   "We had a common enemy": Ibid.

140   Christiane spends the battle: Author's interview with Christiane Boulloche-Audibert, March 25, 1999; Boulloche-Audibert, *Souvenirs*.

141   The Maquis suffer two dead: www.memoiresvivantes.org/histoire_ resistance_dunlesplacesetvermot.php; *Dictionnaire biographique de Paul-Camille DUGENE*; and www.morvan-des-lacs.com/images/ actualites/le%20massacre%20de%20dun2.pdf.

141   "I'm coming back with you": Boulloche-Audibert, *Souvenirs*.

142   Rommel has joined the conspiracy: Shirer, *Rise and Fall of the Third Reich*, p. 1031.

142   To Rommel's chief of staff: General Hans Speidel, *Invasion*, quoted ibid., p. 1039.

143   "Don't you worry": Ibid., p. 1040.

143   Speidel believed that: Ibid., p. 1042.

143   no more than fourteen: Photo and caption in Eparvier, *À sous la botte des Nazis*.

143   ZUR NORMANDIE FRONT: *La Libération de Paris*, documentary, 1944.

144   "The assassination must be attempted": Shirer, *Rise and Fall of the Third Reich*, p. 1043.

145   "The threatened collapse": Ibid.

145   Eisenhower remembers late June: Eisenhower, *Crusade in Europe*, p. 263.

145   Seven weeks pass: Ibid., p. 272.

146   the anti-Hitler plotters get a boost: Shirer, *Rise and Fall of the Third Reich*, pp. 1033–45.

146   By July 1944, the conspiracy: Ibid., pp. 1030, 1034.

146   The thickness of this particular wire: Ibid., p. 1049; Roberts, *Storm of War*, p. 481.

146   "somewhere between a monastery": Ibid.

146   The compound includes: Ibid.

148   Before darkness has fallen: Shirer, *Rise and Fall of the Third Reich*, p. 1060.

148   The conspirators' failure: Ibid., p. 1064.

148   Goebbels initially blames the Allies: *New York Times*, July 21, 1944.

149   "Seized by a titanic fury": Shirer, *Rise and Fall of the Third Reich*,
      p. 1070.

149   "Who says I am not": Churchill, *Second World War*, VI:25.

150   "Although the smell of retreat": Cobb, *Resistance*, p. 258.

150   "A great tide of popular enthusiasm": De Gaulle, *Complete War
      Memoirs*, p. 638.

150   "We had our hands": Boulloche-Audibert, *Souvenirs*; author's interview
      with Christiane Bulloche-Audibert, March 11, 1999.

151   On July 14, a huge: Cobb, *Resistance*, pp. 258–59.

151   "They had a deported son": Boulloche-Audibert, *Souvenirs*.

151   But as the temperature inches: www.meteo-paris.com/bibliotheque/
      documents/3403.txt.

152   He and Rondenay have escaped: www.ordredelaliberation.fr/fr_
      compagnon/426.html.

152   Disaster strikes: Christiane remembers the arrest taking place at
      Passy; Rondenay's official biography says it took place at La Muette,
      www.ordredelaliberation.fr/fr_compagnon/855.html. For de Beafort's
      wound, www.ordredelaliberation.fr/fr_compagnon/426.html.

152   "There was no question": Boulloche-Audibert, *Souvenirs*.

153   "At the same time I felt a trap": Ibid.

153   "At times like this": Ibid.

154   "The conditions of our daily lives" *and* "We are happy to know":
      I found these letters in the family archive maintained by Agnès
      Boulloche, André's daughter. André must have saved them during
      his ten remaining months at the camp and brought them back to
      France after he was liberated.

155   Nothing important is discussed: Boulloche-Audibert, *Souvenirs*.

157   For the next week, the Germans: Ibid.

157   Alone in Paris: Ibid.

157   "I had no choice": Author's interview with Dr. René Cler, March 17,
      1999.

157   "It was not pleasant": Ibid.

159   "Even when motionless": Dallas, *1945*, p. 187.

159   At the first of the three security rings: Collins and Lapierre, *Is Paris
      Burning?*, p. 34.

159   When it ended, only 347: Ibid., p. 32.

160   Then Hitler "began reeling off": Neitzel, *Tapping Hitler's Generals*.

160   "dozens of generals": Collins and Lapierre, *Is Paris Burning?*, p. 35.

160   Hitler orders him to "stamp out": Ibid., p. 36.

161   Right now they are determined: Eisenhower, *Crusade in Europe*, p. 296.

161   "Paris food and medical requirements": Quoted in Collins and Lapierre, *Is Paris Burning?*, p. 20.

161   For all of these reasons: Eisenhower, *Crusade in Europe*, p. 296.

162   Their leaflet exhorts: Cobb, *Resistance*, p. 259.

162   On the night of August 12: http://dora-ellrich.fr/les-hommes-du -convoi-du-15-aout-1944/.

162   Choltitz orders more than two thousand: Cobb, *Resistance*, p. 258.

163   Half an hour after it leaves: Boulloche-Audibert, *Souvenirs*.

163   "You won't go any further": http://memoiredeguerre. pagespro-orange.fr/convoi44/derniers-convois.htm#Pantin.

164   The chief German engineer promises: Collins and Lapierre, *Is Paris Burning?*, pp. 68–69.

164   Since allied bombers are continuing: Ibid., p. 68.

164   "Often it is given to a general": Ibid., pp. 89–90.

165   "Why too soon?": De Gaulle, *Complete Wartime Memoirs*, pp. 636–37.

165   De Gaulle believes it is "intolerable": Ibid., p. 640.

165   De Gaulle also suggests: Ibid., p. 637.

166   By now General Choltitz: Collins and Lapierre, *Is Paris Burning?*, p. 210.

166   "The swastika was still flying": quoted in Cobb, *Resistance*, pp. 260–61.

166   A CHACUN SON BOCHE: Dallas, *1945*, p. 194.

167   "If the American Army": Collins and Lapierre, *Is Paris Burning?*, pp. 178–79.

167   By the time Silbert climbs: Ibid., pp. 178–80.

167   Because they had begun: Eisenhower, *Crusade in Europe*, p. 296.

167   Eisenhower also recognizes: Quoted in Collins and Lapierre, *Is Paris Burning?*, p. 181.

167   Nordling has already convinced: Dallas, *1945*, p. 177.

168   In his place, he sends: Collins and Lapierre, *Is Paris Burning?*, pp. 187–91.

168   "Have the French division hurry": Ibid., p. 208.

168   If there was a strategy: Jackson, *France*, p. 566.

169   When the spectral outline: Collins and Lapierre, *Is Paris Burning?*, pp. 236–37.

169   At last, Free French troops are back: Ibid., p. 255.

169   Within minutes, every block is reverberating: Ibid., p. 257.

170   The Vichy government estimated: Ousby, *Occupation*, p. 237.

170   As Ian Ousby observes: Ibid., p. 238.

170   On the eve of his return: de Gaulle, *Complete Wartime Memoirs*, pp. 645–46.

171   "Gentlemen," he tells his guests: Collins and Lapierre, *Is Paris Burning?*, pp. 258–59.

171   This is the German officer: Dallas, *1945*, p. 176.

171   he had begun to have nightmares: From Choltitz's memoirs, quoted ibid., p. 176.

172   German snipers increase Allied casualties: Ousby, *Occupation*, p. 293.

173   "Why should we hide" *through* "Long live France!": www.emersonkent .com/speeches/paris_liberated.htm.

174   "The Republic has never ceased": De Gaulle, *Complete Wartime Memoirs*, p. 650.

174   Two days earlier: Dallas, *1945*, p. 188.

175   The next day, de Gaulle defies: Collins and Lapierre, *Is Paris Burning?*, p. 331.

175   The French general concedes: Ibid., p 333.

175   "Today we were to revive": De Gaulle, *Complete Wartime Memoirs*, p. 653.

176   De Gaulle thinks Parisians: Ibid.

176   "Since each of all of those": Ibid.

176   "Everyone seemed happy and relieved": Bulloche-Audibert, *Souvenirs*.

177   At midnight on August 26: De Gaulle, *Complete Wartime Memoirs*, p. 659.

178   "I was shocked": Boulloche-Audibert, *Souvenirs*.

178   Christian leaves Paris *through* doesn't want to alarm her: Ibid.

180   "Although letter writing": *Bulletin de l'Association des anciens élèves de l'école polytechnique*, September 1947.

181   When she returns to Paris: Boulloche-Audibert, *Souvenirs*.

182   Just as the Germans had partly ignored: Roberts, *Storm of War*, pp. 505–7.

182   the Germans have lost 120,000 men killed: Shirer, *Rise and Fall of the Third Reich*, p. 1095.

182   "The great difference": Roberts, *Storm of War*, p. 509.

183   In Nuremberg, the sight of gigantic Nazi rallies: Video of the
      explosion at www.ushmm.org/wlc/en/media_fi.php?MediaId=2048.
184   after twelve years, four months: Shirer, *Rise and Fall of the Third Reich*,
      p. 1139.
184   "I was deported": Boulloche-Audibert, *Souvenirs*.
184   Somehow, everyone who survives with him: *Andre Boulloche*, p. 30.
184   "In this way he shared": Ibid., p. 31.
184   "Survival was a constant act": Ibid., p. 33.
186   At dawn on April 16 *through* arrives to liberate the camp: Ibid., p. 32.
187   "Of course he was extremely thin": Author's interview with Christiane
      Boulloche-Audibert, March 19, 1999.
187   "But, when he was finally standing there": Boulloche-Audibert,
      Souvenirs.
187   "If I'd known that": Author's interview with Eric Katlama, March 23,
      1999. "I remember very well that my mother [Jacqueline] told me,"
      Katlama said. "I have no doubt about that memory at all."
191   "My deportation to the camps": Andre Boulloche F.R. 3 radio broad-
      cast, November 23, 1976.
191   "André Boulloche had the longest service": Postel-Vinay, *Un fou
      s'évade*, p. 128.
191   "Did your father André ever talk": Author's interview with Agnès
      Boulloche, December 8, 2001.
193   ten thousand Frenchmen were the victims: Author's interview with
      Claire Andrieu, January 31, 2004.
194   "I went to Macy's": Author's interview with Christiane Boulloche-
      Audibert, March 25, 1999.
196   Christiane thought New York: Ibid.
196   "Fear of the Gestapo": *Washington Post*, April 23, 1946, p. 13.
196   "Why did my life have to be spared": Collection of Agnès Boulloche.
197   "I've always done": Mathilde Damoisel's interview with Christiane
      Boulloche-Audibert, April 7, 1997.
197   "It was when I was deported": André Boulloche interview on
      Radio FR 3, November 20, 1976.
198   "We bourgeois learned some things": Author's interview with
      Christiane Boulloche-Audibert, March 25, 1999.
198   "I was very young": André Boulloche radio interview, November 20,
      1976.

199   killed there in an ambush: www.annales.org/archives/x/
      etienneaudibert.html.

201   "You've never seen two sisters": Author's interview with Eric Katlama,
      March 23, 1999.

201   "It's true. We were always scared": Author's interview with Robert
      Boulloche, March 21, 1999.

202   "camouflaged their unhappiness": Author's interview with Pierre
      Audibert, March 24, 1999.

202   "it was clear that André was suffering": Author's interview with Eric
      Katlama, March 23, 1999.

202   "I remember there was a feeling of meditation": Ibid.

203   "This was the Bolloches": Author's interview with Pierre Audibert,
      March 24, 1999.

204   "It showed that you can do good": Author's interview with François
      Audibert, March 18, 1999.

205   "If one wants people to win": Ophuls, *The Sorrow and the Pity*,
      pp. xiii–xiv.

205   But de Gaulle never literally said *through* outside of institutions:
      Author's interview with Claire Andrieu, January 31, 2004.

207   André told her that if she "wanted to fight": Author's interview with
      Agnès Boulloche, December 8, 2001.

207   Ophuls told me that he thought de Gaulle: Author's interview with
      Marcel Ophuls, March 23, 2004.

208   He chose Clermont-Ferrand: Elliot Wilhelm, "The Sorrow and
      the Pity," *VideoHound's World Cinema* (Detroit: Visible Ink Press,
      1999).

208   "There's something unhealthy": Author's interview with Marcel
      Ophuls, March 23, 2004.

209   teachers from the lycée: Ophuls, *The Sorrow and the Pity*, p. 86.

210   "eating the national tissue": "À la mémoire d'Andre Boulloche."

211   "It was a period when there were terrorist attacks": Author's interview
      with Christiane Boulloche-Audibert, March 25, 1999.

211   In 1967, the Neuwirth Act: www.ined.fr/fichier/t_publication/1336/
      publi_pdf2_pesa439.pdf.

212   "As you can see": Boulloche-Audibert, *Souvenirs*.

212   the Socialist Party had voted against participating: *New York Times*,
      January 12, 1959.

212   Odile rushed to London: Author's interview with Odile Boulloche, March 20, 1999.

213   "He had a terrible violence" *through* "first and foremost, a *polytechnicien*": Author's interview with Jacques Boulloche, April 4, 2004.

214   the secret to his success: *Le Point*, January 9, 1978.

215   "Boulloche was certain that he was working for France": Author's interview with Raymond Forni, June 3, 2003.

215   most people expected Mitterrand: Author's interview with Andrée Vauban, April 23, 2003.

217   "secular monk": Ibid.

217   "an infernal life": André Boulloche radio interview, November 20, 1976.

217   "Are you ever discouraged?": Ibid.

217   "I think I can say without exaggeration": Ibid.

218   Now he climbed into the copilot's seat: Author's interview with Andrée Vauban, April 23, 2003. Investigators apparently determined this by examining the wreckage of the plane.

218   At the same moment: Ibid.

218   A moment later: *Le Monde*, March 19–20; *Le Figaro*, March 18–19, 1978.

220   "This is a very remarkable man": *L'Est Républicain*, March 17, 1978.

221   Their bodies were found: *Le Monde*, March 19–20, 1978.

221   "And on top of everything else": Author's interview with Claudine Lefer, March 24, 1999.

223   "Courage is more exhilarating": www.gwu.edu/~erpapers/abouteleanor/er-quotes/.

224   The death of her sister: Author's interview with Mathilde Damoisel, July 4, 2003.

225   "It was obvious": Author's interview with Christiane Boulloche-Audibert, March 19, 1999.

225   "It was extremely painful": Boulloche-Audibert, *Souvenirs.*

225   "She would read me what she had written": Author's interview with Catherine (Audibert) Dujardin, March 21, 1999.

225   news of Christiane's book: Six years after she published it privately, Christiane's book became part of the collection *Femmes dans la guerre, 1940–1945.*

226   "We did not talk about the Resistance": Author's interview with Michel Katlama, March 14, 1999.

227 "Christiane said she had done": Author's interview with Claudine Lefer,
     March 24, 1999.
227 "she had done her duty": Author's interview with Hélène Dujardin,
     March 24, 1999.
229 German-American Bund: www.ushmm.org/wlc/en/article.php?
     ModuleId=10005684.
229 After the Nazis looted Jewish stores: www.ushmm.org/wlc/en/article
     .php?ModuleId=10005516.
230 "an American reader who honestly recreates": Paxton, *Vichy France*,
     p. xiv.
230 "If one hasn't been through": *The Sorrow and the Pity.* Ophuls told
     me, "I think that's why I put it there. It seems sort of pretentious
     to use Anthony Eden as a spokesman for the author, but he is express-
     ing my sentiments there. The other people, not necessarily. But he
     does. I do associate with that statement. I'm glad that it made an
     impression on you." Author's telephone interview with Marcel Ophuls,
     March 23, 2004.

SELECT BIBLIOGRAPHY

André Boulloche: 1915–1978. Paris: C. Boulloche, 1979.

Andrew, Christopher. *Defend the Realm: The Authorized History of MI5*. New York: Vintage Books, 2010.

Audibert, Etienne. "Notices sur nos morts, Jacques BOULLOCHE (1906)." *Bulletin de l'association des anciens élèves de l'école polytechnique*, no. 9, September 1947.

Boulloche-Audibert, Christiane. *Souvenirs 1939–1945*. Privately published, 1998. Reprinted in Christiane Audibert-Boulloche et al., *Femmes dans la guerre, 1940–1945* (Paris: éditions du Félin, 2004).

British Intelligence file on André Boulloche, National Archives, formerly Public Record Office HS 9/190/6 114106. Declassified at the request of the author.

British Intelligence file on Charles Gimpel, National Archives, formerly Public Record Office HS 9/586/1 114106. Declassified at the request of the author.

British Intelligence File on Eric Katlama, National Archives, formerly Public Record Office HS 9/823/1. Declassified at the request of the author.

Churchill, Sir Winston. *Great War Speeches*. London: Corgi Books, 1965.

———. *The Second World War*. 6 vols. London: Cassell, 1948–54.

Cobb, Matthew. *The Resistance: The French Fight Against the Nazis*. New York: Simon & Schuster, 2009.

Collins, Larry, and Dominique Lapierre. *Is Paris Burning?* New York: Simon & Schuster, 1965.

Cooper, Duff. *Old Men Forget: The Autobiography of Duff Cooper (Viscount Norwich)*. New York: Dutton, 1954.

Dallas, Gregor. *1945: The War That Never Ended.* New Haven: Yale University Press, 2005.

de Gaulle, Charles. *The Army of the Future.* Philadelphia: Lippincott, 1941.

———. *The Complete War Memoirs.* New York: Simon & Schuster, 1964.

Eisenhower, Dwight D. *Crusade in Europe.* Garden City, NY: Doubleday, 1948.

Eparvier, Jean. *À Paris sous la botte des Nazis.* Paris: éditions Raymond Schall, 1944.

Foot, M. R. D. *SOE in France: An Account of the Work of the British Special Operations Executive in France, 1940–1944.* London: Her Majesty's Stationery Office, 1966.

Foot, M. R. D., and J. M. Langley. *MI9: Escape and Evasion, 1939–1945.* Boston: Little, Brown, 1980.

Gilbert, Martin. *Churchill: A Life.* New York: Henry Holt, 1991.

"Hommage à André Boulloche." *Revue Municipale Numero Special.* Montbéliard, March 1979.

Jackson, Julian. *The Fall of France: The Nazi Invasion of 1940.* New York: Oxford University Press, 2003.

———. *France: The Dark Years, 1940–1944.* New York: Oxford University Press, 2001.

Marks, Leo. *Between Silk and Cyanide: A Codemaker's War 1941–1945.* New York: Free Press, 1998.

Marrus, Michael R., and Robert O. Paxton. *Vichy France and the Jews.* Stanford: Stanford University Press, 1995.

Marshall, S. L. A. "First Wave at Omaha Beach." *Atlantic,* November 1, 1960.

"À la mémoire d'André Boulloche (34), compagnon de la Libération, 1915–1978." *La Jaune et la Rouge,* no. 583, March 2003.

Murphy, Brendan. *Turncoat: The Strange Case of British Sergeant Harold Cole, "The Worst Traitor of the War."* San Diego: Harcourt, 1987.

Neitzel, Sönke, ed. *Tapping Hitler's Generals: Transcripts of Secret Conversations 1942–45.* Barnsley, Yorkshire, UK: Frontline Books, 2007.

O'Neill, William L. *The Oxford Essential Guide to World War II.* New York: Berkley Books, 2002.

Ophuls, Marcel. *The Sorrow and the Pity: Chronicle of a French City under German Occupation.* Trans. Mireille Johnston. Intro. Stanley Hoffmann. St. Albans, UK: Paladin, 1975.

Orwell, George. *Diaries*. Ed. Peter Davison. New York: Liveright, 2012.

Ousby, Ian. *Occupation: The Ordeal of France, 1940–1944*. New York: St. Martin's Press, 1998.

Paxton, Robert O. *Vichy France: Old Guard and New Order, 1940–1944*. New York: Knopf, 1972.

Perrault, Gilles. *La Longue Traque*. Paris: J. C. Lattès, 1975.

Perrault, Gilles, and Pierre Azema. *Paris Under the Occupation*. New York: Vendome Press, 1989.

Peschanski, Denis, et al. *Collaboration and Resistance: Images of Life in Vichy France 1940–44*. Trans. Lory Frankel. New York: Harry N. Abrams, 2000.

Postel-Vinay, André. *Un fou s'évade: Souvenirs de 1941–42*. Paris: éditions du Félin, 1997.

Roberts, Andrew. *The Storm of War: A New History of the Second World War*. New York: Allen Lane, 2009.

Rossiter, Margaret L. *Women in the Resistance*. New York: Praeger, 1986.

Shirer, William L. *The Rise and Fall of the Third Reich: A History of Nazi Germany*. New York: Simon & Schuster, 1960.

Speer, Albert. *Inside The Third Reich: Memoirs*. Trans. Richard and Clara Winston. New York: Macmillan, 1970.

Stokesbury, James L. *A Short History of World War II*. New York: Morrow, 1980.

Témoignage de M. André Boulloche, Ingenieur des Ponts et Chaussées, 18 Av. D'Eylau, XVIeme, pseudo Armand et a Londres: Marin-Segment. Recueilli par Madame Granlet le 1 février 1950. French National Archives, box 72AJ68.

PHOTO CREDITS

I gratefully acknowledge the following for permission to reproduce the photographs and documents in this book:

Front endpaper: Photographer unknown, from *A Paris sous la botte des Nazis* (Paris: Éditions Raymond Schall, 1944).

Page 2: Courtesy Rebecca Kaiser Gibson

Pages 8, 14, and 54: Photographs by Roger Schall, courtesy The Image Works.

Pages 32, 42, 185, and 195: Courtesy Agnès Boulloche

Pages 40, 56, 57, 193, and 213: Courtesy Christiane Boulloche-Audibert

Page 49: Photographer unknown, from *Paris Under the Occupation* by Gilles Perrault and Pierre Azema (New York: The Vendome Press, 1989).

Page 59: Courtesy Claire Andrieu

Page 114: Courtesy Musée de l'Ordre de la Libération

Pages 121, 192, and 200: Courtesy Eric Katlama

Pages 173 and 175: Photographs by Albert Seeberger, from *Paris Under the Occupation*. Copyright holder unknown.

Pages 186 and 215: Courtesy Odile Boulloche

Pages 203 and 204: © Joe Stouter

Page 210: Courtesy Pierre Audibert

Page 228: © Tomas van Houtryve

Back endpaper: Photograph by Maurice Jarnoux, from *A Paris sous la botte des Nazis*. Copyright holder unknown.

In cases where the photographer or copyright holder is unknown, every effort has been made to identify such parties, and I ask that anyone with information about these photographs contact the publisher, Other Press.

INDEX

CHARLES KAISER is the author of *1968 in America,* one of the most admired popular histories of the politics and music in the 1960s, and *The Gay Metropolis,* the landmark history of gay life in America, which was a *New York Times* Notable Book of the Year and a Lambda Literary Award winner. He is a former reporter for the *New York Times* and *Wall Street Journal* and a former press critic for *Newsweek.* His articles and reviews have also appeared in the *Washington Post, Los Angeles Times, Rolling Stone, New York, Vogue, Vanity Fair, The Guardian,* and *New Republic.* In 2015 he was inducted into the LGBT Journalists Hall of Fame.